The RANGE CATTLE INDUSTRY

The RANGE CATTLE INDUSTRY

Ranching
on the Great Plains
from 1865 to 1925

by EDWARD EVERETT DALE

UNIVERSITY OF OKLAHOMA
PRESS: NORMAN

BY EDWARD EVERETT DALE:

Territorial Acquisitions of the United States (Privately printed, 1912)
Tales of the Tepee (Boston, 1919)
A History of Oklahoma (with J. S. Buchanan) (Chicago, 1924)
Letters of Lafayette (Oklahoma City, 1925)
The Problem of Indian Administration (with Meriam and others) (Baltimore, 1928)
The Prairie Schooner and Other Poems (Guthrie, 1929)
Outline and References for Oklahoma History (with M. L. Wardell) (Privately printed, 1929)
Readings in Oklahoma History (with J. L. Rader) (Chicago, 1930)
Frontier Trails (ed.) (Boston, 1930)
Grant Foreman: A Brief Biography (Norman, 1933)
A Rider of the Cherokee Strip (ed.) (Boston, 1936)
Cherokee Cavaliers (with Gaston Litton) (Norman, 1939)
Cow Country (Norman, 1942)
History of the United States (with Dwight L. Dumond and Edgar B. Wesley) (Boston, 1948)
History of Oklahoma (with M. L. Wardell) (New York, 1948)
Oklahoma: The Story of a State (Evanston, 1949)
The Indians of the Southwest (Norman, 1949)
Pioneer Judge (with James D. Morrison) (Cedar Rapids, 1958)
Frontier Ways (Austin, 1959)
The Range Cattle Industry (Norman, 1930; New Edition, Norman, 1960)

Library of Congress Catalog Card Number: 60-10552

PREFACE

The Range Cattle Industry was begun in 1924 and the manuscript completed in 1925. The author was at that time a member of the History Department of the University of Oklahoma but had been lent to the United States Department of Agriculture to do a study of cattle ranching in the Trans-Mississippi West since the Civil War. He was accordingly appointed as a research agent in the Division of Statistical and Historical Research of the Bureau of Agricultural Economics. It was expected that the manuscript would be issued as a bulletin of that bureau, but this was delayed, and in 1929 it was released to the University of Oklahoma Press, which published the book in 1930.

The comparatively small edition was quickly exhausted and the price of the volume steadily mounted until it became beyond the reach of the average reader. In 1958 a large firm of rare-book dealers made a survey of the demand for western material which revealed that this was one of the twenty most wanted books on the American West.

The growing demand for the volume and the high price of a copy, when one can be found, seem to justify a second edition, although since its original publication in 1930 several earlier books on ranching have been reprinted and many new ones have appeared. In 1932 came the republication of Joseph G. McCoy's *Historic Sketches of the Cattle Trade West and Southwest,* while two other rare volumes were reprinted in 1959. These are *Prose and Poetry of the Live Stock Industry of the U.S.,* edited by James W. Freeman; and James Cox's *Historical and Biographical Record of the Cattle Industry.*

v

Among the many other books on ranching that have been published since 1930 are *The Cowman's Southwest,* by Angie Debo; *The Cattlemen's Frontier,* by Louis Pelzer; *Cattle Empire* and *The Great Roundup,* both by Lewis Nordyke; *The King Ranch,* in two volumes, by Tom Lea; and a reprinting of *The Day of the Cattleman,* by Ernest Staples Osgood. Other important volumes, all published by the University of Oklahoma Press, are biographies of George Littlefield and Charles Goodnight, and a revised edition of the *XIT Ranch,* all by J. Evetts Haley; *Cow Country,* by Edward Everett Dale; *Shanghai Pierce,* by Chris Emmett; and *Cowboys and Cattle Kings* by C. L. Sonnichsen.

To mention by name all those who gave information and help in preparing the manuscript of this book is obviously impossible. To all of them I am deeply grateful, but especially to the officials of the Bureau of Agricultural Economics and particularly to Mr. Nils A. Olsen, later chief of that bureau, and Dr. O. C. Stine, for many years director of the Division of Statistical and Historical Research. Others whose help will always be gratefully remembered are the officers of the Texas and Southwestern Cattle Raisers' Association, the officials of the Library of the University of Texas, and my wife Mrs. Rosalie Gilkey Dale, who typed the manuscript and aided in reading proof and the selection of illustrations.

EDWARD EVERETT DALE

Norman, Oklahoma
March 30, 1960

CONTENTS

ILLUSTRATIONS

MAPS

INTRODUCTION

Any history of the ranch cattle industry of the Great Plains region is merely a part of the history of a much larger movement, that of the settlement and development of the American wilderness. This is a movement that has been characterized by the appearance of successive stages of society—that of the hunter and trapper, the herder, and the pioneer farmer following one another within the same region in more or less rapid succession according to conditions of topography and climate.

Thus, while the grazing industry in most civilized and well settled countries is carried on largely in areas too dry or too rough and unfertile for the successful production of crops, that has not always been true in the United States. Here ranching has existed as a frontier pursuit ever since earliest times, and often in regions well adapted by the character of soil and climate for other forms of agriculture but so remote from markets as to render the growing of crops unprofitable.

The early English settlers along the Atlantic seaboard brought cattle with them from Europe. These increased rapidly and as land along the coast began to rise in value many men who owned a considerable number of animals removed westward and established themselves along the edge of the wilderness where they could find more abundant pasturage for their herds.

As population increased settlers advanced steadily westward, pushing before them not only the Indians but also those live stock raisers who wished to keep near the border of settlement in order to pasture their animals on the unoccupied and unclaimed lands beyond. Thus, once agricultural occupation was well started in its steadfast march across the continent, there was always to be found along its western edge a comparatively narrow band or border devoted largely to grazing. For a century and more it was there, a kind of twilight zone with the light of civilization behind it, and the darkness of savagery before. The live stock raisers could not move too rapidly nor push too far out into the wilderness because of the savage tribes of Indians that occupied it. On the other hand few of them could linger for a long period of years in one locality. The American people had become "that great land animal." They pushed eagerly westward and occupied lands formerly devoted to grazing, cleared fields, and planted crops, thus forcing the live stock growers again and again to move on to "pastures new." Under such circumstances grew up the idea that grazing is but a transient and temporary occupation to be carried on in any region only until the lands are needed for a more intensive form of agriculture.

As settlement advanced westward into the prairie regions beyond the Mississippi, this border of herding along its western rim varied somewhat in width but was never very broad. However, it is one of the most remarkable features of American economic history during the nineteenth century that soon after the Civil War this border of grazing, hitherto fairly constant in breadth and area, suddenly shot out into the wilderness and spread with a rapidity that was fairly startling until, in less than two decades, it had come to cover an area greater than all that part of the United States east of the Mississippi devoted to crop raising. Thus was formed the so called "cow country" or range cattle area, a region in which ranching was carried on for several years upon a scale vastly larger than ever before had been the case until the homesteaders advancing slowly but steadily westward had invaded nearly every portion of it and taken over most of the land suitable for crop growing.

This brought about a great shrinking of the range and forced the ranchmen into the rougher and more arid areas, and at the same time caused them to reduce their herds and to market animals at an earlier age to feeders in the corn belt to be finished for

xii

market on grain. A growing scarcity of range, the high price of lands, and increased costs of operation at last caused the breaking up of most of the largest ranches and a shift in the industry from large to comparatively small producers. At the same time came changes in the methods of operation due to changed conditions and the experience of the past. Better breeding and better care became the rule. Fenced pastures, food and shelter in winter, the conservation of ranges, and better watering facilities took the place of the old wasteful system under which the cattle were turned out on the open ranges and allowed to shift for themselves.

To relate in brief form the history of the growth and subsequent decline of the ranch industry on the Great Plains, and of the establishment and development of relations between that region and the corn belt farther east is the object of this book.

The task of preparing it has been a peculiarly difficult one. The ranch cattle business as a great industry came into existence within a few years, rose quickly to enormous proportions, and then declined with almost equal rapidity. As a result it never became thoroughly standardized. Carried on in a great area varying much in topography and climate it was inevitable that conditions and, in consequence, methods of operation should also vary considerably in different portions of the range area. A highly technical business, it was never well understood except by the comparatively few persons engaged in it, most of whom have long since died. In many cases lax business methods prevailed. Few records were kept and those that were have in many instances disappeared.

Yet comparatively scanty as are direct records of ranching operations, the volume of material is so great as to be almost overwhelming. It consists of numerous publications of the national and state governments, a vast fund of contemporary newspaper and periodical literature, and a great number of books and articles of more recent date. Diligent search will also discover a considerable amount of manuscript material in the form of old letters, account books, diaries, minutes of meetings of live stock associations, and various other sources. Finally, though their number is growing less each year, there are a few men still living who had an active part in the building of the range cattle industry of the West and whose minds and memories are storehouses of information.

Considerable care must be exercised in the use of much of the above material. Many of the more recent books and articles dealing with ranching are unreliable. Perhaps no great industry has been so little understood by the public at large and yet the picturesque features of range cattle production have served to fire the imagination and awaken the enthusiasm of numerous writers who in many cases have had little conception of the real conditions of ranch life. Obviously reliable statistics are difficult to obtain. Figures with respect to the number of animals in a given area, the volume of cattle driven up the trails, losses in winter or by theft, and numerous other things must usually be regarded as only estimates or approximations.

To find and evaluate the greater part of the available material on this subject is in itself a task involving the expenditure of much time and labor, and no investigator can ever be certain that something of great importance may not have escaped his attention.

While the difficulties of gathering material have been great, the difficulties of dealing with so large a subject within a comparatively limited space have been even greater. The subject of the ranch cattle industry on the Great Plains and its relations with the corn belt has many ramifications and presents numerous phases, any one of which might be made the subject of an entire volume. Condensation has had to be kept in mind at all times. Subjects deserving a full chapter have been accorded one or two pages. Others deserving pages have been dismissed with a single paragraph.

Such matters as breeds and breeding, cattle feeding, the financing of the industry, geographic conditions affecting ranching, transportation, conservation of ranges, the leasing of lands, fencing, watering facilities and many others have each received treatment so brief and incomplete as to prove in all probability disappointing to persons who have made a special study of one or more such subjects.

Inadequate as is the treatment of most of these subjects, it is hoped that the historical account given of their development and of their relations with one another, together with that of the relationships that have grown up between ranching and other forms of agriculture and industry, may prove interesting and instructive. Perhaps, too, such an account may suggest further lines of research and point the way to other and more intensive studies of various phases of the range cattle industry. It is hoped too that this brief history of ranching operations on the Great Plains may have a further and even more practical value.

Ever since the Civil War the cattle industry in the United States has been subject to ups and downs, to periods of prosperity and depression that have served to make the business highly speculative in nature. With due regard to the fact that the conditions under which the industry is carried on are vastly different at present to those of a generation ago, it should nevertheless be remembered that the lamp of experience has ever furnished the chief light by which our feet are guided, and so it seems possible that a study of the history of ranching in the West from the time it first began to assume important proportions may help to reveal causes for these periodical depressions, and even go so far as to suggest means by which they may, in some degree, be avoided in the future.

The RANGE CATTLE
INDUSTRY

1.

TEXAS AT THE CLOSE
OF THE CIVIL WAR

Any history of the cattle industry in the West must begin
with Texas since that state was the original home of ranching on
a large scale in the United States, and from its vast herds were
drawn most of the cattle for the first stocking of the central and
northern plains.

Almost from its earliest settlement Texas had been peculiarly
a cattle country. The first Spanish settlers at the missions and
presidios brought with them cattle of the long horned Spanish
type that had been raised by the Moors on the plains of northern
Africa and of Andalusia for a thousand years.[1] These increased
rapidly under the favorable conditions of range and climate. Some
of them eventually escaped from their owners and ranged the
plains as wild cattle, unbranded and unclaimed by anyone.[2]

The first Anglo-American settlers of Texas were not primarily
live stock raisers but cotton farmers. Yet many of them brought
with them a few milk cows or other cattle mainly of the northern
European breeds which in some cases mixed with the Spanish
breeds already there and soon grew into considerable herds.

Not only were climate and range conditions of Texas ideal
for cattle raising, but the land system also did much to foster that
industry. The Kingdom of Spain and later the Republic of Mexico were both very liberal in their policies of land grants.[3]

In 1825 the state of Coahuila and Texas enacted a law offering
lands to immigrants upon most attractive terms. Families whose

[1] J. W. Thompson Ms., Ch. 7, P. 8.
[2] 10th Census, Vol. III, p. 965.
[3] McKitrick, *Land System of Texas*, pp. 26-27.

[3]

occupation was the cultivation of the soil should receive one labor, or one hundred and seventy-seven acres. Those who should raise a considerable amount of live stock might receive a sufficient amount of grazing land to complete a league, or four thousand four hundred and twenty-eight acres. Those whose exclusive occupation was stock raising were to have four thousand two hundred and fifty-one acres.[4] Premium lands were also to be given to *Empresarios* or contractors who should introduce colonists, in the amount of five leagues of land for every one hundred families so introduced.[5]

When Texas became a republic its first constitution specified that all persons who were living in Texas at the time of the declaration of independence (March 2, 1836), except negroes and Indians, should be regarded as citizens and as such were entitled to certain privileges. Not the least of these was that these citizens who were heads of families should receive one league and one labor of land, a total of four thousand six hundred and five acres. Single men over seventeen years of age were to have one third of a league.[6]

Laws passed later entitled every immigrant who came in before a certain time and who was the head of a family to one thousand two hundred and eighty acres of land, and every single man to six hundred and forty acres.[7] These tracts were later reduced to six hundred and forty and three hundred and twenty acres, but laws were also passed authorizing the president of the Republic to make contracts with immigration agents for the introduction of colonists and providing that such agents might receive two sections of land for every one hundred families so introduced.[8] Other laws were enacted providing for homesteads, for pre-emption claims, and for bounty and donation warrants for soldiers in the Texas War of Independence. Land scrip was also issued and

---

4 Sayles, *Early Laws of Texas* I-64, or Gammel, *Laws of Texas* I-40. Quoted in McKitrick, p. 31.
5 McKitrick, p. 31.
6 Sayles, *Early Laws of Texas* I:205, Quoted in McKitrick, p. 42.
7 *Ibid.*, I:512.
8 *Ibid.*, I:515. Quoted in McKitrick, p. 45.

[4]

used in the settlement of claims held by individuals against the Republic.[9]

When Texas was admitted to the Union as a state, it retained the ownership and control of all unoccupied lands within its borders. The state continued the same liberal policy in the disposal of lands that had been carried on by the Republic, giving out vast areas by bounty and donation warrants, or as homesteads, and selling much more at a low price and upon liberal terms of payment. As a result of these policies the average size of Texas farms by 1850 was nine hundred and fifty-one acres.[10] This was far larger than the average size of farms in any other state in the Union with the single exception of California, which had been but recently admitted and was covered with huge Spanish grants.[11] Texas also had in 1850 the smallest percentage of cultivated land per farm of any state in the Union except California.[12]

While these conditions did not quite hold true a decade later, yet the size of farms, even at that time, remained relatively large and the acreage of improved land comparatively small.

However, the size of the farms does not give a very clear conception of conditions in Texas at the time of the outbreak of the Civil War. As the number of cattle steadily increased, many men owning a comparatively small acreage controlled a much larger area of the state's public domain which they held by "range right" and used as pasturage for their herds of cattle.

As a matter of fact most cattle raisers ranged their live stock largely upon the unoccupied public lands. Men with thousands of head frequently did not own a single acre of land.[13] Men of small means coming to this region were advised not to buy land, but to invest all of their capital in cattle and depend upon the open range for pasturage.[14]

As the raising of live stock began to show profits, the industry

9 Sayles, *Early Laws of Texas,* I, pp. 210, 211, 224, 235, 238, 257, 283, 472 and 576. II, pp. 254, 321, 452, 510, and 532. Also McKitrick, pp. 47-52.
10 9th Census, Vol. III, p. 341.
11 *Ibid.*
12 *Ibid.*
13 *A Six Year Resident, Texas, the Australia of America,* p. 22.
14 *Ibid.,* p. 24.

grew rapidly. Men came to Texas from many parts of Europe and commenced to engage in it.[15] The expense of raising cattle was slight. They lived the year around upon the open range which was entirely free. Caring for the animals cost little, as co-operation was extensively practiced. Pens were built through co-operative effort at convenient places for branding, and drovers and laborers to do the rounding and branding could be employed at from twenty to forty dollars a month.[16] Also men were often employed to brand calves "on shares," usually receiving one calf out of every four branded.[17] Many men reaching Texas with little or no capital had started herds of their own by branding calves on shares for others.[18]

Live stock raisers with large herds of cattle, who in consequence were obliged to ride the range regularly and brand their own calves, would frequently agree to brand for others having but few animals at rates regarded as unreasonably low.[19] How often and to what extent they took advantage of the opportunities offered by such a system is an interesting question.

For many years the chief problem which the cattle raisers of Texas had to face was that of market. Yet many cattle were sold as work oxen for use in freighting upon the plains, and for local consumption as beef.[20] In 1842 driving cattle to New Orleans began, and this city soon became the chief market for Texas cattle.[21] Cattle were often driven to Shreveport and from there shipped down Red River to New Orleans. The cost of the drive was slight and the freight from Shreveport to New Orleans about five or six dollars a head.[22] Others were sent by sea from Galveston and other Gulf ports, and not a few were sent by sea from Galveston to Mobile or Cuba.[23]

[15] *Ibid.*, p. 41.
[16] *Ibid.*, p. 201.
[17] *Ibid.*, p. 19
[18] *Ibid.*, p. 20.
[19] *Ibid.*, p. 42
[20] *Ibid.*, p. 184.
[21] 10th Census, Vol. III, p. 965, or *A Six Year Resident*, pp. 27-28.
[22] *Report of the Patent Office*, 1850, p. 189.
[23] *A Six Year Resident, Texas, the Australia of America*, p. 184.

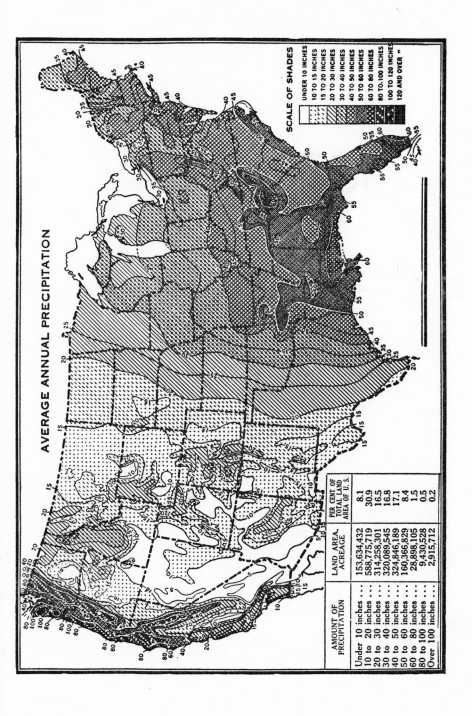

AVERAGE ANNUAL PRECIPITATION

SCALE OF SHADES

UNDER 10 INCHES
10 TO 15 INCHES
15 TO 20 INCHES
20 TO 30 INCHES
30 TO 40 INCHES
40 TO 50 INCHES
50 TO 60 INCHES
60 TO 80 INCHES
80 TO 100 INCHES
100 TO 120 INCHES
120 AND OVER "

AMOUNT OF PRECIPITATION	LAND AREA, ACREAGE	PER CENT OF TOTAL LAND AREA OF U. S.
Under 10 inches	153,634,432	8.1
10 to 20 inches	588,775,719	30.9
20 to 30 inches	314,258,301	16.5
30 to 40 inches	320,089,545	16.8
40 to 50 inches	324,846,189	17.1
50 to 60 inches	160,366,829	8.4
60 to 80 inches	28,898,105	1.5
80 to 100 inches ...	9,430,528	0.5
Over 100 inches	2,915,712	0.2

Texas cattle were also driven north to Chicago and other northern markets or to the Atlantic seaboard.[24] As early as 1846 Edward Piper drove a thousand head of Texas steers to Ohio, where he fed and sold them.[25] In 1850 were the first drives to California, while by 1853 a considerable movement of cattle northward had begun, and this reached Chicago by 1856.[26]

Unfortunately this movement of southern cattle northward brought on an epidemic of Texas fever among the native cattle along the roads over which these herds passed.[27] Many persons lost nearly all their cattle within a few days. The inhabitants of south-western Missouri held conventions in several places to consider the situation and formed armed bands or patrols to turn back all Texas droves that might try to pass.[28]

By 1858 the drive northward through Missouri had been checked and was not resumed very much until after the war. Some of the later drovers passed around Missouri to the west going through Indian Territory, Kansas, a corner of Nebraska and Iowa.[29] Moved by the hope of large profits a number of northern men came in and bought herds to drive to market. In 1856 one herd of seven hundred head driven to Chicago is said to have yielded a net profit of ten thousand dollars.[30] Yet many northern men did not succeed so well, partly owing to the fact that they bought a poor grade of cattle and were inexperienced in handling them. [31] Before the outbreak of the Civil War the trade had lessened very much as it was said not to be profitable.[32]

The checking of the movement of cattle northward must have meant a rapid increase in the number of animals in Texas during the last two or three years before the war, and a consequent steady decrease in the price of cattle per head.[33] In 1860 the average price

[24] *Year Book* of Department of Agriculture, 1908, p. 228.
[25] 10th Census, Vol. III, p. 965.
[26] *Ibid.*
[27] 8th Census, Agriculture, p. CXXXIV.
[28] *Ibid.*
[29] *A Six Year Resident, Texas, the Australia of America*, p. 221.
[30] *Ibid.*, p. 180.
[31] *Ibid.*, p. 41.
[32] *Prairie Farmer*, July 14, 1866, p. 23.
[33] 10th Census, Vol. III, p. 965.

of cattle in Texas was about six dollars a head though fat beeves sometimes sold for as much as sixteen or eighteen dollars.[34]

Various companies were engaged in the business of shipping or driving fat cattle to market, usually to New Orleans or some of the other Gulf ports. These companies employed beef buyers whose duty it was to purchase and collect herds of fat cattle for shipment or for placing on the trail.[35]

By 1860, Texas with a population of 604,215 had, according to the eighth census, cattle to the number of 3,533,768 head,[36] or nearly six head per capita of population.[37] However, since most of these cattle were upon the open range and scattered over an enormous region, it seems certain that the census figures are but the roughest sort of an approximation, and are probably far too low. Careful estimates made by men who have given much time to research in the matter indicate that the number of cattle in Texas in 1860 was probably more than four and a half millions.[38]

The land area of Texas is 262,398 square miles, which would indicate a population in 1866 of less than 2.5 to the square mile. However, in 1860 this population was most unevenly distributed, by far the greater part of it lying in the eastern third of the state. Two-thirds of it was east of the ninety-seventh meridian while west of the ninety-ninth meridian there was only a very small area that had a population of more than two to the square mile.[39]

The extreme eastern part of the state was occupied largely by cotton farmers. To the west of these was a region of mixed farming and cattle raising, while along the western border, as has often been the case on the American frontier, lay a strip of great ranches.

In the southwestern portion of the settled region of Texas was San Antonio, the metropolis of the state, a city of a little over seven thousand five hundred people.[40] Galveston had a little more

34 *A Six Year Resident, Texas, the Australia of America,* p. 221.
35 *Ibid.*
36 8th Census, Pop., p. IV. This is cattle on farms. The total number was over 800,000 more.
37 *Ibid.,* Agriculture, p. CVIII.
38 10th Census, Vol. III, p. 965.
39 Henry Gannett, *Gazetteer of Texas,* p. 14.
40 8th Census, Pop., pp. 486-7.

than six thousand people, Houston about three thousand seven hundred, Austin and Brownsville each a little over twenty-five hundred.[41] These were the only towns with more than two thousand people each, while only eighteen more had a population of as much as one thousand.[42] Along the lower reaches of the Rio Grande was a scattered fringe of people mostly Mexican, while far to the west lay El Paso, the gateway to Mexico, a town of only a few hundred inhabitants.

Between the western frontier line of settlements and the border of Mexico and New Mexico lay a vast uninhabited region consisting largely of level, grassy plains. Over it roamed herds of buffalo and numerous wild horses and cattle. Men living along the border of settlement frequently engaged in catching wild horses and cattle either for sport or profit. Pens into which they might be driven were built upon many of the extensive prairies and Texas "mustang ponies" when broken and gentle were sold at from ten to twelve dollars a head.[43]

Over these plains also roved scattered bands of Indians who preyed upon the frontier settlements, stealing horses and taking scalps, rendering it unsafe for live stock raisers to venture too far beyond the border of settlements.

The Civil War came, and most of the able bodied men of Texas hurried away to join the armies of the Confederacy. During the four years of civil strife Texas remained the least touched of any southern state by that struggle. While the armies of Sherman swept through Georgia and the Carolinas leaving little in their wake, while the border states were being devastated by the forces of both sides, and while the fields of Alabama and Mississippi lay fallow and waste or grew up in bushes and briers from want of laborers to till them, the cattle on the broad plains of Texas grew mature and fat, and in many places increased rapidly in numbers.

It is true that some Texas cattle were used to feed southern armies, particularly during the early part of the war, but after

41 *Ibid.*
42 *Ibid.*
43 *A Six Year Resident, Texas, the Australia of America,* pp. 37-40.

the Mississippi River had fallen into the hands of the North through the capture of New Orleans and Vicksburg the provision storehouse of Texas was virtually closed to the South except for the use of the limited number of troops in the Trans-Mississippi Department.[44] A few herds were marketed early in the war by swimming them across the Mississippi below Vicksburg and then hurrying them east to the Confederate armies, but the vigilance of the Union gunboats rendered such operations extremely hazardous, even from the first, and soon stopped them entirely.[45] Of course the blockade stopped all shipments by sea, and while a few herds may have been driven to California,[46] the number must have been so small as to be almost negligible. It seems certain, therefore, that but few Texas cattle were consumed during the four years of war except those used to feed the civilian population of the state itself, and the comparatively small number of troops within its borders. As a result, when the war closed and the Texas soldiers released from the Confederate armies returned to their homes, many of them found their ranges overflowing with fat, mature cattle for which there seemed to be no market.

It is impossible to state with any degree of accuracy the number of cattle in Texas at the close of the Civil War. The Department of Agriculture estimated the number in 1866 to be 3,111,-475,[47] a decrease of nearly twelve per cent since 1860. When we consider that many calves had escaped branding during the years of war, and in consequence numerous cattle raisers did not themselves know how many animals they possessed, it must be obvious that this estimate is at best only an approximation.

As a matter of fact the figures given are probably far too low. Men who have made a careful study of the subject usually agree that the number of cattle in Texas increased greatly during the war.[48] Associations and live stock agencies of various kinds had

44 "The Texas Cattle Trade," *Year Book* of Department of Agriculture, 1870, p. 348.
45 McCoy, *Historic Sketches of the Cattle Trade*, p. 20.
46 10th Census, Vol. III, p. 966.
47 Monthly Reports of Department of Agriculture, 1866, pp. 350-351.
48 10th Census, Vol. III, p. 966.

been established during the years of warfare to ride the ranges, round up and brand calves and keep an account for absent parties.[49] It seems probable that instead of a decrease of nearly twelve per cent the number of cattle in Texas actually increased greatly during the four years of war, particularly in some localities, and at its close numbered not less than five and probably eight head per capita of population.[50]

Trustworthy figures with respect to the number of live stock in various states during the period immediately following the war are extremely difficult to obtain. However, even by 1870 when live stock raising had had some time in which to recuperate from the destructive years of warfare, New York had on farms but .46 head of cattle per capita of population, Ohio .53, Iowa .84, Kentucky .51, Illinois .67, Missouri .67, and Massachusetts .15.[51]

In 1865 the percentages must have been even lower since many states, particularly those of the South and the border, had suffered a frightful depreciation in their stocks of cattle. Georgia in 1866 had but a little more than half as many as in 1860, Arkansas less than half, Louisiana less than half, and Missouri but a little more than half, while nearly every state showed a considerable loss.[52]

Obviously the isolation of Texas during the four years of war was not without great influence upon prices. In 1865 cattle could be bought in Texas at almost any price offered. Mature animals could be purchased at three to four dollars a head and fat beeves at five or six dollars.[53] Stocks of cattle were often offered for sale upon the range at from one to two dollars a head, and that too without finding a purchaser.[54]

Yet at this time the prices of cattle and of beef in the North and East were high. Round steak was selling at retail in the New York markets at twenty to twenty-five cents a pound, sirloin at

49 *Ibid.*

50 D. E. McArthur, A History of the Cattle Industry in Texas, (Ms.), or Thompson Ms., Ch. 11.

51 Figures from 9th Census.

52 Monthly Reports of the Department of Agriculture, 1866, pp. 247 and 350-351.

53 10th Census, Vol. III, p. 966.

54 McCoy, p. 20.

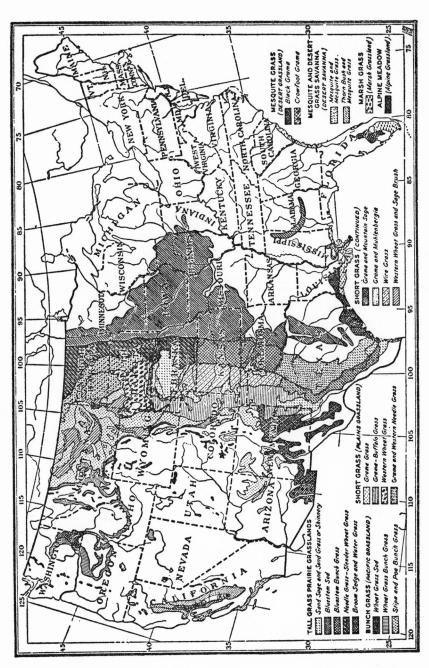

Vegetation of the Great Plains Region

twenty-five to thirty-five and rib roast at twenty-eight to thirty cents.[55] On the live stock market of the eastern cities cattle were quoted at $5.00 to $10.00 per cwt. and sometimes even higher.[56]

In 1867 the price of three-year-old steers and oxen in Massachusetts was given as $86.00, in New York as $68.57, in New Jersey as $70.58, Illinois $40.19, Kansas $38.40, Nebraska $46.32, Missouri $32.83, while in Texas it was given at $9.46.[57]

Such a situation could produce but one result. The Texas soldiers released from the armies of the Confederacy in 1865 returned to their homes, in many cases ragged and penniless, to find their ranges overflowing with mature, fat cattle which were worthless at home but of great value in the North and East. Texas in 1865 was a vast reservoir fairly overflowing with cattle. To the north lay markets, to the north Texans must go with the only movable property left to them, their great herds of cattle. In the years following the Civil War this flood of Texas cattle pent up within the state through the four years of conflict burst its bonds and flowed northward in a great stream that was not to lessen until the eastern markets had been fully supplied with beef and enough animals furnished to stock the ranges of the northern and central plains.

[55] New York *Tribune,* June 23, 1866.
[56] New York *Times,* December 22, 1866, p. 1.
[57] Monthly Reports of Department of Agriculture, 1867, pp. 108-109.

2.

THE CENTRAL
AND NORTHERN PLAINS

At the time of the Civil War there lay to the north and west of Texas a vast and nearly uninhabited region extending from Red River to Canada and from the edge of agricultural settlements on the east to the Rocky Mountains and on beyond to the settlements along the Pacific coast. The frontier line, beyond which there was a population of less than two inhabitants to the square mile, extended in 1860 from Red River north along the eastern boundary of Indian Territory to the Southeast corner of Kansas. Thence the line ran west along the southern boundary of Kansas to about the ninety-seventh meridian, and then north through Kansas to Nebraska, most of which was unoccupied except a little of the eastern part from which long tongues of settlement extended westward up the river valleys. The frontier line then swung northeast into Iowa, the northwestern portion of which was little settled, and crossed into Minnesota, most of which was unsettled with the exception of the region along the Mississippi River centering about St. Paul. Largely speaking, there was but little settlement in Minnesota west of the ninety-fifth meridian or north of forty-six degrees and thirty minutes north latitude.[1] By 1870 the frontier line had advanced very considerably, though most of this advance had come in the five years following the war, or the second half of the decade.

At the close of the war there were to be found along this frontier line a number of towns that were outfitting points for emigrants across the plains to the Pacific Coast, or fur markets and distributing points for goods for the Indian trade. Prominent

[1] See map, or 12th Census, Statistical Atlas, pp. 9-10.

among these were Fort Smith on the border of Arkansas and Indian Territory, Leavenworth, Kansas City, St. Joseph, Council Bluffs, and St. Paul. To the west of these towns lay the wilderness, a great region of varied topography and climate. It consisted largely of broad stretches of rolling plains sloping gently upward to the foot of the Rocky Mountains. Beyond those mountains lay the arid region of the Great Basin followed by other mountain ranges, and finally the Pacific Coast area. However, the Pacific Coast states seldom produced a great surplus of cattle and in fact often drew a large number of animals from the next tier of states to the east. This chapter, largely speaking, omits not only the Pacific Coast states, but also Arizona, Nevada, Utah, and Idaho, and is devoted to Montana, the Dakotas, Wyoming, Colorado, Kansas, Nebraska, and Indian Territory. These states came to form the greater part of the so called "cow country," and their relations were largely with the East rather than with the Pacific Coast. Ranching in the Indian Territory and New Mexico is considered in some detail in the study of Texas and the Southwest.

The rolling plains of the region under consideration were broken in many places by large areas of rough and hilly lands. Among these were the Flint Hills of Kansas, the Sand Hill region of western Nebraska, and the Black Hills and the Bad Lands of Dakota, Wyoming and Montana. Also there were many mountainous areas in Colorado, Wyoming and Montana since parts of these states are in the Rocky Mountain region.[2] The mountains were in many cases covered with a growth of stunted pine trees, and there was also a fringe of timber along most of the streams. With these exceptions the greater part of this vast territory consisted of prairies on which the traveler might in many cases ride for hours without seeing a single tree.

This lack of timber had considerable influence upon settlement. Hitherto, the American pioneers had frequently found the forest an impediment to their advance, because of the great labor that must be expended in clearing fields, but it had also furnished

2 See topography map.

[16]

material for building houses, barns, and fences, as well as abundant fuel, and so had proved a help as well.

It is true that considerable areas of prairie land had been encountered east of the Mississippi River, but these were comparatively small, and in most cases no part of them was remote from sufficient timber for fuel and the building of necessary improvements. The plains regions to the west of the Mississippi, however, were different. Here were wide stretches of territory with almost no timber for hundreds of miles. It is therefore small wonder that settlement was checked at the border of this region and, when it later did begin to advance, moved cautiously, at first extending tongues of population up the timber-bordered streams.

Of these water courses there were many, some of the largest being the Arkansas, Smoky Hill, Platte, Niobrara, and the Missouri and its upper tributaries.

Climatic conditions were almost as varied as was topography. The rainfall, which was fairly abundant in the eastern portion, grew less toward the west until it became so slight as to leave large regions that were almost real deserts. In the lower altitudes of the southern plains the winters were fairly mild, while in the North and in the higher altitudes of the mountains and the elevated plains at their foot they were long and cold. Severe blizzards and snow storms were here of frequent occurrence, causing great suffering and loss to the buffalo and other wild animals and later among the herds of cattle, though there were numerous sheltered valleys where animals might find protection and some food even in coldest weather.[3]

Unsettled though it was, the entire Great Plains and Rocky Mountain area was at the time of the close of the Civil War by no means unknown. Explorers sent out by the American government, fur traders, trappers, and travelers interested in science, or merely in adventure, had traversed nearly every part of it between 1804 and 1850. The Santa Fe trade, the migration of the Mormons and of settlers to Oregon, together with the great rush

3 See map.

to the gold fields of California and of Colorado, had made numerous and well marked trails throughout this region.[4]

Among these was the old Santa Fe Trail, which led southwest from Kansas City across Kansas, No Man's Land, and northeastern New Mexico to Santa Fe. Starting at the same point the Oregon Trail led northwest to the Platte River, up that stream, following the north branch, to a little past the one hundred and sixth meridian, thence up Sweetwater and through South Pass, and on past Forts Bridger, Hall, and Boise to the Columbia, and down that stream to the Pacific. First broken by the fur traders, largely between 1810 and 1930, it had been traveled much by emigrants between 1840 and 1855. Between Fort Bridger and Fort Hall the California trail branched off to the southwest. It became a well marked highway in the years following the gold discoveries of 1849. Other prominent trails led from Westport to the gold fields of Colorado, from St. Paul to Oregon, from Nebraska City to Fort Kearney, and from Fort Smith to Santa Fe. Numerous other trails made by the military, by emigrants, traders, or trappers led westward across the plains from the border towns or connected the forts and fur trading posts of that region. Some were plain and often traveled, others dim and but little used.

Scattered about at strategic points on the plains and near the foot of the mountains were a number of military posts whose garrisons were to watch the Indians and protect emigrants or other travelers. A rather clearly defined line of forts had been established along the frontier between 1820 and 1840 but the gold discoveries and consequent rush westward had made it expedient to abandon some of these and to establish others farther west along the trails or at other points of vantage. No list of military posts can be of much value since they were established, garrisoned, abandoned and regarrisoned as need required, and in consequence generalizations are difficult. However, some prominent posts in this part of the West during the Civil War period and the years following were Forts Gibson, Reno and Sill in the Indian

4 See Marcy, *The Prairie Traveler,* Edited by R. F. Burton, for descriptions of trails, list of itineraries, pp. 181-251.

[18]

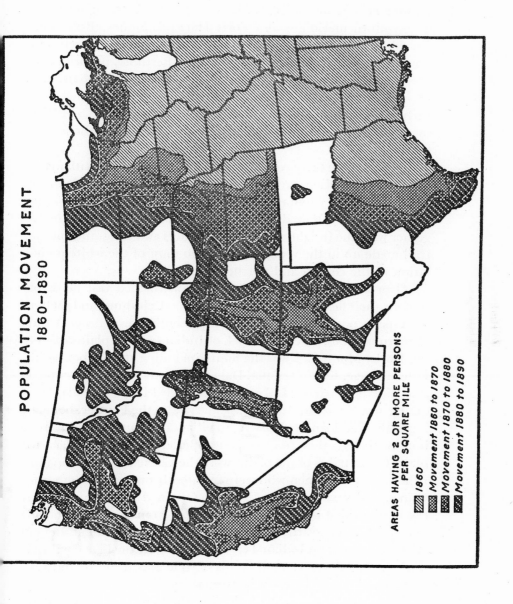

POPULATION MOVEMENT
1860-1890

AREAS HAVING 2 OR MORE PERSONS
PER SQUARE MILE

1860
Movement 1860 to 1870
Movement 1870 to 1880
Movement 1880 to 1890

Territory, Forts Dodge, Larned, Wallace, Riley and Hays in Kansas and Fort Kearney, Nebraska, on the Platte River near the ninety-ninth meridian; also Forts Hartsuff, Sidney, Robinson, Sheridan and Niobrara, Fort Laramie, Fort D. H. Russell and Fort Bridger in Wyoming, Forts Randall, Berthold, Buford, Bennett, and Union in Dakota, and Forts Benton, Peck, Shaw, and Missoula in Montana. Some of these had been established very early. Others were founded in the years following the Civil War to watch over the Indians and prevent or check outbreaks of hostilities.

Besides these there were numerous others together with many fur posts and trading stations, and a few mining towns particularly in Colorado and Montana. About these forts, fur posts and mining camps was gathered a small number of people and these together with the freighters, trappers, traders and emigrants on the trail made up in the years 1865 to 1870 most of the white population of the central and northern plains.

Over almost the entire plains region roamed vast herds of buffalo, their flesh and skins furnishing food, clothing, and shelter for a sparse population of Indians representing several stocks and numerous tribes. The chief stock of Indians on the plains east of the Rocky Mountains was the Sioux including such tribes as the Ponca, Osage, Kaw, Ogalalla, Dakota and others. They occupied a considerable part of Dakota and extended into Montana, Wyoming and Nebraska. In Nebraska were also the Pawnee, belonging to the Caddoan stock, living in villages of round, turf covered houses, though they frequently wandered about from place to place. Other tribes of the plains were the Cheyenne and Arapaho, wild, savage horsemen who were frequently on the war path, the Crows, and various others. Kansas contained numerous Indian reservations that had been given to tribes from the East who had been pushed westward by the advance of white settlement. Below Kansas lay the great Indian Territory owned by the Five Civilized Tribes, though some small bands of Wichitas, Kiowas, and Comanches occupied lands in its western part.

The years immediately following the close of the Civil War

are marked by certain distinct and important movements upon the plains to the west of the frontier line. One of these was the gathering up of these wild tribes of Indians and the placing of them upon reservations in the Indian Territory and elsewhere. Another was the slaughter of the buffalo and the replacing of these animals with herds of cattle. About the same time came the building of the Pacific railways, and a comparatively rapid advance of the agricultural population westward.

These various movements were simultaneous and were somewhat dependent upon one another. The Indians could not be kept upon reservations so long as there was a plentiful supply of buffalo to be found, a potential source of food, clothing and shelter that constantly tempted them to leave their reservations and wander about hunting these animals. Nor could the ranchmen occupy the plains in any great safety with their herds as long as there were bands of Indians roaming about. Of course the building of the Pacific railways soon after the Civil War not only caused a rapid advance of the agricultural population but also furnished shipping facilities for buffalo hides, and so rendered the speedy destruction of the great herds inevitable.

All of these movements began immediately after the Civil War. Scarcely had that struggle closed before the government of the United States determined to make great changes in the Indian policy, due in part to the insistence of Kansas and other western states that had many Indians whom they wished to see removed. The Five Civilized Tribes of Indian Territory had all joined the Confederacy.[5] As a punishment for participation in the rebellion and in order that the new policies of the government might be carried out, they were forced in 1866, with the exception of the Cherokees, to cede the western half of the Indian Territory to the United States as a home for other friendly tribes.[6] The Cherokees ceded to the United States their Neutral Lands, a tract of 800,000 acres in Kansas; and agreed to allow the United States

[5] See Official Records of Rebellion, Fourth Series, Vol. I, pp. 426-527 and 636-687 for treaties of alliance between the Five Civilized Tribes and the Confederate government.

[6] 14 *Stats.*, pp. 755-799.

to locate friendly tribes on their Outlet, the title to the Outlet lands to remain with the Cherokees until such tribes were so located.[7]

In accordance with the provisions of the treaties of 1866 there were placed in the next few years upon reservations in western Indian Territory a large number of tribes mostly from Kansas or Nebraska or in some cases from the plains north and west of those states. In the Cherokee Outlet were located the Osage, Kaw, Ponca, Otoe and Missouri, a band of Nez Perces and the Pawnee.[8]

In the territory ceded by the Creek, Seminole, Choctaw and Chickasaw there were placed, besides the small bands of Wichita and other Indians already residing there, the Sac and Fox; Shawnee; Potawatomi; Kickapoo; Iowa; Kiowa; Comanche; Apache; Cheyenne; Arapaho; and broken fragments of other tribes as the Caddo, Keechi, Waco, Towaconi and some others.[9]

Reservations were set aside in Nebraska for the Niobrara, Winnebago and Omaha, while the large Wind River reservation was formed in Wyoming, and the Ute reservation in Colorado. Montana and Dakota had more and larger reservations than any of the other states or territories except the Indian Territory.[10] In the former were reservations known as the Blackfeet, Crow, Fort

[7] *Ibid.*

[8] Chief Joseph's band of Nez Perces were later permitted to return north. The Pawnee reservation lay partly in the Cherokee Outlet and partly in the western lands ceded by the Creeks.

[9] These Indians were located in Indian Territory as follows:

Osage and Kaw, 1872, 17 *Stats.*, p. 228.

Ponca, 1872, 17 *Stats.*, p. 228.

Pawnee, 1876, 19 *Stats.*, p. 28.

Otoe and Missouri, 1882, 21 *Stats.*, p. 380.

Sac and Fox, 1867, 15 *Stats.*, p. 495.

Kickapoo, Ex. Order 1883, Kappler, *Indian Laws and Treaties,* Vol. I, p. 844.

Iowa, Executive Order, 1883, *Ibid.*, p. 843.

Potawatomi, 1867, 15 *Stats.*, p. 591.

Cheyenne-Arapaho, 1869, Ex. Order, Kappler, *Indian Laws and Treaties,* Vol. I, p. 839.

Comanche-Kiowa and Apache, 1867, 15 *Stats.*, p. 581.

Tonkawa, formerly Nez Perces reservation, 1884, 20 *Stats.*, p. 63.

The Wichita were given their lands by an unratified agreement in 1872, but had been living in that region for a century of more.

[10] See map on page 29.

PRINCIPAL TRAILS, FRONTIER TOWNS, AND MILITARY POSTS
SOON AFTER THE CLOSE OF THE CIVIL WAR
(GREAT PLAINS AREA)

THE RANGE CATTLE INDUSTRY

Belknap, Fort Peck, and Northern Cheyenne, while in Dakota were the Fort Berthold, Standing Rock, Cheyenne River, Pine Ridge, Rosebud, Lower Brule, Crow Creek, Lake Traverse, and Yankton.

During the fifteen years following the Civil War there was considerable shifting of the Indian population of the plains area and generalizations are difficult. In 1869 the new policies of the Grant administration with respect to Indians were inaugurated. Heretofore the superintendency system had been the rule. Each superintendent had from two to ten agencies under his charge, the agent reporting to the superintendent who in turn reported to the commissioner of Indian affairs.[11] Under the new policy the superintendencies were abolished and the agents made their reports directly to the commissioner at Washington. Also a board of ten men was provided for known as the Board of Indian Commissioners. These were to serve without pay and to co-operate with and advise the Indian office in matters of policy and administration. Finally, various church organizations were asked to recommend men for appointment as Indian agents.[12]

By 1880 these policies were in full operation, the hostilities among the Plains Indians had ceased and most tribes were permanently located upon reservations. At this time within the area under consideration there were outside of Indian Territory, that is Colorado, Dakota, Kansas, Nebraska, Montana and Wyoming, twenty-three Indian agencies with reservations containing a total area of 125,835 square miles on which lived an Indian population of 58,401.[13] These reservations and Indian population were by 1880 distributed as follows:

RESERVATION		INDIAN POPULATION
Colorado	2	2,530
Kansas	1	684
Nebraska	4	4,306

[11] 11th Census, Indians, p. 63.
[12] 11th Census, Indians, p. 63.
[13] Report of Commissioner of Indian Affairs, 1880, pp. IV, and 228-237.

[24]

Wyoming	1	2,063
Dakota	10	27,168
Montana	5	21,650

Indian Territory, to which had been brought numerous plains tribes had, outside the territory of the Five Civilized Tribes, an area of about 35,000 square miles and an Indian population estimated at 17,398, while the Five Civilized Tribes also occupied an area of about 35,000 square miles and had a population of 59,187.[14]

It will be seen that the Indians of the Great Plains region north of Indian Territory occupied reservations whose aggregate area was only a little less than the combined areas of New York, Pennsylvania and Ohio.[15]

The Indians had been placed upon these reservations in the decade following the Civil War with much difficulty and bloodshed. In the summer of 1868 the Cheyenne were raiding in western Kansas and during the fall and winter following, General Custer conducted a campaign against them and fought the battle of the Washita in the western part of Indian Territory. The Kiowas, Sioux and Northern Cheyennes also caused much trouble during the years following the Civil War. Custer's command was wiped out at the battle of the Big Horn in 1874, while the Fetterman Massacre and numerous other encounters gave eloquent testimony as to the ability of the Plains Indian as a warrior. However, by about 1880 most hostilities had ended and the Indian had become somewhat resigned to his life on the reservation.

The chief factor in making it possible to place the Indian upon a reservation and keep him there was the slaughter of the buffalo. At the close of the war these animals ranged by hundreds of thousands over almost the entire plains region from Mexico to the Canadian border, and even beyond.

14 *Ibid.*, p. IV.

15 New York has 47,654 square miles, Pennsylvania 44,832, and Ohio 40,740, a total of 133,226 square miles as compared with 125,835 as the total aggregate of all Indian reservations in Montana, Dakota, Nebraska, Kansas, Wyoming and Colorado in 1880.

The end of the war brought to the West many adventurous young men eager for any enterprise that promised profit and adventure. Some of these engaged in scouting for the United States government, others in freighting or the Indian trade, and not a few began the pursuit of buffalo hunting.

There had been systematic buffalo hunting for profit on a considerable scale by white hunters ever since about 1820 or probably even before, and many animals had been killed for their flesh and hides by frontier settlers, travelers, and emigrants across the plains.[16] Soon after the Civil War however began the systematic slaughter that within a comparatively few years was to result in the virtual extermination of this animal.

The profits of the business were for some years very great, as the number of animals was enormous. In 1870 it is estimated that there were in the United States about four million buffalo south of the Platte River and about one and a half million north of it.[17] Robes and hides were usually in great demand and sold on the range at prices ranging from sixty-five cents to ten dollars depending upon the time taken and the locality of the market.[18]

The gold rush to California and later the building of the Union Pacific Railway served to divide the buffalo of the plains into two great herds. The center of range for the southern herd was not far from the site of Garden City, Kansas, from which they ranged north to Wyoming and south into Texas. The northern herd though much smaller was spread over larger area, and in consequence lasted several years longer than did the southern herd.

The slaughter of the buffalo was hastened by the advance of the railways. In 1865 the Union Pacific began construction west from Omaha. By November, 1867, it had reached Cheyenne and in 1869 the line was opened for traffic over its entire length.[19] By 1867 the southern branch of the Union Pacific, later known as the

16 Hornaday, *Extermination of the American Bison,* pp. 436-437, and 489-490.
17 *Ibid.,* p. 504.
18 *Ibid.,* p. 444.
19 *Ibid.,* p. 492.

Kansas Pacific, had been built west as far as Salina, and was soon extended across Kansas. By 1872 the Atchison, Topeka and Santa Fe had been built southwest from Atchison to Dodge City, and branch lines extending to Wichita and other points cut the southern buffalo range to pieces. These roads furnished an easy ingress to hunters as well as excellent shipping facilities, with the result that the rush of hunters to the plains was second only to the rush to the California gold fields some twenty years before.[20] The frontier towns of Dodge City, Wichita, Leavenworth and many others did an enormous business in furnishing guns, ammunition and supplies to hunters. Cordons of camps were established by the buffalo hunters along the Arkansas, South Platte, Republican and Smoky Hill rivers and other streams, and the animals were shot down by thousands as they came to drink.[21] From 1871 to 1875 the slaughter was enormous. By this time the great southern herd was about gone. Those left fled south to the plains of Texas, but the hunters and Indians followed them. By 1880 they were virtually gone and buffalo hunting ceased in the Southwest.[22]

The hunters quickly turned their attention to the northern herd already much depleted by Indians and white hunters. The great slaughter in the North did not begin however until about 1880. The Northern Pacific Railway had reached Bismarck, Dakota, in 1876 which had remained the terminus until 1880. It furnished transportation for hides and robes which before its construction had been mostly sent down the Missouri River by boat. By 1882 it was estimated that there were five thousand hunters and skinners on the northern plains, and by 1884 the animals had virtually all been killed and buffalo hunting as a business came to an end forever.[23]

During the few years of its existence the business was a very

20 *Ibid.*, p. 493.
21 *Ibid.*
22 *Ibid.*, p. 502. The disappearance of the buffalo can be traced through the reports of the agents for the Indian tribes of western Indian Territory. In 1876 the Indians of the Kiowa-Comanche agency sold to traders buffalo robes to the amount of $70,400. In 1877, $64,500, in 1878 the amount was $26,375, and in 1879 the amount was $5,068. *Report of the Commissioner of Indian Affairs*, 1879, p. 65.
23 Hornaday, p. 513.

considerable one. From 1872 to 1874 inclusive the Atchison, Topeka and Santa Fe Railway carried 459,453 buffalo hides and robes over its lines penetrating the southwestern plains, and it is estimated that other railways carried twice as many more or a total of 1,378,359 in three years.[24] From 1876 to 1884 a single firm in New York, J. and A. Boskowitz, purchased 246,175 hides and robes for which they paid $924,790.[25] When it is considered that there were many firms handling buffalo hides and robes it is obvious that the business was one of very considerable proportions, and it is also certain that in addition to the buffalo slaughtered for their hides an enormous number of animals had been killed wantonly for mere sport.

Criminally wasteful as was the destruction of the buffalo the rapid disappearance of these animals from the plains rendered much less difficult the carrying out of the new policies of the United States government with respect to keeping the Indians upon definite reservations. The buffalo was for the Plains Indian the chief source of food, clothing and shelter. So long as there was an abundance of these animals he was comparatively independent and could roam about at will or take the war trail at any time which might suit his fancy. Quite naturally he at first refused to remain regularly upon the reservation assigned to him, but instead wandered away buffalo hunting. The United States government sought to discourage this as much as possible by beginning at once to issue to reservation Indians regular rations of beef, flour, and other food as well as quantities of blankets, clothing and dry goods.

It was at first difficult to change the habits formed through many generations. Even after buffalo were growing scarce and a long journey was necessary in order to reach their feeding grounds, hunting parties of Indians would be forced two or three times a year to travel westward in search of them. These hunting trips were frequently turned into raiding expeditions in which horses were stolen and people murdered. As a result the Indian

24 *Ibid.*, p. 479.
25 *Ibid.*, p. 439.

INDIAN RESERVATIONS
1885

QUINAIELT
COLUMBIA
COLVILLE
WASHINGTON
DOEUR D'ALENE
JOCKO
YAKIMA
UMATILLA
SILETZ
GRAND RONDE
LAP WAI
WARM SPRING
OREGON
IDAHO
LEMHI
KLAMATH
FORT HALL
HOOPA VALLEY
DUCK VALLEY
ROUND VALLEY
NEVADA
PYRAMID LAKE
WALKER RIVER
UINTAH
UNCOMPAGHRE
UTAH
CALIFORNIA
TULE RIVER
HUALPAI
MOQUI
ARIZONA
MISSION INDIAN RES
COLORADO RIVER
SALT RIVER
GILA RIVER
YUMA
WHITE MOUNTAIN
PAPAGO
UTE
NAVAJO
ZUNI
INDIAN PUEBLO GRANTS
NEW MEXICO
MESCALERO APACHE
GROS VENTRE, PIEGAN, BLOOD, BLACKFEET AND RIVER CROW
MONTANA
CROW
NORTH CHEYENNE
FORT BERTHOLD
WIND RIVER
WYOMING
TURTLE MOUNTAIN
DEVILS LAKE
RED LAKE
BOIS FORTE
WINNIBIGOSHISH
WHITE EARTH
LEECH LAKE
FOND DU LAC
MINNESOTA
SIOUX
LAKE TRAVERSE
DAKOTA
OLD WINNEBAGO
CROW CREEK
YANKTON
PONCA
NIOBRARA
WINNEBAGO
OMAHA
IOWA
NEBRASKA
COLORADO
POTTAWATOMIE
KANSAS
PUBLIC LAND
INDIAN TERRITORY
TEXAS

agents soon established the custom of allowing the Indians to go only after a definite permit had been issued, and of sending a white man with them to restrain any inclination toward raiding and horse stealing.[26]

As the buffalo became increasingly scarce the Indians became more and more dependent upon the government rations of beef and flour, which in consequence had to be increased. The money hitherto spent in costly military expeditions to put down hostilities was now expended for more rations and annuity goods, and the Indian gradually accepted the inevitable and settled upon his reservation to live upon the supplies issued to him, supplies which the agent took care to inform him would be stopped at once if he left the reservation or engaged in any outbreaks against the whites.

Within a little more than ten years after the close of the Civil War the Indians had been largely reduced to submission and confined to their reservations while the buffalo were in a fair way toward extinction. Without these animals to consume it, the grass on the plains and in the rich meadows of the river valleys was growing up rank and luxuriant, affording a pleasing prospect to anyone who might wish to pasture herds of cattle. Also the railroads had by this time penetrated the plains area, rendering many parts of it much more accessible than it had been but a few years before. Finally, there was by this time a great stream of Texas cattle flowing northward over the trail and that state was reputed to have millions more that could be bought at very low prices.

It is not surprising, therefore, that many men who had come to the plains to engage in freighting, hunting, or railway construction work should now begin to think of establishing themselves on these rich pasture lands for the purpose of raising cattle. Within a few years after the close of the war the business was well started, a business destined to grow within fifteen years to such colossal proportions as to have an enormous and far reaching influence upon the United States as a whole. However, before taking up ranching on the central and northern plains it will be neces-

[26] *Report of Commissioner of Indian Affairs,* 1877, p. 82.

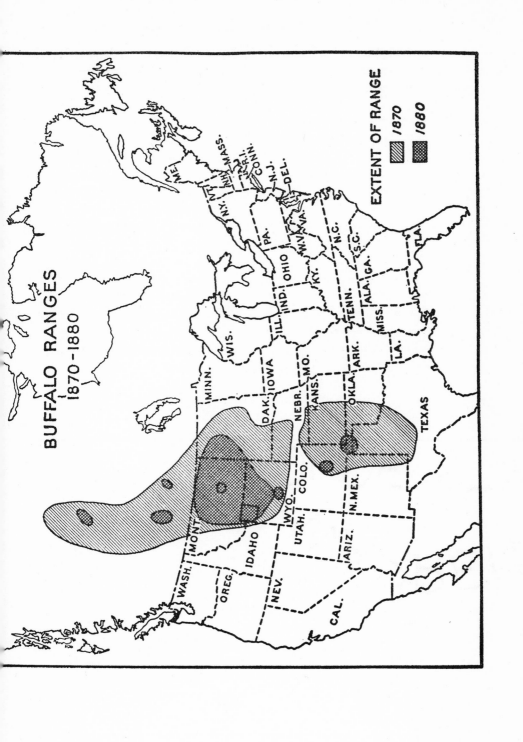

BUFFALO RANGES
1870-1880

EXTENT OF RANGE

1870

1880

sary to direct our attention to the Texas cattle trade since it was from that state that most of the animals were brought for the stocking of the northern ranges.

3.

THE NORTHERN DRIVE

The Civil War closed too late and the conditions of the country were too unsettled for any serious attempt to be made to market Texas cattle during the summer of 1865. However, the Texas stock raisers were keenly alive to the possibilities offered by the high prices of cattle and beef in the North, and during the winter of 1865–6 large herds were collected preparatory to driving north as soon as grass should be sufficiently advanced to make a start possible.

Not only did the Texans realize that large profits might be made by a trade in Texas cattle, but a number of men in the North, particularly in Iowa and Illinois and other portions of the corn belt, determined to engage in driving cattle from Texas to these states. During the late winter of 1865–6 several of these men came to Texas and purchased herds of beeves and stock cattle to drive northward.[1]

The usual procedure in such cases was to journey from St. Louis down the Mississippi River by steamer to New Orleans from which city a ship was taken to Galveston. Landing at Galveston, the cattle buyer proceeded northward to the interior and bought a herd somewhere in the neighborhood of Austin or San Antonio. A trail outfit was then purchased including wagons, mules, horses, and equipment. A number of men were hired and the drive northward began as soon as spring was sufficiently advanced to make it practicable.[2]

[1] See George C. Duffield's Diary in *Annals of Iowa*, Vol. XIV, No. 4, pp. 243-262 for an account of one of these drives.
[2] Duffield's Diary, *op. cit.*, pp. 246-250.

The start was usually made late in March or early in April. Naturally the bulk of the drive was by Texans seeking market with their herds though there was also a considerable number of these northern men who had purchased herds for speculative purposes or to stock their lands in the corn belt. Just how many cattle were started north in the spring of 1866 is, of course, uncertain, but estimates made a few years later by men who had made a careful study of the subject, give the number as 260,000 head.[3]

Largely speaking, the drive this year was disastrous in the extreme. The route generally pursued was north from central Texas passing just west of Fort Worth and traversing the strip of prairie lying between the upper and lower "cross timbers," past Pilot Point, Denton and Sherman to Red River. Across Indian Territory the route was north past Boggy Depot, thence northeast across the two Canadians and on past Fort Gibson to Baxter Springs.[4]

Virtually all of the northern men and many of the Texans were inexperienced in driving cattle long distances on the trail. The line of travel led through a region entirely unfamiliar to most of them, and one in which frequent rough and wooded areas made the driving of large numbers of cattle very difficult. The war had but recently closed and conditions within the Indian Territory and along its border were lawless and unsettled. As a result the entire drive from central Texas to the Kansas or Missouri border was, for many men, a seemingly endless succession of troubles and delays. The earlier part of the season was rainy. Mud, swollen rivers, stampedes, lack of provisions, and dissatisfied men who quit work at the time when they were most needed are but a few of the troubles complained of before crossing Red River.[5] Once beyond that stream there was added to all of these difficulties much annoyance from the Indians, who stampeded the cattle in order to collect money for gathering them again, demanded payment for the grass consumed by the herds in passing over their

---

3 McCoy, p. 23, or Nimmo, *Range and Ranch Cattle Traffic of the U. S.*, p. 28.
4 Duffield's Diary, *op. cit.*
5 *Ibid.*, pp. 250-252.

lands, and generally proved themselves a constant source of worry and vexation.[6] White thieves and outlaws, as well as pilfering Indians, also caused much trouble by stealing horses, mules, and cattle, thus rendering it necessary for the drovers to watch their property closely at all times.[7]

When they reached the Kansas and Missouri border below Baxter Springs, the trail drivers encountered fresh difficulties. The settlers of southwestern Missouri and southeastern Kansas had by no means forgotten their heavy losses from Texas fever during the years preceding the war, and were fully determined not to risk any repetition of such disasters. Armed bands of farmers were quickly formed to stop the herds of Texas cattle at the border, and to warn the drovers that they would not be permitted to proceed farther until cold weather.[8]

Some of the drivers were assaulted and beaten or even killed by these men. Others who insisted upon proceeding had their cattle stampeded or shot down and killed.[9] Some turned back into the Indian Territory to await the coming of cold weather, but prairie fires destroyed much of the grass and it was found very difficult to hold the cattle so long in the Indian country. Discouraged by the hardships and difficulties, not a few men abandoned their herds or sold them for anything that might be offered, and rode back to Texas. Still others turned west through the Cherokee country and after driving in that direction until they had passed the western limits of settlement in Kansas, again turned north across Kansas and a corner of Nebraska to Iowa or, in some cases,

[6] Duffield's Diary, *op. cit.,* pp. 253-257.

[7] *Ibid.,* pp. 256-257.

[8] Biographic Sketch of Joseph G. McCoy, *Kansas Magazine,* Dec. 1909, pp. 48-49, or *Second Annual Report of Missouri State Board of Agriculture,* p. 20.

[9] J. T. Botkin in Topeka *Daily Capitol,* Feb. 6, 1915. This gives an account of the slaughter of a small herd of Texas cattle by Kansas farmers. See also *Prairie Farmer,* Aug. 25, 1866 for a statement that cattle from Texas have been killed in Kansas and Missouri as a protection to the native animals. The writer states that if drovers persist in advancing after they have received warning, killing his cattle is the only alternative. He states that a man driving Texas cattle north in warm weather is considered by the border settlers of Kansas and Missouri as no better than a horse thief.

to St. Joseph from which point the cattle were shipped to Chicago.[10]

Apparently a few of these men met with some success, but in most cases the losses on the trail had been so heavy as to leave only a fraction of the number of animals with which they had started from Texas, and even these were so poor and thin from the long and arduous journey as to be of little value, in most cases not selling for enough to pay the expenses of the drive and the freight charges to the point at which they were at last sold.[11] Of the 260,-000 head of cattle driven north from Texas in 1866 very few reached a profitable market.

There can be little doubt that many of the difficulties of the drovers in 1866 were due to lack of experience, yet even at the best taking a herd up the trail was a most difficult undertaking.

The discouraging experiences of the year before prevented any considerable drive in 1867. Many men, however, turned their attention to an attempt to reach market by way of the Mississippi River. Even in 1866 a number of herds were driven to Red River, shipped down that stream by steamer to the Mississippi, and up the Mississippi to Cairo. Here they were unloaded and sent by rail to various parts of Illinois, Iowa, and other states.

In 1867 this trade was resumed in an increased volume. The live stock growers of Texas had been accustomed before the war to send many cattle by steamer down Red River and the Mississippi to New Orleans, and so had had some experience in that kind of traffic. Naturally, after four years of war New Orleans afforded little market since the impoverished South was in no position to purchase large numbers of cattle. But it seemed at first quite practicable to drive east over the old routes used before the war and ship by steamer up the Mississippi to the corn states. In this way the cattle raisers would avoid the hostile population of southeastern Kansas and southwestern Missouri. However, before many shipments had been made other difficulties presented themselves. The long journey by steamer and railway was not only

10 Duffield's Diary, *op. cit.,* pp. 257-259, or McCoy, p. 29.
11 McCoy, p. 23.

expensive, but the loss was heavy, and those cattle reaching their destination were frequently bruised, lame, or sick and nearly always poor and thin from the hardships of the journey.

Moreover, it was soon found that such cattle transmitted fever to a much greater extent than did those animals that had spent some months on the trail. Texas fever broke out in several places in Kentucky to which southern cattle had been brought in the summer of 1866. It also appeared in Grundy and Perry counties, Illinois, and in several other places.[12] The cause of the disease was unknown except that it was brought by Texas cattle and many absurd theories were advanced as to the manner in which it was transmitted from southern native animals.[13]

By 1867 fever was causing great loss in parts of Illinois, and by 1868 it was said that the disease was "rapidly becoming a public calamity."[14] During several weeks of that summer, Texas cattle were coming into Illinois mostly by way of Red River and the Mississippi, at the rate of fifty carloads a day and the disease spread rapidly.[15]

The business of grazing and feeding Texas cattle centered about Tolono where thousands of head were delivered in the summer of 1868.[16] In the spring of that year a firm of Chicago cattle buyers had gone to Texas and contracted for 40,000 head to be delivered at the mouth of Red River. These were shipped to Cairo and mostly sent by rail to Tolono and grazed with native cattle. A frightful epidemic was the result.[17] Public opinion was aroused and the farmers of Illinois organized in some localities, and refused to allow any more Texas cattle to be unloaded from the cars, or gathered up those that had been recently brought in and forced the owners and railways to take them away at once.[18] By 1869 great and widespread indignation prevailed in Illinois

[12] *Monthly Reports of the Commissioner of Agriculture,* 1867, p. 140.
[13] See *Second Annual Report of Missouri State Board of Agriculture,* pp. 16-18, or *Prairie Farmer,* Aug. 15, 1868, for some of these theories.
[14] *Country Gentleman,* Aug. 20, 1868, p. 124.
[15] *Ibid.,* July 2, 1868, p. 13.
[16] *Ibid.,* Aug. 13, 1868.
[17] McCoy, p. 149.
[18] *Country Gentleman,* Vol. XXXIII, p. 94.

against dealers in Texas cattle, and the trade by way of Red River and the Mississippi was virtually broken up.[19]

In the meantime, a great impetus had been given to driving herds up the trail. In 1867 the southern branch of the Union Pacific Railway, later called the Kansas Pacific, was building westward from Kansas City up the valley of the Kaw River. Joseph G. McCoy, a prominent cattle dealer of Springfield, Illinois, had become much interested in the Texas cattle trade. McCoy was the youngest of three brothers who had been engaged for some years in buying and shipping cattle. They did an enormous business and were men of wealth and influence in the community in which they lived.[20]

In 1867 McCoy came to Kansas City and made a trip up the Kansas Pacific Railway, the western terminus of which was at this time Salina. Keenly alive to the possibilities of the Texas cattle trade, McCoy had determined either to establish a cattle depot and shipping point on the Mississippi from which cattle might be sent north by steamer, or to locate such an establishment on the railway far to the west of all agricultural settlement. To this, cattle might be driven from Texas without interfering in any way with the agricultural population of Kansas farther east.[21]

The visit to the plains of Kansas convinced him that the latter plan was best. He chose as the site of his shipping point the little town of Abilene in Dickinson County, a mere village consisting of a dozen rude huts.[22] Having made a contract with the railways for favorable freight rates and an arrangement whereby he should have a percentage of the freight charges on all cattle shipped from Abilene, McCoy built shipping pens to accommodate three thousand head of cattle, a hotel, barns and livery stables. The region about was entirely unsettled and was well supplied with grass

19 McCoy, p. 149.

20 Historical and Biographical Sketch of Joseph C. McCoy, *Kansas Magazine*, Dec. 1909, pp. 48-49.

21 Harger, "Cattle Trails of the Prairies," *Scribner's Magazine*, June 1892, p. 732, or McCoy, pp. 40-41.

22 McCoy, p. 44.

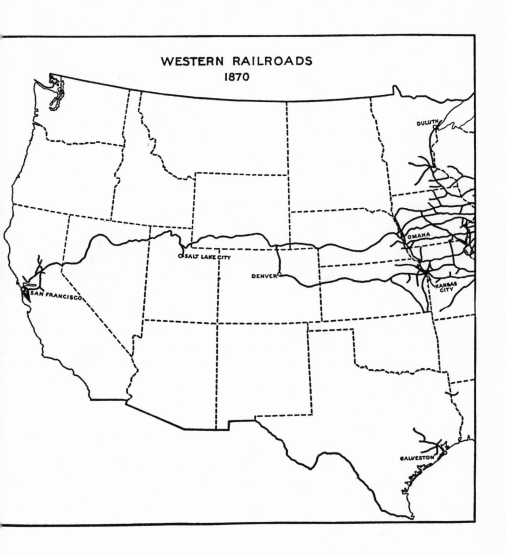

WESTERN RAILROADS
1870

and water. As soon as work was started on these various buildings a rider was sent south with instructions to seek as far as possible all herds on the trail in southern Kansas or the Indian Territory, and to tell the drovers of the shipping facilities prepared at Abilene. The man chosen for this mission was W. W. Sugg, an Illinois man by birth who had had much experience in the West and had driven a herd of cattle north from Texas in 1866.[23]

Sugg started south in July which was too late to increase the drive from Texas that season. Still, several herds were picked up on the trail with the result that about thirty-five thousand head of Texas cattle were shipped from Abilene that season.[24]

McCoy was a man of energy and business ability. Late in the summer of 1867 he arranged for an excursion of Illinois feeders and cattle dealers to Abilene, and a large number came out to see the beginning of the shipment of Texas cattle from that point.[25] News that the cattle shipped from Abilene had yielded their owners handsome profits quickly reached Texas and the spring of 1868 saw the drive more than doubled. Yet the trying experiences of 1866 were hard to forget and it was not until 1869 that the northern drive really reached great proportions.

The advantages of McCoy's plan of reaching market were soon manifest. The route followed was far to the west of the old trail to Baxter Springs, and so avoided the wooded and mountainous areas of the eastern part of Indian Territory, and the settlements of the Five Civilized Tribes. The rivers were crossed at points far above the crossing on the old trail and so proved a less difficult problem. Finally, the plains of Kansas were traversed to the west of all settlements and so the drovers no longer met interference from the farming population of that state.

True the drive was still an arduous one. Water was sometimes scarce while the plains tribes of western Oklahoma were frequently a source of considerable annoyance, often demanding beef for

23 *Ibid.,* pp. 122-123.
24 *Ibid.,* pp. 50-51.
25 *Ibid.,* p. 52.

the privilege of driving across their lands and stampeding the herds if they were refused. However, their reservations were so large and the Indians so few in number that serious trouble could usually be avoided. In any case the difficulties were much less than they had been when the drives were made over the rough and wooded country of the Five Civilized Tribes, where herds had been subject to interference from these Indians and had been almost certain to be stopped at the border of Kansas or Missouri and forced to await the coming of cold weather.

As the years went by the drive increased in volume. Abilene was for only a short time the chief shipping point. McCoy advertised the town very extensively. Two men were sent to Texas to travel over that state, meet the cattlemen and tell them of the advantages of Abilene as a shipping point. Many circulars were also distributed throughout Texas and newspapers all over the state reprinted these. McCoy also spent several thousand dollars in advertising in the northern papers, urging cattle dealers in need of stockers and feeders to come to Abilene for such animals.[26] The summer of 1868 saw many cattle buyers gathered at this point. They came not only from the states of the corn belt, but there were some from Colorado, Montana, and Utah as well as a number of Indian beef contractors seeking to buy herds with which to fill their contracts with the United States government for feeding the Indians of the western and northern reservations.[27] However, in 1868 McCoy sold his interests in the town of Abilene to a group of men from Mendota, Illinois.[28]

By this time a few settlers were coming into this region and by 1871 Abilene had lost its position as chief shipping point for Texas cattle, and the trade had shifted farther west. In the spring of 1871 the Atchison, Topeka and Santa Fe Railway was com-

[26] *Ibid.*, p. 115. McCoy captured some buffalo and sent them east to Chicago via St. Louis with great placards on the cars advertising Abilene. In 1868 an auction sale of herds of Texas cattle was held at Abilene which was well attended by buyers from many states. McCoy, pp. 179-180.

[27] *Ibid.*, p. 124.

[28] *Ibid.*, pp. 229-231.

[41]

pleted far enough west to enter into active competition with the Kansas Pacific. Newton, on this line of railway about sixty-five miles southwest of Abilene, became a great shipping point as did also Wichita and various other towns, but the greatest of all was Dodge City, founded in 1872 on the Santa Fe Railway not far from the one hundredth meridian, and about fifty miles north of the southern boundary of Kansas.[29] The central branch of the Union Pacific also sought to attract part of this trade to its stations in Nebraska west of Omaha, and Ogalalla became an important market and shipping point.

These points of marketing and shipping cattle were known as "cow towns." Far out on the plains to the west of all agricultural settlement, they soon became notorious because of the rough and lawless element that flocked to them. Each became for a time a rendezvous for gamblers, saloon keepers and the riff-raff of the underworld. Owing to the fact that agriculture was at first not profitable in this region these towns came to present a curious reversal of ordinary frontier conditions. Out upon the plains beyond the edge of settlement would be found these wild, busy, little cities where money was plentiful and business profitable. However, once agricultural settlement had crept up and engulfed them, they were immediately deserted by most of the population. Business stagnated and grass grew in the streets, while farther west sprang up a group of new "cow towns" as busy, as prosperous and as wicked at the first ones had been.[30]

Just how many cattle were driven up the trail to Kansas each year during the period following the Civil War no one can say with any degree of accuracy. However, the following table made in 1885 from careful estimates may serve to give some idea of the volume of the drive during the fifteen years following the Civil War, or up to the time when the range cattle industry reached its height.

[29] See Wright, *Dodge City, the Cowboy Capital,* for an account of this town and its importance in the cattle trade.

[30] For ten years Dodge City was the greatest market for trail driven cattle in the world.

1866	260,000	1876	321,998
1867	35,000	1877	201,159
1868	75,000	1878	265,646
1869	350,000	1879	257,927
1870	300,000	1880	394,784
1871	600,000	1881	250,000
1872	350,000	1882	250,000
1873	405,000	1883	267,000
1874	166,000	1884	300,000
1875	151,618	1885	220,000 (estimate)[31]

The numbers given are but rough approximations and most drovers who took part in the movement of cattle northward during these years insist that they are far too low. Colonel Ike T. Pryor of San Antonio estimates that the average annual drive northward from Texas from 1870 to 1890 was half a million head.[32] Manuscript records show that from June 9 to July 20, 1880, there crossed the Arkansas River at Trail City fifty-seven herds aggregating 126,951 head.[33] When we consider that this was but a single trail and that the period is only forty-two days, we get some idea of the magnitude of the drive, and this at a time when it had clearly begun to decline.

The fat, mature animals from this great stream of Texas cattle were usually shipped from the "cow towns" to Chicago or Kansas City for slaughter, while many young steers were shipped to the corn states of Iowa, Illinois, and Missouri as stockers and feeders. The experience of Illinois cattle dealers with Texas cattle brought up the Mississippi by steamer served to discourage importations from Kansas, but a law was passed by the Illinois legislature that cattle that had been wintered in Kansas might be admitted without inspection. Proof of wintering was to be a certificate sworn to before a notary public.[34] Certificates that cattle had been wintered

31 The figures 1866 to 1884 are from Nimmo, p. 28.
32 Manuscript Statement of Ike T. Pryor, p. 1.
33 Manuscript records of C. H. Marselus, Inspector of Trail Herds at Trail City, 1886.
34 McCoy, pp. 188-190.

in Kansas were easily obtainable and Illinois buyers made large purchases in Abilene and the other cow towns.[35]

However, as the years went by the larger part of the cattle driven from Texas to Kansas were sold for the purpose of stocking the northern ranges. As the buffalo were killed and the Indians confined upon reservations the northern plains became increasingly attractive for ranching. It was soon found that not only would cattle live the year around upon the open ranges of Wyoming, Dakota, Montana and the other western territories, but that they grew larger and fatter there than did cattle in Texas.[36]

There is an old story that a government freighter, caught in a heavy snowstorm on the Laramie Plains about the time of the close of the Civil War, abandoned his work oxen to die of cold and hunger, but the following spring found them grazing on the plains fat and sleek despite the fact that the winter had been a very severe one. This incident may well have taken place, but the story that this was the way in which it was discovered that cattle would live throughout the winter in these regions without feed may be dismissed as a pleasing bit of fiction.

As a matter of fact many men had wintered cattle upon the northern ranges long before the Civil War,[37] and it was well known that cattle would thrive throughout the year in any region that had supported herds of buffalo.[38] Freighters, trappers and army officers had wintered cattle on these ranges between 1850 and 1860 and possibly before the first date.[39] Alexander Majors had wintered 15,000 heavy work oxen on the plains of the North in the winters of 1857 and 1858, and stated that cattle frequently gained in weight during the winter, and were fat enough for beef in the early spring.[40]

[35] *Ibid.*

[36] Statement of George B. Loving, Nimmo, *Range and Ranch Cattle Traffic,* p. 106, Mr. Loving states that a Texas steer removed to Nebraska when one or two years old would weigh when four years old 1,100 to 1,300 pounds, while the same steer if matured in eastern or southern Texas would not weigh at four years of age more than 850 to 950 pounds. *Ibid.*

[37] Nimmo, p. 5.

[38] Whitfield to Manypenny.

[39] "The Pastoral Lands of America," *Report of Commissioner of Agriculture,* 1870, p. 303.

Even before the close of the Civil War there were some men with stocks of cattle on the northern plains. Iliff established a ranch in Colorado in 1862 and other men were holding cattle in the Northwest before the close of the war.[41]

The rush to the West that followed immediately after the conclusion of that great struggle was very great. Many men were quick to see the opportunities of profit to be found in buying young cattle and pasturing them upon the prairies of Kansas, Nebraska, Wyoming, Colorado, Dakota and Montana, and even farther west. A few animals were brought east from Oregon and Washington, but nearly all the cattle in this region were young Texas steers brought up the trail. The drive to Dodge City frequently became but the first part of a longer drive to ranges in these northwestern territories. The Texans themselves also saw the possibilities of the northern ranges as feeding grounds for their young steers and many of them established ranches there to supplement those ranges they held in the South.[42]

Besides the Texas cattle sold for slaughter at the packing centers, for feeders in the corn states, and for stocking the northern ranges, there was also a considerable sale to contractors who were supplying the reservation Indians with beef under contracts made with the government of the United States. In 1871 there were 265,-940 Indians on reservations in the United States. All but 28,302 of these were west of the Mississippi, where they occupied reservations aggregating over ninety-seven million acres exclusive of the territory of the Five Civilized Tribes.[43] Most of these Indians were fed, in part at least, by the government of the United States and the amount of the beef issue had to be increased as the buffalo grew increasingly scarce due to the operations of the hide hunters. By 1879 the total quantity of beef furnished the western Indians

40 *Ibid.*

41 *Ibid.*

42 Reynolds of Fort Worth, or Dickey Bros. are examples of men with large numbers of cattle both in the North and South. See John Clay, *My Life on the Range*, p. 88.

43 *Report of Commissioner of Indian Affairs*, 1872, p. 416.

annually had risen to over forty-three million pounds, requiring some fifty or sixty thousand head of cattle.[44]

As the years went by and the northern drive grew in volume, the Texans learned by experience much regarding the easiest and most economical methods of handling cattle on the trail. Herds at first were of various sizes, but experience soon taught the drovers that about 2,500 was the most convenient number for a long drive. If the herd contained more than three thousand head it was likely to prove cumbersome and difficult to handle, while two thousand or less required almost as much expense for labor and equipment as did the larger number.[45] Of the fifty-seven herds previously mentioned as having crossed the Arkansas River from June 9 to July 20, 1886, the largest contained 3,300 head and the smallest 70 head, only five had less than 1,000 head, fifteen between 1,000 and 2,000, and five 3,000 head or more. The remaining 32 herds had from 2,000 to 3,000 each, with the average about 2,500.[46] Herds of four, five or even six thousand were occasionally driven, though usually with much trouble and difficulty, and there is one recorded instance of a great herd combined from the cattle of several ranches which numbered twenty-five thousand head. This vast herd was merely grazed northward at the rate of a few miles a day rather than actually driven on the trail as were the smaller ones. It was said at times to be five miles in width and, when fairly well strung out, extended a distance of nearly twenty miles from leaders to drags.[47]

A herd of two thousand five hundred head required about twelve men with four to six horses each, together with four mules and a "chuck wagon" to haul the food and bedding. These cattle would travel ten or fifteen miles a day or 300 to 500 miles a month and gain in flesh while on the trail if carefully handled. Five hundred dollars a month was a fair estimate of the expense of driving such a herd, or about fifteen hundred dollars for a drive of twelve

44 *Report of Commissioner of Indian Affairs,* 1879, pp. 272-273. Andy Adams, *The Outlet,* or *Wells Brothers* tell something of Indian contracts.
45 Manuscript statement of R. C. Tate, p. 1, or Ike T. Pryor, p. 1.
46 Manuscript Records of C. H. Marselus, Trail Inspector at Trail City, 1886.
47 R. C. Tate Manuscript Statement, p. 1.

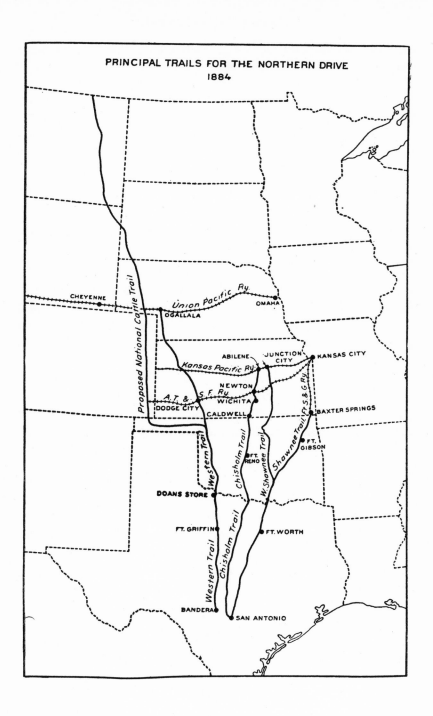

PRINCIPAL TRAILS FOR THE NORTHERN DRIVE
1884

to fifteen hundred miles.[48] An account book for a drive of 2,500 head made in 1892 from X I T Ranch in western Texas to Miles City, Montana, gives the expense of the drive as follows:[49]

Wages	$1,340.00
Chuck bill	386.27
Watering expenses	48.00
Other expenses	27.23
Total	$1,801.50

The loss on the trail in the drive was sixty head, twenty-three of which were frozen to death in a severe blizzard in eastern Colorado the latter part of May.[50] Not counting loss, or interest on the money invested in horses, wagon and equipment, the cost was about seventy-five cents a head for the trip. Other estimates indicate that cattle could be driven 1,200 to 1,500 miles at a total cost of sixty cents a head, or from one dollar to one dollar and twenty-five cents for every mile traveled with a herd of 2,500 head.[51]

Within two or three years after the drive was well under way certain clearly defined trails had been established. Perhaps the best known and longest used of these was the old western trail to Dodge City and Ogalalla, Nebraska. It started somewhere about Bandera, Texas, and ran north past Fort Griffin to Red River. Crossing that stream at Doan's store it passed through Greer County, a corner of the Kiowa-Comanche Indian reservation, the Cheyenne-Arapaho reservation, and through the Cherokee Outlet and on through Kansas to Dodge City, and past this to Ogalalla.[52]

East of this lay the Chisholm, or Chisum Trail, said to have

48 Manuscript Statement of Col. Ike T. Pryor, p. 1.
49 J. E. Moore's Diary and Log Book in Texas University Manuscript Collections.
50 *Ibid.*
51 The foreman kept an account with each man, noting down the date he began work and any money paid him in tobacco or other things purchased for him by the foreman. The bulk of the wages was not paid until the end of the journey. Colonel Ike T. Pryor, Manuscript Statement, p. 1.
52 See maps. Also see map in Nimmo.

Wild Buffalo Herd

After the Buffalo Hunt—Drying the Hides

From a photograph taken in 1870

been named for John Chisum, a Texas ranchman who made one of the earliest drives north. Chisum's first herd crossed Red River near the mouth of Mud Creek at the northwest corner of Cooke County, Texas. He followed that stream to its source, crossed the Washita at Elm Springs, and thence went due north to the Canadian. Crossing that stream, he followed the Kingfisher Creek valley to the Cimarron, and on to the Salt Fork of the Arkansas, crossing into Kansas near Caldwell. He crossed the Arkansas near Wichita, then drove northeast past the site of Newton and over the divide between the Arkansas and the Smoky Hill to Abilene.[53] This route became the famous Chisholm Trail. It is said to have been opened in 1866, and so was perhaps the earliest trail except the one leading to Baxter Springs.[54] The Chisholm Trail gave off a western shoot at Elm Springs which ran northwest and connected with the western trail. Farther east was the West Shawnee Trail leading to Junction City, and still beyond that was the old Shawnee Trail, the approximate route followed by the herds driven to Baxter Springs in 1866.

For some years much of the driving north was done by professional drovers who purchased herds of Texas cattle usually on six or eight months credit and drove them north to market. Later many Texas ranchmen drove their own herds or sent them up the trail under a competent trail boss.

The customary procedure was to gather the herd and pass the animals through a chute where each received the "road brand." Each cowboy furnished his own saddle and bedding, but horses were supplied by the owner of the cattle. The bedding, food, and camp equipment were loaded in the chuck wagon driven by the cook, while a "horse wrangler," often a boy, was employed to look after the band of horses usually called the "saddle band," "remuda," or "caballado." Cowboys were commonly paid twenty-five to forty dollars a month, and the cook about five dollars a month

[53] McArthur Manuscript, pp. 152-153.

[54] The Chisholm Trail has been the subject of much dispute both as to the origin of its name and as to its location. It may have been named Jesse Chisholm, the noted scout and guide. Its off shoots and cut offs have caused much confusion and disputation as to which was the real trail.

[49]

more, while the trail boss, who had full responsibility of the herd on the drive, would receive a monthly salary of about $125.[55]

The cattle were moved very slowly at first, in order to get them accustomed to travel on the trail, and were watched closely at night. After a few days or weeks, they could be pushed along a little more rapidly and two men at a time were usually sufficient for night duty. These usually stood guard in three shifts, the first until about eleven o'clock ,the second from eleven until two, and the third from two until daylight.[56]

It was most important to move slowly and carefully at first, or until the cattle were "road broken." Herds that became frightened and stampeded once or twice early in the drive did not recover from the experience for a long time. The cattle became "spoiled" and in the future would stampede upon the slightest provocation, and so give the drivers endless trouble.[57] When camp was broken early in the morning the herd was drifted slowly away from the bedding ground toward the north, grazing as it went for an hour or two. By this time it was well "strung out" on the trail and moved along at a good rate of speed until noon. In the meantime, the cook had driven on ahead to a place agreed upon, usually on some stream, where he had formed camp and prepared dinner. When the herd arrived the animals were thrown along the stream in loose herd or "at ease" for a couple of hours. When the drive was resumed the cook again pushed on ahead with the chuck wagon to establish camp at a point designated by the trail boss.[58] The movement of a herd of cattle on the trail is best shown by the diagram.

The post of honor was the "point" covered by two men who

55 See J. E. Moore's Diary.
56 J. B. Cranfill's *Chronicle*, p. 148.
57 Statement of J. H. Waters and others.
58 Of course, no definite position can well be assigned to foreman, wagon or remuda and wrangler. The foreman was any place where he was most needed and frequently left the herd altogether to ride ahead and observe the condition of grass and water, or to confer with the foremen of other herds. The remuda usually trailed along ahead of the herd or beside it, while the wagon starting behind the herd after breakfast was usually several miles ahead when the cook stopped and established camp in order to prepare dinner or supper.

were usually old and experienced hands and whose duty it was to direct the herd, to prevent a mixup with other herds, and to check instantly any tendency to run. In the rear was always a group of lazy, slow or lame cattle and this post of "bringing up the drag" was the most disagreeable of all since the riders here were exposed to the dust raised by the entire herd and frequently had their patience sorely tried by the slow or perverse animals that fell back to that position in the herd. Young and inexperienced men were often placed at drag.

At the end of the drive the men were paid, and usually returned to Texas with the wagon and a part or all of the remuda. In many cases the horses were also sold except one for each man who wished to ride back to Texas. Some drovers who also owned ranches in the North would send two or three men with a remuda of horses from the northern ranch to meet the herd halfway up the trail. The Texas horses would then be returned to the home ranch in the South.[59]

Besides the drive to Kansas and Nebraska and beyond, a considerable drive was begun soon after the war westward from Texas to New Mexico and then north to Colorado or in some cases on west to Arizona and California. Driving to California began before the Civil War,[60] but was checked by hostile Indians and resumed later.

Following the war the trail-breaker in this direction was Colonel Charles Goodnight, and the trail west to New Mexico and Colorado came to be called the "Goodnight Trail."[61]

The cattle were gathered near Fort Concho and driven up the Concho River to its source, thence southwest about ninety miles to Horsehead Crossing of the Pecos. The route then followed up the Pecos and crossed into New Mexico near Pope's Well. Here the trail divided, one branch going west along Delaware River and on past El Paso and across west to Arizona and California.

[59] J. E. Moore's Diary. Moore relates the experience of Reynolds Brothers of Fort Worth, whose northern horses met the trail herd at Bovina, Col.

[60] See Erskine, "Journal of a Trip to California," 1854, Texas University Manuscript Collection.

[61] McArthur Manuscript, pp. 155-156.

The other branch followed up the Pecos to about thirty-five degrees north latitude, thence across the divide to the Canadian River, up that stream and north into Colorado through the Trinchera Pass, or northwest across the Raton Mountains.[62]

The drive in this direction began about 1865 to supply beef to army posts and to the Navajo Indians or to miners and later for stocking these ranges.[63] It is estimated that this drive west annually amounted in volume to from twenty to twenty-five per cent as much as the drive north.[64] In 1874 the number passing west and northwest up the Pecos is estimated at 110,000 head.[65]

As the plains became stocked with cattle various complications arose with regard to trail driving. A state law of Texas was eventually passed requiring herds driven north to be inspected before they left the state in order that strays or cattle not belonging to the trail driver might be cut out and returned to their rightful owner.[66] Live stock associations were formed and these employed inspectors to remain at certain river crossings or other points of advantage on the trails to inspect herds bound northward and cut out all cattle belonging to members of the association.[67] Such cattle were returned to their owner or, if he was so far distant as to render this impracticable, were sold and the proceeds sent to him.[68]

The fear of Texas fever was always present among the settlers and stock raisers in Kansas, northern Texas and Indian Territory, and this frequently caused the trail drivers much difficulty. In 1884 Kansas enacted a law forbidding any Texas cattle to be brought into the state except between December 1 and March 1.[69]

62 10th Census. Vol. III, p. 990.

63 *Ibid.*, p. 989.

64 Statement of Col. Ike T. Pryor.

65 10th Census, Vol. III, p. 990.

66 J. B. Cranfill's *Chronicles*, p. 151.

67 Manuscript Proceedings of Southwestern Cattle Raisers' Association, 1877 to 1892, or Manuscript Statement of R. C. Tate.

68 *Ibid.*

69 Nimmo gives much discussion relative to this law, See pp. 32, 104, 105, and 132-133.

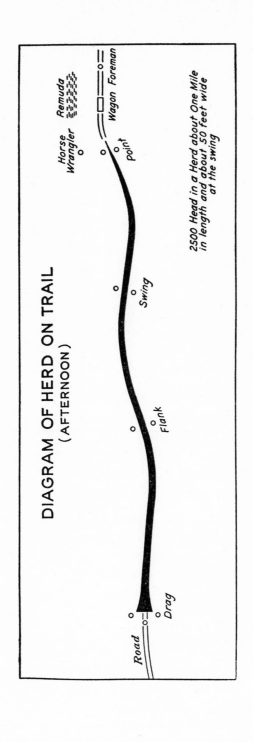

DIAGRAM OF HERD ON TRAIL
(AFTERNOON)

Horse Wrangler

Remuda

Wagon Foreman

Point

Swing

Flank

Drag

Road

2500 Head in a Herd about One Mile
in length and about 50 feet wide
at the swing

Since this prohibition covered the entire season of the drive the law was a terrible blow to the cattle drivers. The price of cattle in Texas immediately declined and the Texans protested bitterly against this legislation.

Out of this controversy grew the agitation for a national cattle trail extending from the northern boundary of Texas to the Canadian border. A bill was introduced in Congress by Representative James F. Miller of Texas, providing that such a trail, not to exceed six miles in width, be laid out by three commissioners to be appointed by the Secretary of the Interior for that purpose.[70] This trail was to have grazing grounds and quarantine grounds at various places, and at certain points there were to be crossings for native cattle. At these crossings the trail was to be only two hundred feet in width. All lands required for this trail and for quarantine and grazing grounds were to be withdrawn from settlement or sale for a period of ten years.[71]

The people of Texas were almost unanimous in their support of such a measure, but it was from the first doomed to failure. By this time the northern plains were well stocked with cattle. The settlers of Kansas feared Texas fever while the ranchmen of Wyoming, Dakota, and Montana, who were in most cases grazing cattle upon the public domain, feared that such a trail would bring in numerous Texas ranchmen who would occupy their ranges and over-stock the entire region.[72] As a result most people north of Texas opposed the measure. The northern ranchman wanted congress to enact legislation providing for the leasing of lands for grazing purposes over a long period of years. If the Texans would support this measure they would in turn support the national cattle trail.[73] This the Texas ranchmen, largely speaking, refused to do and both the plan for a cattle trail and for leases of the public domain came to nothing.

The quarantine act of Kansas in 1884 seriously checked the

[70] See Nimmo, pp. 27-31.
[71] Ibid.
[72] Statement of A. T. Babbit, Nimmo, pp. 35-36.
[73] Ibid.

northern drive. By this time the northern plains were well stocked and also some trunk lines of railway had been built south into Texas thereby furnishing opportunities to reach market by rail. There was much driving north after this date through Colorado, but the volume of the drive steadily decreased, and before 1900 had virtually ceased.

4.

RANCHING ON THE CENTRAL AND NORTHERN PLAINS TO 1880

As has been indicated the great stream of Texas cattle which flowed northward in the years following the Civil War brought about the rapid spread of the cattle industry over the central and northern plains. Simultaneously, as cattle raising began to show increased profits owing to the market for animals to stock these northern ranges, the ranchmen of Texas advanced westward upon the high plains of that state. Within a few years the range cattle industry had spread itself over a great region reaching from the Rio Grande to the Canadian border and from the edge of agricultural settlement on the east to the Rocky Mountains and far beyond. This was the so called "cow country" that was to play so important a part in the economic life of the entire country.

For convenience the range cattle area may be divided into two parts: the Southwest, including Texas, Indian Territory and a part of New Mexico and the central and northern plains including Kansas, Nebraska, Dakota, Montana, Wyoming and Colorado. The first was primarily a breeding ground producing hundreds of thousands of calves each year, while the second was, largely speaking, a feeding ground to which were brought young steers from the Southwest to be matured and fattened on the rich pasturage of these northern ranges.

Any such division is naturally more or less artificial and must be regarded as only general in its nature. Large numbers of cattle were matured and fattened in the Southwest and a considerable number of calves were raised on the northern plains, but, largely speaking, this classification of the two regions holds true, and became increasingly so as the business spread and grew in volume.[1]

The spread of the range cattle business over this enormous region was one of the most significant events in the economic history of the United States during the latter half of the nineteenth century and the influence of the "cow country" and the ranching industry upon the United States as a whole can hardly be over estimated.

It provided an outlet for the energies of many young men released from military service at the close of the Civil War, or of those who came to manhood in the decade following the close of that struggle. Also it furnished a field of investment for millions of dollars of eastern and foreign capital. From the broad ranges of the ranch cattle area were drawn animals to consume the surplus grain of the corn belt states as agriculture in that region advanced rapidly westward upon new prairie lands and grew in its volume of production due to the return of soldiers from the war and to the increased use of improved farm machinery. It caused in a large measure the great development of the packing industry and the resultant growth of the packing centers, provided cheap meat for the fast growing manufacturing cities of the East, and made possible a great export trade in cattle and dressed beef.

The range cattle business also affected American life in numerous other ways that were less obvious, but none the less important. Carried on largely either upon the public domain or upon Indian lands, it early attracted the attention of Congress and of certain executive departments of the federal government. However, its rapid rise had given governmental officials but scant time to become familiar with the details of an industry so technical in its nature as is ranching. As a result, legislation and departmental orders with respect to the range cattle business showed

[1] Many men in the North who started with cows and stock cattle soon began to replace these animals with young steers from Texas and within a few years had nothing but steers.

that the men responsible for such measures did not always have a clear conception of the ranchmen's problems and difficulties.

The cattlemen quickly realizing this and, moreover, finding themselves in many cases in a region remote from the protection of law and the courts, formed among themselves extra-legal organizations whose rules had for their members all the force of law. Such organizations were designed to facilitate the carrying on of the business and above all to protect each individual's cattle, valuable property that was scattered over a wide area and was by its nature peculiarly vulnerable to attack.[2] These institutions were economic in their nature and foreshadowed the future associational arrangements of "Big Business" that sought to act as corporate persons in accordance with frontier ideals. They were often closely associated with Territorial or State governments and their rules and regulations were in some cases translated into actual law by State or Territorial legislatures or at least made the basis of legislation.[3]

In addition to the rules of more or less local live stock associations, there gradually grew up in the range cattle area a body of precedents, customs, and principles, the whole forming a kind of unwritten law of the range known as "cow custom" which was in force and respected throughout the entire region.[4] Some of the principles of this unwritten law, as the rules of live stock associations, in time found their way into statutes, or at least influenced the lives and conduct of many people of the West even after cattle ranching had long since disappeared in their particular community. As the farming population moved westward the relations of settlers and ranchmen produced some interesting results. The ranchmen, even while seeking to discourage the advance of the

[2] A prominent Englishman, Baillie-Grohman, states the ranchman's position as follows: "In no business is a man so dependent upon his neighbors, so open to petty annoyances, and so helplessly exposed to vindictive injury to his property as in stock raising out West." Baillie-Grohman, *Camps in the Rockies*, p. 364.

[3] It was illegal in Wyoming at one time to brand cattle in advance of the regular spring round-up of the Wyoming Stock Growers' Association. Also the *Statutes of Texas* are filled with provisions respecting marks, brands, driving of cattle, etc. that are the results of the influence of stock associations.

[4] See testimony of Ben. S. Miller before Senate Investigating Committee, 1885.

homesteaders, were nevertheless in many respects the "advance agents" of crop raising. Unconsciously, and often unwillingly, they pointed the way to the men dependent upon cultivation of the soil for a livelihood. In the struggle that eventually took place in many areas between "range and grange," there was developed much of the antagonism later manifested by the western farmer toward the so called "money power" and wealthy corporations, and so were sown the seeds of populism that were later to yield so bountiful a harvest in some of the newer agricultural states of the West.

Finally the "cow country" furnished in time a wealth of material for the writer of fiction as well as themes for the artist and poet. Stories, pictures, and songs of the range region were produced in great abundance, and given a wide circulation serving to advertise the cattle business and in many cases to give an entirely false conception of the industry and the region in which it was carried on.

Apart from the influence of the range cattle industry upon the country at large, its history presents certain phases that are not without interest. Like most other forms of agriculture the business was characterized by ups and downs, by periods of prosperity and others of adversity, the reasons for which are not always easy to perceive.

Broadly speaking, the business started in a comparatively small way with small operators and grew with astonishing rapidity. It was soon seen that, under conditions then existing, efficiency and cheap production of beef could be best achieved by large scale operations. As a result many of the smaller ranchmen pooled their interests or sold out to large cattle companies, or in some cases by good luck and good management expanded a small business to large proportions. For a brief period the great cattle companies and individual ranchmen with large holdings were the rule. Then came heavy losses due to cold winters, over-stocking the range, and poor business management. Homesteaders came flocking west to take up much of the best land. Conditions in the range country began to change. Land values increased enormously and it became impossible longer to control large areas of the public domain. As conditions changed the cattle business changed also. Many of the large companies failed. Others went out of business voluntarily, breaking up their large holdings of land and selling them out in smaller tracts to men with a small number of cattle. Eventually the large operator came to be the exception rather than the rule, and that portion of the "cow country" still left largely for grazing was occupied again by comparatively small operators.

Unlike Texas, which was the cradle of the ranch cattle industry of the United States, the central and northern plains had almost no cattle until after the Civil War. It is true that in the settled regions of eastern Kansas and Nebraska there were often small herds of milch cows, and also along the western border of these settlements was to be found that narrow rim of stock raisers characteristic of the American frontier from very early times. In this particular region, however, the presence of wandering bands of Plains Indians but a short distance to the west rendered the possession of property in cattle hazardous since these Indians possessed numerous ponies and in consequence could move rapidly over a wide range of territory. Also the great herds of buffalo on the plains could be made to furnish beef and hides for the use of the frontier settlers, and so the possession of cattle except for use as milch cows was less important. After the discovery of gold in California there was always a considerable number of work oxen used on the plains either in the trains of the emigrants and gold seekers, or by professional freighters like Alexander Majors, who, as has been indicated, often wintered thousands of head of work oxen at some convenient spot on the plains. The Mormons, of course, took animals with them to Utah, while in 1857 General Johnston moved an army to Utah and wintered all the animals in sheltered valleys on the grass alone.[5]

Perhaps some of the forty-niners journeying across the plains

5 "The Pastoral Lands of America," *Report of Commissioner of Agriculture,* 1870, p. 303.

to California realized the possibilities of the region for grazing but there is little record of any attempt to establish ranches. In the late '50's, however, came the gold rush to the Pike's Peak region and some of these argonauts, disappointed in their effort at finding gold, turned their attention to cattle.

One of these who may be regarded as typical and who became very prominent was J. W. Iliff, later known as the Colorado and Wyoming "cattle king."[6] Iliff journeyed to Colorado with the gold seekers of 1859 and, failing to find gold, settled on a small tract of land near Denver and began raising vegetables for sale at the mining camps. Having accumulated a little money from his season's work, he removed farther north and established a little store near the site of the present city of Cheyenne on the trail leading to California and Oregon. Here he bartered with the emigrants passing along the trail for poor, lame, and footsore cattle, frequently securing such animals for a mere pittance. In this way he acquired a considerable herd which he pastured in this region in spite of Indian attacks and other difficulties. Eventually the Union Pacific Railway was pushed westward through this territory passing near Iliff's store and ranch, and he found a profitable market for cattle in supplying the railway construction camps with beef. Other animals were purchased from Texas after the drive from that state had begun, and Iliff became the richest and most influential cattleman of this section of the West.[7]

Col. J. D. Henderson, another of the Pike's Peak gold seekers, established one of the first ranches in Colorado. Like Iliff, Henderson established a little store. It was located on an island in the Platte River and here he purchased the lame and footsore cattle of emigrants. In time "Henderson's Island" became a famous stopping place and its owner a well-known ranchman with thousands of head of cattle.[8] A few other men established ranches and grazed cattle in Colorado or Wyoming in the days before the

6 *National Live Stock Journal*, Aug. 1877, p. 351.
7 Baillie-Grohman, pp. 351-353.
8 *Ibid.* p. 353.

Civil War, or during that struggle. Among them was Edward Creighton, later president of the First National Bank of Omaha, who began grazing cattle in that region in 1859.[9]

Such men were but pathbreakers, however, whose operations were too small in these early days to be of any considerable importance though they doubtless pointed the way to later comers. The real history of ranching in these regions did not begin until after the Civil War, and the cattle for stocking the northern plains came for the most part up the trail in the northern drives from Texas.

As has been indicated some 260,000 head of cattle were driven north from Texas in 1866, but few of these ever reached a profitable market. Most of those that did were sent to Kansas City, St. Joseph, Chicago, or some other point for slaughter. The same was true of the small herds driven north in 1867, but by 1868 other markets had been opened on the plains. The railroads that were building west required a considerable number of cattle for use by the construction camps while the military posts established to restrain the Indians and aid in carrying out the government's new Indian policy also furnished a market for a considerable quantity of beef. Moreover, as the Indians were placed upon reservations, it was found necessary to feed them, especially as buffalo grew increasingly scarce owing to the slaughter of these animals and the driving of those remaining farther and farther west by the hide hunters. The Indians of the Five Civilized Tribes, torn by feuds and factions and with their country ravaged by armies of both sides, were in a deplorable condition while many of the tribes farther north were in a state of destitution owing to the disappearance of the buffalo from the region in which these Indians were accustomed to hunt. As a result many tribes were restless and at times hostile, and could be kept upon the reservations set aside for them only when given a liberal supply of beef and other food. As a result the supplying of beef to the Indians under government contracts soon became an important business

[9] See Board of Immigration Publication: *The Territory of Wyoming*, 1874, pp. 14-15.

affording a market on the plains for many thousand head of Texas cattle each year.

Exact figures as to the quantity of beef supplied to the Indians during the three or four years following the close of the war are difficult to obtain owing to the fact that conditions on the plains were very unsettled and special appropriations were often made and the money placed in the hands of individual agents to be expended as they thought best for the subsistence of the Indians under their charge.[10]

At first there was carelessness and perhaps a certain amount of graft connected with Indian beef contracts, but in 1869 the Board of Indian Commissioners was created and this body exercised supervision over Indian contracts, and conditions gradually improved. Scales were provided for weighing the cattle instead of depending upon merely guessing at their weight as had been the former method. Bids were required for contracts and contractors were bonded. Their operations were scrutinized closely and an earnest effort was made to safeguard the interests of the Indians and of the government.[11]

In 1870 the government purchased for the Indians 12,669,790 pounds of beef on the hoof besides some small special purchases to meet emergencies. The average price paid was $4.39 a hundred pounds. In 1871 the purchase amounted to 27,441,750 pounds and the price had dropped to $2.60 per hundred, the reduction being in part due to the lower price of cattle, but mainly to closer supervision of the business and greater care in the awarding of contracts. By 1880 the quantity purchased for the Indians had

10 *Report of Commissioner of Indian Affairs,* 1869, p. 29. Also *Ibid.,* p. 389 for an account of purchase of beef by the agent at Fort Cobb at three cents a pound net.

11 From September, 1868, to February, 1869, the average weight per head of cattle issued at one of the Sioux agencies as certified by the agent was 1,577 pounds. From September to November, 1872, the average weight per head of the cattle issued at the same agency was 1,021 pounds. In the former case in which the weight of the cattle was merely estimated by the agent, it seems that the government paid for 36 per cent more beef than the Indians actually received. *Fourth Annual Report of Board of Indian Commissioners,* 1872, pp. 4-5.

increased to about forty million pounds requiring some fifty thousand head of cattle.[12]

Competition for these beef contracts was keen particularly for the big Sioux contracts which amounted to over 26 million pounds annually. In spite of the efforts of governmental officials to prevent it, a certain amount of fraud persisted for several years and the purchase of beef was attended by difficulties and vexations. Contractors formed combinations in order to keep up prices, or submitted "straw bids" and in some cases sought to deliver cattle below the specifications required by their contracts.[13] The profits of these Indian beef contracts must have been great at times as it was estimated that the contractor for the Sioux agencies made a net profit of $117,500 in a single year.[14]

Cattle to supply the Indians were usually bought in Texas by these northern contractors and driven up the trail, or in some cases herds were purchased from Texas drovers at the cow towns of Kansas, or contracts were made with Texas drovers for the delivery of herds near the agencies where the cattle were to be consumed. The most in Texas in the seventies was seven to eight dollars for cows and twelve or thirteen dollars for beeves, and it cost in this earlier period about two dollars a head more to drive them from Texas to Montana or Dakota.[15] Cattle delivered near the northern agencies, according to one contemporary writer, usually

[12] The following table gives the quantity of beef purchased for the Indians at the annual awarding of contracts from 1870 to 1880. In addition there was a considerable quantity purchased each year under special contracts to meet emergencies, amounting in value in 1872 to $58,716.

1870------12,660,790	1874------36,000,000	1878------37,230,000
1871------27,441,750	1875------47,020,000	1879------42,878,000
1872------27,850,000	1876------30,790,173	1880------39,160,900
1873------28,645,000	1877------29,173,000	

The high price of cattle in the years following 1880 raised the total expenditure for beef very considerably so that for many years it amounted to over a million dollars annually.

[13] Seventh Annual Report of Board of Indian Commissioners, 1875, pp. 23-33.

[14] Ibid., p. 23

[15] Ibid., pp. 33 and 36. It was said that the cost of the earliest drives was two or three times as much per head as the later ones but before 1875, methods of trail driving had become so efficient as to reduce the cost very greatly.

Scene During the Opening of the Cherokee Strip

Cutting Out a Calf

Erwin E. Smith photograph
Library of Congress

cost eleven to twelve dollars for cows, and eighteen to twenty dollars for beeves.[16]

Indian contractors usually received their cattle in the autumn and pastured them on the reservation near the agency, delivering at specified times and under the direction of the agent a number of the animals to the Indians for slaughter. In this way the contractor became after a fashion a ranchman upon Indian lands since he must pasture large herds throughout the year and maintain a force of cowboys, together with horses, wagons, and full ranch equipment. These Indian beef contractors were among the first men grazing herds of cattle on the central and northern plains and their operations pointed the way to others as to the possibility of raising cattle there, or maturing them for sale in the eastern markets.

The rapid peopling of Kansas and Nebraska and the advance westward of the Pacific railways served to foster the growth of ranches. The population of Kansas had increased from 107,206 in 1860 to 364,399 in 1870 and Nebraska had in the same time grown in population from 28,841 to 122,993.[17] As has already been stated the Union Pacific Railway pushed rapidly westward in the years following the war. By November, 1867, it had reached Cheyenne, the southern branch or Kansas Pacific, was by the summer of that year built west as far as Salina. Many of the cattle driven from Texas after 1867 were marketed for stocking ranches on the plains. In 1868 it was stated that stock raising was very profitable in central Kansas and it seemed uncertain whether agriculture ever would be.[18] The same year it was reported that numerous ranches had been started in the valley of the Big Laramie River and that grazing in that region was excellent.[19] In 1870 it was reported that many thousands of head of Texas cattle were coming to Nebraska to be fattened and that the profits of the industry were very great.[20] The town of Schuyler, Nebraska, was

16 *Ibid.*
17 9th Census, Population.
18 *Prairie Farmer,* Aug. 22, 1868.
19 *Report of Commissioner of General Land Office,* 1868, p. 227.
20 *Ibid.,* 1870, p. 400.

laid out about this time as a concentration point for Texas cattle and perhaps 50,000 head were marketed there in the summer of 1870, stock cattle selling at twelve dollars and beeves at about twenty-five dollars a head.[21]

As has been indicated, the drive from Texas steadily increased in volume after 1867 until by 1871 it reached a total of 600,000 head or perhaps more. Records made ten years later of 164 Texas trail herds aggregating 384,147 head showed them to be composed of the following classes of animals:

Yearlings	124,967
Twos	116,824
Threes	66,078
Fours	43,237
Dry Cows	30,060
Cows with calves	2,972

This would indicate that out of a total of 384,147 head, 241,-791 or nearly two thirds, were yearlings and two-year-old steers. Virtually all of these were sold for stocking the northern ranges and it was estimated that one third of the remaining animals, or seventy-five per cent of the whole number driven, were for the same purpose, leaving but twenty-five per cent for shipment to the markets for slaughter or for Indian contracts.[22] It seems probable that the proportion of young steers for stocking the northern ranges was about the same in the earlier drives and it may have been somewhat greater owing to the rapid spread of ranching in the North and the consequent demand for animals to stock new ranges.

The men first establishing these new ranches were of several types and came from various sections of the country. Some were beef contractors who, after supplying Indian agencies for a few years with cattle from Texas, at last secured permanent ranges and began raising or maturing cattle for the eastern markets.

21 *National Live Stock Journal*, 1870, Vol. I, pp. 11-12.
22 10th Census, Vol. III, p. 21.

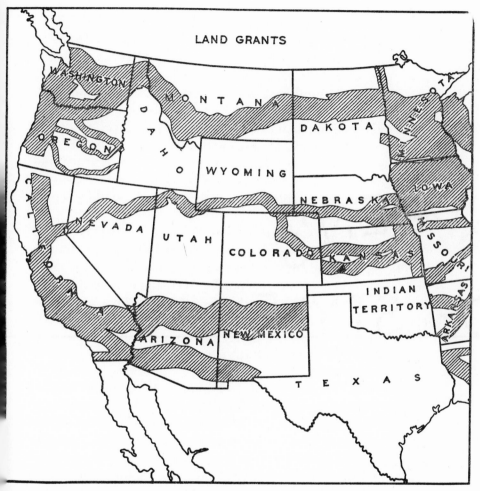

Land Grants by the United States to Railroads, Western Half

Others were originally stock farmers of the corn belt who came west and, seeing the possibilities of grazing on the plains, remained permanently in that region. Edward Creighton, whose operations have already been mentioned, was engaged for many years in stock raising in the corn states but after a few years of ranching in the West transferred all his live stock interests to the plains, declaring that profits there were three times as great as in the corn states.[23] Other early ranchmen were former freighters, trappers, buffalo hunters or railway contractors, while not a few Texans who drove herds north to Kansas or beyond found themselves forced to hold their cattle for several months while awaiting a purchaser. Becoming in this way somewhat familiar with the business in this region, many of these men later returned and established permanent ranches, thus providing feeding grounds for maturing the surplus young steers raised on their home ranches in Texas.

Besides the Texas cattle marketed in Kansas and Nebraska for stocking the ranges west and northwest of these states, it must also be borne in mind that there was a smaller but not inconsiderable stream of cattle flowing northwest from Texas up the Pecos into New Mexico and across the Raton or Trinchera passes into Colorado, and in some cases on into Wyoming or Montana.[24] Also there was at first a comparatively small number of cattle driven eastward from Oregon across the mountains into the western part of the plains region.[25]

Of course the building of the Union Pacific Railway through western Nebraska and across Wyoming brought many stock raisers into that region. In the summer of 1869 it was stated that within two months the banks of Denver had sold drafts aggregating nearly $500,000 for the purchase of Texas cattle to stock the region along the railway west of Cheyenne or in some cases to the east of it.[26] By 1871 there were some fifty ranchmen or ranching

23 See *Report of Commissioner of Agriculture*, 1870, p. 305, or *The Territory of Wyoming*, published by the Wyoming Board of Immigration, 1874, pp. 14-15.
24 See J. L. Hill, *The End of the Cattle Trail*, pp. 23-31 for an account of one of these early drives. Also 10th Census, Vol. III, pp. 989-990.
25 Baillie-Grohman, p. 346.

firms in eastern Wyoming south of the North Platte River pasturing a total of nearly 100,000 head of cattle.[27] Many of these held ranges comparatively near the railroad. Most of them were small operators with but a few hundred head though there were two or three comparatively large ones each owning about 10,000 head or more.[28] Most of these cattle had been brought in very recently. On the Laramie Plains east of the Laramie Mountains were ranging numerous small herds of from one hundred to five hundred head.[29] Nearly all of the cattle in Wyoming at this time had been brought from Texas, and that state supplied very many more in the years following.

The great drive of 1871 proved disastrous to most of the Texas trail drivers. Many of the cattle were not of age or quality for profitable sale in the eastern markets, while the more accessible ranges of the central and northern plains region had by this time become fairly well stocked, and the expansion into new and remote areas was not sufficient to absorb the great volume of Texas cattle driven up the trail in that year. As a result many drovers held their herds on the Kansas plains awaiting a buyer until fall was well advanced. Despairing then of making a profitable sale, some established winter quarters in central or western Kansas, or pushed on north or west into Colorado, Wyoming or Nebraska. Others drove back into Indian Territory to pass the winter in the Cherokee Outlet. It is estimated that 300,000 of the 600,000 head of cattle driven north in the summer of 1871 were unsold and put by the drovers upon ranges for the winter.[30]

The winter of 1871–2 was unusually severe. Snow fell early and was followed by a succession of blizzards and long periods of intensely cold weather. The Texas cattle, accustomed to warm climate and in some cases thin from the long drive and from be-

26 *Prairie Farmer*, July 10, 1869.

27 The *Report of the Commissioner of General Land Office*, 1871, p. 263 gives a list of these ranchmen with the number of cattle owned by each.

28 Of the fifty herds there were only two with over 10,000 head. Three more had 5,000 or over, twelve were between 1,000 and 5,000 and thirty-three less than 1,000. *Ibid.*, p. 263.

29 *Ibid.*, 1871, pp. 262-264.

30 McCoy, p. 227.

ing held for months on the closely grazed prairies in the vicinity of the cow towns, died by thousands. Estimates have placed the loss of cattle in Kansas and a part of Nebraska, in the winter of 1871–2, as high as 250,000 head. It was said that 50,000 hides were shipped from a single Kansas railway station and that two others shipped 35,000 and 25,000 respectively though perhaps not more than one-third to one-half of the animals that died were skinned.[31]

The disastrous experience of 1871 checked very much the drive of 1872, but the market that year was fairly good, and 1873 saw a heavy drive to Kansas. But few buyers came from the Northwest, however, except Indian beef contractors and as a result many stock cattle again had to be held on the range. The winter of 1873–4 proved a rainy one and again heavy losses ensued.[32] Moreover, many drovers were forced to borrow heavily in order to hold their herds over the winter in Kansas. The Panic of 1873 came in the autumn of that year and numerous banks refused to renew the drovers' notes with the result that these men were forced to ship their young and, in some cases, thin cattle to market. Prices went down and many men found themselves facing financial ruin.[33]

Prominent cattlemen urged that the ranges of the northern plains were now largely stocked and advised the Texas cattlemen to fatten their steers at home and ship to market over the Missouri, Kansas and Texas Railway which had by this time been built from St. Louis into north central Texas.[34]

The experience of the Texas drovers and the general influence of the panic were reflected in the volume of the drive during the next two years, since it dropped from 405,000 head in 1873 to 166,000 in 1874 and to about 151,000 in 1875. However, it

[31] McCoy, pp. 227-228. Also see *Report of Commissioner of Agriculture*, 1872, pp. 26-30. This reports that 75 per cent of some Texas herds died.

[32] *Ibid.*, p. 250.

[33] *Ibid.*, p. 251. McCoy writing in 1874 states that the Texas drovers lost two million dollars in the Panic of 1873 and that nearly every man who drove cattle that year shared in this loss. Cows and thin, rough steers sold in some cases at from $1.00 to $1.25 a hundred.

[34] *Ibid.*, pp. 424-425. Out of this idea no doubt grew the packing industry of Fort Worth.

was by no means true that the northern plains were stocked with cattle in 1874. The vast ranges of Montana and Dakota were at that time almost untouched while there was ample room for more cattle in many other portions of the plains region. Also the men operating in well stocked areas were by this time finding that these ranges were better suited for maturing and fattening steers than for raising calves. As a result they soon began to sell their cows and to fill the place of these animals and of the fat beeves shipped to market with yearlings and two-year-old steers from Texas.[35] As a result the drive had increased to large proportions again by 1876 and continued large for many years.[36]

From January, 1874, to September, 1875, the Union Pacific shipped 763 cars of cattle out of Wyoming and the volume grew steadily.[37] By this time most of the land along the streams and water courses had been taken up by ranchmen though not many of these had sufficient capital to stock all the range controlled by their river frontage.[38]

In the meantime, while cattle had been spreading over Kansas and Nebraska as a result of the drives from Texas to those states and extending westward into Wyoming on either side of the Union Pacific Railway, they had also been spreading into Colorado and north into Montana and Dakota. The beginnings of ranching in southern Colorado were closely associated with stock raising in New Mexico and were influenced by the Mexican occupation of that region. Prior to the Civil War a considerable number of Mexicans had small bands of sheep and possibly a few cattle in Colorado.[39] Also a few cattle were doubtless grazed in Colorado following the Pike's Peak gold rush of 1859 and sold for

[35] The herds of the first small ranchmen in Kansas, Nebraska, Wyoming, Montana and Dakota were often composed of mixed stock cattle, but as the years went by this condition changed and most men had nothing but steers, usually bought when one or two years old.

[36] To about 1890 and even later there were many herds driven up the trail.

[37] *Report of the Commissioner of General Land Office,* 1875, p. 368.

[38] *The Territory of Wyoming,* Published by the Territorial Board of Immigration, 1874, p. 50.

[39] 10th Census, Vol. III, pp. 1003-1004.

local consumption in the mining camps. About the time of the Civil War, Charles Goodnight and a few other Texans brought herds of cattle up the old Pecos Trail through New Mexico for sale at the military posts and for Indian contracts, and some of these men established ranches near Trinidad and Pueblo and farther north on the plains near the foot of the Rocky Mountains.

In 1868 George A. Binkleman established a ranch on the Kiowa east of Denver removing farther north to the Republican River in 1875.[40] Other early ranchmen were R. G. Webster, who established a ranch near Denver in 1872, and F. P. Ernest, who began operations in New Mexico in 1871 and removed to Colorado four years later, settling on one of the tributaries of the Platte.[41] John Hitson of Texas began driving to Colorado over the Pecos Trail at the close of the war and eventually settled there and became one of the principal ranchmen of the state.[42] From the region along the Union Pacific Railway other men, including Iliff, extended their operations south into Colorado. By 1874 the Arkansas Valley for a hundred miles east of Pueblo had nearly all been occupied by ranchmen.[43] By this time the Kansas Pacific Railway was furnishing excellent transportation facilities and a line had been built connecting Denver with Cheyenne. The latter town had before this time become an important live stock market to which were brought numerous herds from Texas to be sold for stocking the ranges of Montana, Idaho, Utah and Nevada.[44]

Montana, far to the north of the Union Pacific Railway, developed more slowly as a ranching area than Wyoming. Yet there were a few small herds in the Bitter Root Valley as early as 1854 or 1855 consisting mostly of cattle bought from emigrants on the trails to Oregon,[45] or in some cases brought east from the Oregon settlements. The owners[46] of most of these were French Canadians

---

40 Richthofen, Baron Walter Von, *Cattle Raising on the Plains*, p. 69.
41 *Ibid.*, pp. 67-68.
42 McCoy, pp. 345-346.
43 *Ibid.*, p. 380.
44 *Report of Commissioner of General Land Office*, 1872, pp. 258-259.
45 10th Census, Vol. III, p. 1021. See also J. L. Hill, p. 50.
46 *Ibid.*

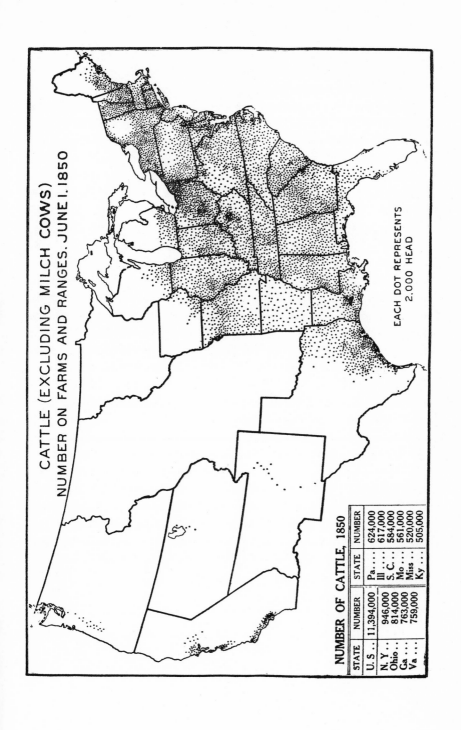

CATTLE (EXCLUDING MILCH COWS)
NUMBER ON FARMS AND RANGES. JUNE 1. 1850

EACH DOT REPRESENTS
2,000 HEAD

NUMBER OF CATTLE, 1850

STATE	NUMBER	STATE	NUMBER
U. S . . .	11,394,000		
N. Y . . .	946,000	Pa	624,000
Ohio . . .	814,000	Ill . . : . .	617,000
Ga	763,000	S. C . .	584,000
Va	759,000	Mo	561,000
		Miss	520,000
		Ky	505,000

or half-breed Indians. There were also a few cattle in the Deer Lodge Valley very early though the number was small.[47]

The development of gold mining in Idaho and western Montana during the years of the Civil War caused some slight demand for beef and caused small herds of cattle to be gathered and driven to these mining camps. In 1862 Granville Stuart, who had gone to Montana from California, collected a herd of cattle and drove them to the Bannock Diggings.[48] The same year there came to this region Conrad Kohrs, who was later to be one of the greatest of the northwestern ranchmen. Kohrs started from Iowa in 1862 for California but at Salt Lake City he left the California emigrants and joined a group from Denver en route for the mining camps of Idaho. At Bannock he established a butcher shop and supplied the miners with beef and with candles made from the tallow of the animals slaughtered. By 1864 he had gathered a small herd of cattle purchased mostly from emigrants on the trail farther south. This herd he gradually increased and in 1867 went to Denver and formed a partnership with Joseph Bell and Captain Roberts to bring Texas cattle to Montana.[49] In 1871 Kohrs removed from the Deer Lodge Valley to the Sun River region where he established a large ranch. His operations there pointed the way, and other men began to bring in Texas cattle in large numbers.

Dakota, largely a region of broad prairies lying remote from the emigrant trails across the plains to the Pacific, and inhabited by the warlike Sioux, was one of the last portions of the cow country to be occupied. There was little mining in the early days to attract prospectors, while in 1862 the Sioux drove out most of the few inhabitants. In consequence it was not until the building of the Northern Pacific Railway which was completed to Bismarck by 1873 that many settlers began to enter the state.[50] All construction work was stopped on this road by the Panic of 1873 and was not resumed until 1878 after which it was pushed rapidly, open-

47 Hill, pp. 49-50.
48 10th Census, Vol. III, p. 1021.
49 Hill.
50 10th Census, Vol. III, p. 1019.

ing western Dakota and eastern Montana to ranching by affording these regions shipping facilities.[51] In 1875 there were perhaps not 50,000 people in what is now the two Dakota's. But in that year came the discovery of gold in the Black Hills and a rush to that region which, coupled with the advance of this railroad, brought in some 85,000 more people by 1880.[52]

By this time the depression following the crisis of 1873 had entirely passed away and the cattle area was entering upon a period of unprecedented prosperity. Railroads had penetrated to many parts of it, opening up new districts. Some of these railway companies had drilled artesian wells to furnish water along their lines and had shown to the ranchmen a method of making ranges remote from water available for grazing by means of wells and windmills.[53] The drives from Texas, much reduced for the years immediately following the Panic of 1873, had again assumed large proportions and were supplemented somewhat by the influx of a considerable number of well bred bulls and other cattle shipped west from the corn belt to improve the quality of the herds of the breeders.[54] The buffalo were about gone and the Indians had been reduced to the position of peaceful occupants of reservations.

Moreover, by 1880 the business of ranching was becoming better understood and more efficient methods of operation had been established. The live stock associations that had been formed were doing much to promote the industry through intelligent cooperation. Prices were rising and profits increasing. Eastern and foreign capital was beginning to be poured into the industry with the result that the small operators were giving place to large ones, either corporations or individuals.

By this time much of the Great Plains area was stocked and some of it over-stocked, but the number of animals brought in

[51] *U. S. Geological Survey Bulletin* 611, p. 51.

[52] 10th Census, Vol. III, p. 1019.

[53] *Report of the Commissioner of General Land Office,* 1872, p. 259.

[54] See Hopkins, Manuscript, The Economic History of the Production of Beef Cattle in Iowa, pp. 344-345.

steadily increased.[55] Kansas, which in 1860 had 93,455 head of cattle on farms and in 1870 had 373,967 head, had in 1880, including the estimated ranch stock, 1,533,133 head.[56] Nebraska had, including the estimated number of ranches, 1,113,247 head as compared with 37,197 on farms in 1860 and 79,928 in 1870.[57] Wyoming had increased from 11,130 on farms in 1870 to 521,213 in 1880, including estimated ranch stock.[58] The number of Montana cattle had grown from 36,738 on farms in 1870 to 428,279 in 1880, including estimated range cattle.[59] Dakota had increased from 12,467 in 1870 to 140,815 in 1880.[60] Colorado had on farms in 1870, 70,736 head and on farms and ranches in 1880, 791,492 head.[61]

Great as had been the growth of the cattle industry on the Great Plains in the decade before 1880 the years following were to see a much greater one. That date marks the beginning of a tremendous boom in the ranch cattle business, which had by this time begun to attract the attention of numerous investors in the East and in Europe. During the next few years an enormous volume of capital was to be poured into the industry. Numerous books and magazine articles had appeared detailing in glowing terms the profits of ranching. For a few years such profits were undoubtedly realized by many operators. But the over expansion of the business and the over-stocking of the ranges could have but one result. It was not long until there came the bursting of the bubble, a collapse of prices and a general decline in the whole movement, which brought to the ranchmen dire distress and, in many cases, complete financial ruin.

[55] 10th Census, Vol. III, p. 1022-1023.
[56] *Ibid.*, p. 1001.
[57] *Ibid.*, p. 1009. The figures for 1860 and 1870 are for cattle on farms.
[58] *Ibid.*, p. 1015.
[59] *Ibid.*, p. 1028.
[60] *Ibid.*, p. 1019.
[61] *Ibid.*, p. 1008. The Census figures for cattle on farms on these states and territories in 1870 and in 1880 are as follows:

	1870	1880		1870	1880
Kansas	373,967	1,452,057	Dakota	12,467	140,815
Nebraska	79,928	738,550	Montana	36,738	172,837
Wyoming	11,130	278,073	Colorado	70,736	346,839

5.

RANCHING ON THE CENTRAL AND NORTHERN PLAINS, 1880 TO 1900

E ven before 1880 the ranch cattle industry on the western plains of the United States had grown to such proportions as to attract national and even world wide interest. The increased meat supply due to the growth of ranching in the West led to experiments in improved methods of refrigeration, and in the autumn of 1875 Timothy C. Eastman of New York began sending dressed beef to England.[1] By the spring of 1877 the business had grown to such proportions as to cause grave alarm among the live stock growers of England and Scotland lest the continued importation of American beef reduce the price of that commodity in Great Britain to such an extent as to interfere seriously with their business.[2]

[1] The first shipments of dressed beef in quantities to Europe by Mr. Eastman were in October 1875. See statement of T. C. Eastman in Nimmo, p. 172. Apparently a small shipment or two had been made earlier by Nelson Morris of Chicago perhaps in 1868, but this reached England in bad condition. *Ibid.*

[2] This was accompanied by a great increase in shipments of live cattle also. That the British had some reason to fear the competition of American meat may be seen by the following table which shows the exports of beef and live cattle from the United States for ten years.

YEAR	NO. OF OF CATTLE	VALUE	FRESH BEEF IN POUNDS	VALUE
1875	57,211	$ 1,103,085	----------	----------
1876	51,593	1,110,703	----------	----------
1877	50,001	1,593,080	49,210,990	$ 4,197,956
1878	80,040	3,896,818	54,046,771	5,009,856
1879	136,720	8,379,200	54,025,832	4,883,080

Accordingly in 1877 the *Scotsman*, a Scotch newspaper devoted to the agricultural interests of North Britain, sent to America an agricultural expert who was a member of its staff to inquire into the live stock business of the country and to make reports in the form of letters for publication.[3]

There can be little doubt that these letters and the other publicity given to the ranching business in America through the columns of the British press had considerable influence in arousing the interest of Scotch and English investors in possible profits in ranching on the Great Plains. In 1880 the government of Great Britain sent two commissioners to America to investigate the range cattle industry with special reference to the amout of British capital invested in it. The men chosen were Clare Sewell Read and Albert Pell, both members of Parliament, who were dispatched in response to a parliamentary resolution passed in 1879. They spent several months on this mission and their report, which stated that a profit of thirty-three and one-third per cent annually was ordinarily made in ranching, attracted much attention.[4]

About this time came a great and widespread interest in the range cattle industry on the part of numerous people in the eastern part of the United States as well as in some of the countries of continental Europe. The price of cattle and beef began to rise soon after 1880 and within two years had reached a level never

1880	182,756	13,344,195	84,717,194	7,441,918
1881	185,707	14,304,103	106,004,812	9,860,284
1882	108,110	7,800,227	69,586,466	6,768,881
1883	104,444	8,341,431	81,064,373	8,342,131
1884	190,518	17,855,495	120,784,064	11,987,331

See Nimmo, p. 170. The greater part of these exports were to Great Britain. In 1884 Great Britain and Ireland received live cattle to the value of $17,336,606 out of the total export value of $17,855,495, and fresh beef to the value of $11,516,369 out of the total of $11,987,331. *Ibid.*, p. 171. In that year Great Britain and Ireland received 88.7 per cent of the total exports of cattle and cattle products from the United States including canned and salted beef, hides, tallow, etc. *Ibid.*, p. 190.

[3] McDonald, James, *Food from the Far West*, p. XV. The imports of fresh beef into the United Kingdom in March, 1877, was 6,016,200 pounds, nearly six times the amount imported in March, 1876. *Ibid.*, p. XII.

[4] Read and Pell, *Reports for Commissioners and Inspectors*, 1880, Vol. XVIII, Serial 856.

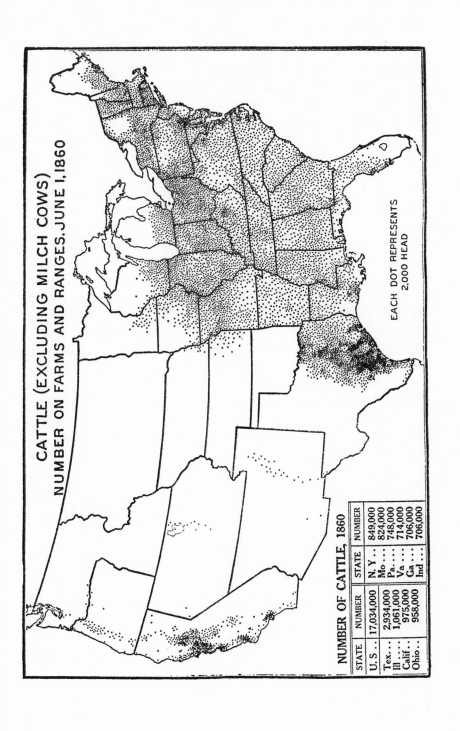

CATTLE (EXCLUDING MILCH COWS)
NUMBER ON FARMS AND RANGES, JUNE 1,1860

EACH DOT REPRESENTS
2,000 HEAD

NUMBER OF CATTLE, 1860

STATE	NUMBER	STATE	NUMBER
U.S.	17,034,000	N.Y.	849,000
		Mo.	824,000
Tex.	2,934,000	Pa.	748,000
Ill.	1,061,000	Va.	714,000
Calif.	975,000	Ga.	706,000
Ohio	958,000	Ind.	706,000

attained before in the United States if we take into consideration the premium on gold in the latter part of the Civil War. Choice steers sold on the Chicago market in the summer of 1882 at above nine cents a pound and good Texas steers brought five and a half or more while good well bred milch cows sold for as much as eighty dollars a head.[5] Prices continued high during the entire year as well as during 1883 with the result that the export trade fell off nearly fifty per cent, both in live cattle and dressed beef.[6] Of course, prices on the plains were correspondingly high. Beef contracts for the Rosebud and Pine Ridge Indian agencies in Dakota aggregating twelve and a half million pounds were awarded at $2.73 1/4, and $2.83 3/5 in 1880 while the big contracts in Indian Territory for seven and three-fourths million pounds were let at $2.64.[7]

In 1881 the Pine Ridge and Rosebud contracts were awarded at $3.87 and $3.91 respectively and the big Indian Territory contracts at $3.32.[8] In 1882 the figures were $3.84 and $4.09 for Pine Ridge and Rosebud and $3.64 for Indian Territory,[9] while in 1883 contracts for the big Dakota agencies ranged from $3.73 to $4.09 and ten and a half million pounds of beef were purchased for Indian Territory agencies at $3.73.[10]

The rapid rise in prices and the fact that they remained at a high level for a comparatively long period of time resulted in enormous profits especially for the men who had purchased young cattle at a relatively low price. A fever of excitement swept over the country and extended to Europe. Books and magazine and newspaper articles dealing with the range cattle industry were published in ever increasing abundance, detailing in glowing

---

[5] *Breeder's Gazette,* June 8, and July 6, 1882.

[6] See tables. Also *Breeder's Gazette,* Aug. 3, 1882, p. 179.

[7] *Report of Commissioner of Indian Affairs,* 1880, pp. 285-286.

[8] *Ibid.,* 1881, pp. 338-339.

[9] *Ibid.,* 1882, pp. 373-374.

[10] *Ibid.,* 1883, pp. 323-324. Even in 1884 the price was from $3.23 to $3.55, and in 1885 from $3.17 to $3.53. See *Reports of Commissioner of Indian Affairs* for those years, pp. 352-356 and 416-420. These prices are very high when we consider the quality of beef cattle furnished, and the fact that an Indian contract virtually carried with it grazing privileges on the reservation for the herd used to supply the Indians.

and unmeasured terms the immense profits of the business.[11] Even some years earlier extravagant claims had been made for ranching. In 1874 the Wyoming Territorial Board of Immigration published a pamphlet in which they gave figures to show that $25,000 invested in the ranch cattle business would in five years yield a net profit of over $80,000.[12] After 1880 the stories as to ranch profits became even more startling.[13] It was stated in 1883 that in northern and western Texas no capital had been invested since 1880 that had not returned a net profit of more than 50 per cent.[14] Tables of figures were given to show profits of 30 to 40 per cent annually and even more over a long period of years,[15] while the life of the ranchman was described in numerous books and magazine articles as an almost ideal existence.[16]

The effect of the widespread circulation of such reports was very great. The desire to engage in ranching became almost a craze. Prominent lawyers, bankers and other business men throughout the East began the formation of cattle companies in order to take advantage of the wonderful opportunities pointed out to them. Every great city in the East had men interested either directly or indirectly in ranching. Boston, New York, Philadelphia and Washington, together with many lesser cities, all had a number of prominent men who invested money in ranching enterprises and who in some cases hastened west to give their personal attention to the details of the business. Members of Congress and senators or former senators of the United States, not only from the West but in several cases those from the eastern states, invested large sums in the range cattle industry.[17] In the

11 Some of the best known of these books and articles are: Brisbin, James, *The Beef Bonanza*, 1881; Aldridge, Reginald, *Life on a Ranch*, 1884; Baillie-Grohman, *Camp Fires in the Rockies*, 1880; McDonald, James, *Food from the Far West*, 1878; Richthofen, Baron Walter von, *Cattle Raising on the Plains of North America*, 1885. The quantity of magazine material is enormous and space cannot be given to attempting to list it.

12 *The Territory of Wyoming*, 1874, pp. 9-11.

13 See Baillie-Grohman, p. 428.

14 *National Live Stock Journal*, July 1883, p. 301.

15 Richthofen, p. 72, also Brisbin, or Baillie-Grohman, p. 428.

16 Baillie-Grohman, p. 428.

17 Senator P. B. Plumb of Kansas was for many years closely identified with

western cities bankers and capitalists did a large business in helping to finance cattle companies or made heavy loans to individuals for the purchase of cattle or for expenses of operation.

As has been indicated, Europe also furnished a great flood of capital for the development of the range cattle industry. In 1872 the Scottish American Investment Company had been formed in Scotland, founded by W. J. Menzies. Its shares were $50 each of which $10 was paid and the subscribers were made liable for a call of $40. Its promoters were men of undoubted financial standing and were able to borrow large sums at four and a half per cent interest which was reloaned in the United States and Canada at six to eight per cent.[18] Another large Scotch syndicate formed quite early was the Scottish American Mortgage Company which founded the Prairie Cattle Company, one of the largest ranching enterprises in the West.[19] The operations of the Prairie Cattle Company were carried on largely in Colorado, New Mexico, and Texas and it was said to own nearly 150,000 head of cattle in 1885, and to have paid heavy dividends.[20]

The high prices of 1882 caused a renewed interest in the range cattle industry of America on the part of Scotch and English capitalists and that year saw the organization of many British companies to engage in the business.[21] Even at that time ranching was a comparatively new industry except in Texas and many men

----

the ranching interests of his state. Former U. S. Senator T. C. Platt of New York was also financially interested in ranching. See Platt to Secretary of the Interior, Jan. 27, 1883. *House Ex. Doc.* 54, 48 Cong., 1 Sess., Vol. IV. The Standard Cattle Company ranching in Wyoming was a Boston corporation. Its president was William G. Weld and its treasurer, Nathaniel Thayer. See *Senate Rep.* 1278, 49 Cong., 1 Sess., Vol. VIII.

18 Clay, pp. 91-92.

19 *Ibid.*

20 Richthofen, pp. 48-50 and p. 55.

21 Clay, p. 21. Some of the leading Scotch companies were the following: Hansford Land and Cattle Company; The Matador Cattle Company; The Prairie Cattle Company; The Texas Land and Cattle Company; The Western Land and Cattle Company; The Wyoming Cattle Ranch Company; and many others. Richthofen, p. 55. It was stated by the Wyoming Stock Growers' Association in 1882 that six million pounds of English and Scotch capital had been invested in ranching largely in Wyoming and the Texas Panhandle. See *By Laws and Reports of the Wyoming Stock Growers' Association,* 1882, p. 19.

embarked in it with little conception of the difficulties confronting them.[22] The usual procedure was to purchase a few sections of land from the railways or from individual homesteaders or, in some cases, employees of the company were induced to take up homesteads, thus giving complete control of a limited area which was fenced. Upon this the buildings and corrals were constructed and the remainder was used as hay land or pasture for the saddle horses while most of the cattle were ranged outside upon the public domain. "Line camps" were established at convenient places along the border of the range and at these the cowboys lived, spending their days in riding over the range or along its border to watch over the cattle and keep them within the bounds of the area claimed by their owners.[23] Since most of the operations were carried on upon the public domain or, in some cases, on Indian reservations, the improvements were naturally of the cheapest and most temporary character. The line camps were mere huts or "dugouts" and even the ranch headquarters usually consisted of buildings, corrals, and other improvements of a very inexpensive character. A prominent English writer of this time estimated that sixty to one hundred pounds was sufficient to erect all buildings necessary to start an ordinary ranching enterprise.[24] Fencing the public domain was forbidden by the United States government, though it was stated that there was no objection to grazing cattle or cutting hay on government lands so long as they were left open for the use of all alike.[25]

All cattle were marked and branded and stringent laws were passed by most of the range states and territories relative to brands and branding. All brands must be recorded either by the county or state or territory. The killing of unbranded animals was usually prohibited by law and the alteration of a brand was severely pun-

[22] Clay, pp. 22-23.

[23] Barb wire began to be used quite extensively on the northern plains soon after 1875, and within a few years had almost revolutionized the cattle business in some areas.

[24] Baillie-Grohman, p. 328.

[25] Departmental Circular of April 5, 1883. *House Ex. Doc.* 232, 50 Cong., 1 Sess., Vol. 28.

ished. Experienced men chose very carefully the symbols to be used as a brand, always seeking something that could not be easily altered. The brand of a large operator frequently came to be widely known and was regarded by his employees with somewhat the same feeling as was held in the middle ages by knights and men at arms for their overlord's coat of arms.[26]

As the business grew and every part of the plains area became covered with cattle, co-operation among the men engaged in ranching became increasingly necessary. It was important that measures be taken to prevent a newcomer from bringing cattle upon a range already occupied and stocked to its full capacity and close co-operation was also necessary in caring for the animals, branding calves, gathering beeves for shipments and in preventing loss from predatory animals or by theft or straying. The first men establishing ranches in any region usually sought to safeguard their ranges so far as possible by the homestead or purchase of the lands controlling the water supply, but this was not in all cases practicable. Moreover, as the demand for grazing increased many large areas hitherto impossible to use as ranges for cattle because of distance from water were made available for pasturage by the drilling of deep wells or the construction of reservoirs to catch the rainfall. Such methods of providing a supply of water not only made possible the grazing of large areas for-

[26] This attitude is shown by the song, *The Brand of X I T,* once quite popular in the Southwest particularly among the employees of the "Capitol Syndicate Ranch" commonly known from its brand as the X I T Ranch. Some men found their brands became attached to their names in curious fashion. The brand of B. H. Campbell, one of the best known ranchmen of the Southwest, was B̄ Q̄ and he soon became widely known as "Barbeque Campbell." While most brands consisted of combinations of letters and figures, many were pictures of some particular object. Well known brands of this type were the spur, pitchfork, frying pan, milking stool, and rocking chair. As ranching grew in importance almost every imaginable device came to be used. Brand books of the period when ranching was at its height show such brands as a bridle bit, spectacles, hat, hatchet, pipe, flask, jug, apple, heart, parasol, watch, andiron, scissors, ox yoke, plow, wrench, keystone, ladder, spear head, crown, crossed swords, pistol, gun, ship's wheel, star, moon, glove, duck, bird's head, steer, hammer, anvil, pocket book, question mark, dollar mark, English pound mark, horsehead, clover leaf envelope, house, and many others equally curious. See Colorado Brand Book, 1886-1906. Also Cherokee Strip Live Stock Association Brand Books, 1882-1888, and Wyoming Stock Growers' Association Brand Books, 1880-1890.

merly useless, but also helped to break the monopoly of the men who held the land along the water courses.

Live stock associations began to be organized as soon as ranching on the plains had reached any considerable proportions and these organizations grew in numbers and power with the growth of the industry. They were of two kinds, local and general. The former usually consisted of all the ranchmen in a single region who organized for the purpose of mutual protection against fire, thieves, wolves and other destructive agencies, and for mutual aid in the round-up and branding of cattle.[27]

These local or district associations were united to form a territorial or state association, the power and influence of which was in many cases very great. Not infrequently the great territorial, state, or regional association was the only one of any importance in a large area, and the territory covered by the operations of its members was subdivided into "round-up districts" over each of which was placed a "round-up foreman" who was an officer of the association and whose powers during the fall and spring round-ups were enormous. Rules were formulated by the association relative to methods of working the range, the branding of calves, the bringing of cattle upon a range already occupied, and many other things. Rewards were offered for the arrest and conviction of stock thieves, or for the scalps of wolves and other beasts of prey. Surveyors were employed to designate the boundaries of each man's range, inspectors were appointed to watch the trails, shipping points and markets for strayed or stolen cattle belonging to association members, and courts of arbitration were sometimes provided to settle disputes between members.[28]

Such organizations eventually became extremely powerful and very efficient in their methods of operation. Through their influence many of the state and territorial legislatures enacted laws similar in character, if not identical with the rules of the stock associations. Laws of the range states and territories in many

27 Nimmo, p. 79-89.
28 See *Senate Report*, 1278, 49 Cong., 1 Sess., Vol. 8, p. 187 for testimony of J. A. Blair relative to surveyors. *Ibid.*, p. 468 for members of Cherokee Strip Live Stock Association's Board of Arbitration.

cases provided much heavier penalties for the theft of live stock than for that of other property of equal value.[29] Other laws provided for the recording of brands, the inspection of cattle, and the offering of a bounty for wolf scalps, and forbade under a severe penalty the allowing of any inferior bull to run at large.[30]

One of the greatest of these organizations, and one that was very successful in getting its rules translated into statute, was the Wyoming Stock Growers' Association. Organized in 1873 with a membership of ten men owning some twenty thousand head of cattle, within twelve years it had extended its operations into Colorado, Nebraska, Montana, and Dakota, and had a membership of four hundred, its members owning about two million head.[31] Largely through its influence, stringent laws were passed by the Territory of Wyoming relative to branding and driving cattle and even as to the time and manner of holding round-ups.[32] Eventually this legislation went so far as to make the Wyoming Stock Growers' Association almost an instrumentality of the territorial government. The general time of its annual meeting was fixed by a law which provided that two round-ups should be held each year, and which created a machinery for carrying on this work. All cattle, regardless of age, running at large in the Territory without a mother and without a brand were known as "mavericks," and the round-up foremen were by law charged with the duty of branding these cattle with the association brand and of selling them at auction to the highest bidder. The money from such sales, less ten per cent retained by the round-up foreman as his fees, was placed in the treasury of the association for operating expenses.[33] It was also made unlawful to brand any cattle

29 Under the Texas law the theft of ordinary property of less than fifty dollars in value was punishable by confinement in the county jail for not more than two years. Theft of a horse was punishable by five to fifteen years imprisonment in the state penitentiary and of a cow by from two to four years. See *Texas Stats.*, 1895.

30 McCoy, p. 238. Also *Colorado Statutes.*

31 Clay, p. 338. See also *By Laws and Reports of Wyoming Stock Growers' Association.*

32 Among other stock laws an act was passed providing for a fine from fifty to one hundred dollars for the running of cattle belonging to another with dogs.

33 *By Laws and Reports of Wyoming Stock Growers' Association*, 1884, pp. 97-102. See also *Wyoming Statutes.*

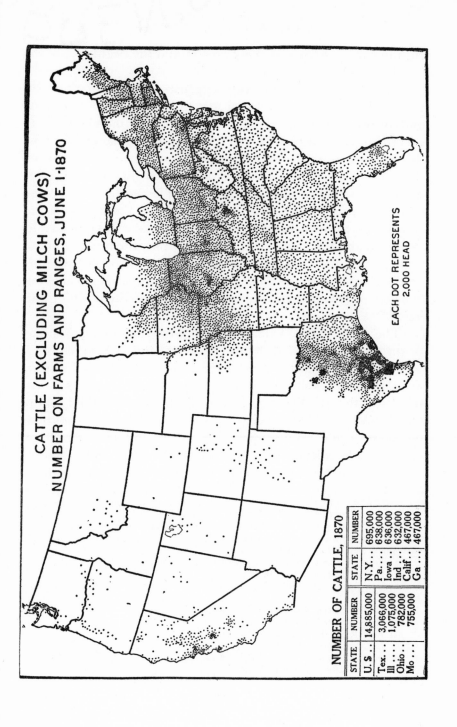

CATTLE (EXCLUDING MILCH COWS)
NUMBER ON FARMS AND RANGES, JUNE 1·1870

EACH DOT REPRESENTS
2,000 HEAD

NUMBER OF CATTLE, 1870

STATE	NUMBER	STATE	NUMBER
U.S...	14,885,000	N.Y...	695,000
Tex...	3,066,000	Pa...	638,000
Ill...	1,075,000	Iowa...	636,000
Ohio...	782,000	Ind...	632,000
Mo...	755,000	Calif...	467,000
		Ga...	467,000

running at large between February 15 and the beginning of the spring round-up.[34]

Other funds for the operating expenses of the association were provided by an initiation fee of $15, the sum of $10 a year dues, and assessments which might be laid upon its members not to exceed one cent for each head of cattle owned.[35] Inspectors, whose duty it was to watch for strayed or stolen cattle belonging to members of the association, were employed and placed at all large markets as well as at shipping points and along the trails. When such animals were found they were seized by the inspector and returned to the owner or, if too far away to make this practicable, were sold and the money sent to him. In 1883 the number of cattle inspected, including the trail herds passing through Wyoming on their way north, was 298,838 and 1,910 strays, valued at about $76,000, were recovered, not including the strays cut out of trail herds.[36]

The work of the Wyoming Stock Growers' Association may be regarded as typical. Colorado, Montana and Dakota had similar organizations, while there were other large regional associations in Kansas, Nebraska, Indian Territory, and Texas. All were similar to that of Wyoming in organization and methods of operation. All provided inspectors to watch for the property of their members, made arrangements for spring and fall round-ups, adopted rules with respect to marks and brands, and sought to encourage the breeding of better animals. Also all used their in-

[34] *Ibid.*, 1884, pp. 102-103. See also *Wyoming Statutes, Session Laws of 1884.*

[35] *By Laws and Reports of Wyoming Stock Growers' Association*, 1884, pp. 7-8. See also *Wyoming Statutes, Session Laws of 1884.*

[36] *Ibid.*, 1884, p. 37. A detailed statement as to these inspections is of value as indicating the volume of Wyoming cattle going to market over the various roads. Such inspections were made as follows:

At Council Bluffs covering shipments over the Union Pacific, 110,138.

At Pacific Junction over Burlington and Missouri Railway, 11,825.

At Valentine, Neb., and Clinton, Iowa, over Sioux City and Pacific Railway, 4,679.

At St. Paul, over Northern Pacific Railway, 21,969.

At Rosebud Indian Agency, 10,888.

At Pine Ridge Indian Agency, 22,333.

At Military Posts, 7,450.

Killed by Union Pacific Railway trains, 656.

On trail leading north, 100,000.

fluence in securing legislation helpful to the live stock interests, as well as in seeking to secure lower freight and interest rates and higher prices for cattle. Organization was no doubt made easier by the tendency of the range cattle business to become more and more consolidated in the hands of large operators.

There can be no doubt but that such organizations were an economic necessity in carrying on a business such as ranching. Yet these associations perhaps tended to enhance the formation of a class consciousness that was later to show itself at times in the struggle between cattlemen and sheepmen and also between ranchmen and the settlers. Also when certain matters affecting the ranch cattle interests, such as the disposal of the public domain or the opening of Indian lands to settlement, became the subject of congressional or departmental action, it was hardly possible for these organizations to avoid being drawn into political controversies. As a result they were sometimes accused of having been formed largely for political purposes and later became, for a time, objects of suspicion on the part of many governmental officials and a great portion of the public at large.[37]

The bad feeling that grew up toward the ranch cattle interests was further intensified by the fact that so much foreign capital was invested in the industry. In 1884 speakers on the floor of Congress gave figures to show that more than twenty million acres of land, mostly in the range cattle area, had been acquired within a few years by foreigners, mostly citizens of Great Britain, and declared that these great holdings by foreign capitalists were a menace to the best interests of the American people especially in the West.[38] Ranchmen were referred to as "cattle barons," and much criticism was launched against "rich and insolent foreigners who sought to monopolize the public lands and to keep American citizens from securing homes on the public domain."[39]

[37] See Noble to Fairchild, Oct. 26, 1889, *House Report* 3768, 51 Cong., 2 Sess., pp. 9-16, also Memorial of the Cherokee Strip Live Stock Association, for a presentation of the ranchman's views.

[38] See speech of N. W. Nutting of New York, *Congressional Record*, March 27, 1884, 48 Cong., 1 Sess., p. 2359.

[39] *National Live Stock Journal*, Aug. 1885, p. 337.

Not only was there a large amount of foreign capital invested in ranching but, as has already been indicated, a considerable number of Europeans, in some cases members of the nobility, came over and gave their personal attention to the business. In Dakota the Marquis de Mores, a French nobleman, had large cattle interests. He built the town of Medora on the Northern Pacific and established a slaughtering plant and a line of refrigerator cars with the intention of supplying dressed beef to the eastern markets. His scheme collapsed, however, within a few years.[40] In Colorado Baron von Richthofen, a German nobleman, was one of the leading cattle raisers while in every part of the range cattle area were to be found young men of European birth, members of good families, who were engaged in ranching.[41]

By 1884 the ranch cattle industry had become a minor South Sea bubble. Large sums of money were borrowed, in many cases at ruinously high rates of interest, for investment in cattle. Fearful that the advance of the homesteaders would soon crowd them off their ranges on the public domain, many men resolved to take full advantage of present opportunities with the result that large areas were terribly over-stocked. No provision was made for feeding or shelter. In fact, in most cases, none was possible under existing conditions. Through the use of high grade bulls the quality of the cattle on the range had been greatly improved, but at the same time the animals were rendered less hardy than the old time Texans had been, and in consequence not so able to care for themselves when the fierce storms of a severe winter should sweep over the over-stocked ranges of the northern plains.[42]

[40] Clay, p. 196. Also Richthofen, p. 51. De Mores' scheme was economically unsound since he could secure but one class of animals for slaughter, grass fed steers, and these only for a few months in the year.

[41] Baillie-Grohman, pp. 321-323. Farmers, trappers and guides were sometimes loaned money for a small ranching venture by English gentlemen whom they had guided on hunting expeditions. *Ibid.*, p. 349.

[42] Clay, p. 37. The range cattle area furnished a market for a large number of well bred bulls to improve its herds and so had a great influence in promoting the breeding of fine stock in the corn belt. At first Shorthorns were in great demand, but this soon changed to a demand for Herefords owing to the superior ability of the latter to adapt themselves to the range conditions of the plains. While these high grade bulls in time brought a vast improvement in the quality of cattle on

The year of 1884 marks the peak of prosperity for the range cattle business. In that year there was held at St. Louis a great cattleman's convention attended by some two thousand delegates from every part of the range cattle area. The most prominent ranchmen, breeders, and feeders from every part of the country were present as well as a number of leading packers, bankers and railroad officials, and not a few prominent men in public life. It was hoped that much good to the live stock interests would result from such a meeting, but such hopes were not realized. It was soon seen that the convention was divided into two rival groups, each with a single particular interest. The southern wing of the convention, consisting mostly of men from Texas, New Mexico, and Indian Territory, was deeply interested in the proposal to establish a national cattle trail extending from the northern boundary of Texas to Canada. As agricultural settlement had extended westward in Kansas and Nebraska, the Texas trail drivers found themselves beset by ever increasing difficulties. It was, therefore, proposed that the United States government set aside land for the national cattle trail which has been previously mentioned.[43]

The men of the northern group, composed largely of men from Wyoming, Montana and Dakota, were on the other hand not particularly eager for a national cattle trail, especially since their ranges were now largely stocked and they no longer felt the imperative need for more Texas cattle. What they did wish very much, however, was an act by Congress providing for the leasing of the range lands of the public domain in the West for a long term of years.[44] This was a proposition that had been made many times before and was to be made many times in the future. The northern ranchmen felt that if they could secure greater perma-

the range, it should be borne in mind that the Texas cow in transmitting to her offspring some of her own hardy qualities and ability to live under the worst possible conditions was also a most important factor in meat production in the West.

[43] See Nimmo, p. 160. Such a trail extending from Texas to Canada would be 690 miles long and have an area of 2,070 miles since it was proposed to make the average width three miles. *Ibid.*, pp. 27-33.

[44] *Ibid.*, p. 46.

nence of tenure on their ranges, they were willing to see the cattle trail created. Otherwise they felt that such a trail would only serve to bring more and more Texas cattle to the North, still further over-stocking many areas in that region, and would result in the establishment of many new ranches by men from the South to compete with them in their business.[45]

It is doubtful if either proposal could have been enacted into law even if supported by the full force of the influence of the ranchmen of the West. The division in their ranks, however, destroyed any possible chance of success, and neither movement apparently ever received great support in Congress. Yet the proposal to lease the grazing lands of the public domain was discussed again and again and always had a considerable number of adherents besides the ranchmen themselves.[46]

Early in 1885 Kansas enacted a law quarantining the entire state against Texas cattle from March 1 to December 1.[47] The result was to lessen enormously the importance of Dodge City as a market and shipping point and to cause the Texas drive to be pushed farther west through Colorado. The quarantine laws of that state, however, were also made more rigid in 1885, thus increasing the difficulty of moving cattle northward by trail.[48]

The winter of 1885–6 was a very severe one in the South. Losses in Texas, New Mexico, and Kansas would in such a winter have normally been very heavy, but were made additionally so in some areas by the fact that in 1885 the ranchmen on the great Cheyenne-Arapaho reservation in Indian Territory were ordered by President Cleveland to remove their herds, and troops under

45 Cox, James, *Historical and Bibliographical Record of the Cattle Industry in Texas and Adjacent Territory*, p. 108. Also *Ibid.*, pp. 102-118 for an account of this convention and a list of stock associations and of states represented.

46 Even the experts of the Bureau of Animal Industry created in 1884 were divided in opinion on this question. Some asserted that such leases should be made and others that they should not. See *First Report of Bureau of Animal Industry*, 1884, and *Second Report*, 1885, p. 315.

47 Nimmo gives a copy of the Kansas law, p. 134.

48 *Ibid.*, p. 136 for the Colorado Quarantine law of 1885. The Kansas law nearly caused war in the summer of 1885 between the Texas drovers and men from western Kansas. See Clay, pp. 183-184.

General Sheridan were sent to execute this order.[49] More than two hundred thousand head of cattle from this Indian reservation were thrown, at the beginning of a severe winter, upon the already over-stocked ranges of the neighboring states. As a result the loss was frightful. Ranchmen later averred that the range cattle interests never recovered from the effects of President Cleveland's order.[50] As a matter of fact the decline of the ranching industry had already begun, and the removal of the herds from the Indian lands was only an added but probably comparatively minor factor in the general depression which was past due.[51]

About the time of the removal of the ranchmen and their herds from the Cheyenne-Arapaho reservation in the Indian Territory there came aggressive action on the part of the United States government to stop the fencing of the public domain by cattlemen, and to remove such fences as had already been erected.

This, as well as grazing on Indian lands, had been the subject of bitter complaint on the part of numerous people in the West and had eventually resulted in investigations by Congress.[52] In February, 1885, an act of Congress had been approved giving the President authority to take whatever means might be necessary to remove or destroy inclosures on the public domain.[53] Accordingly, two weeks after his proclamation ordering all cattle to be removed from the Cheyenne-Arapaho reservation, President Cleveland issued another proclamation ordering the removal of all fences from the public lands and calling upon United States officials throughout the West to assist in the execution of this

49 Proclamation of July 24, 1885, 24 *Stats.*, p. 1023. See also Sheridan's Report, *House Ex. Doc.* No. 1, 49 Cong., 1 Sess., Vol. II.

50 Memorial of Cherokee Strip Live Stock Association.

51 This depression began by 1885. *The Report of the Bureau of Animal Industry* of the next year stated that prices of beef cattle were less by fifteen dollars a head throughout the plains area than they had been when highest and that this had prevented additional men entering the industry and so caused stagnation. *Report of Bureau of Animal Industry*, 1886, p. 105.

52 A lengthy Senate investigation with respect to grazing on Indian lands had taken place late in 1884 and early in 1885. See *Senate Report No. 1278,* 49 Cong., 1 Sess., Vol. VIII.

53 *23 Stats.*, p. 321.

order.[54] As far as possible this was done but the added convenience and reduced expense in ranching operations afforded by wire fences tempted many men to replace the fences removed under the President's order as soon as they deemed it safe to do so. The subject came up again and again and was the source of much trouble to the government for many years.[55]

The winter of 1885–6 was not severe in the North and the loss in Wyoming, Montana, Dakota, and throughout the northern range area was slight. Prices were lower in 1886, but the business still seemed prosperous on the northern plains. Ranges, however, were in many places over-stocked and yet a large number of southern cattle were brought in during the summer of 1886 and spread out over the range in most reckless fashion.[56] The result was that cattle in large areas by no means were in good condition at the beginning of cold weather, which came early.

The winter of 1886–7 was terrible. Deep snows and heavy winds were followed by intense cold such as even the men who had been pioneers in the ranching business in that region never had seen before and had hardly believed possible. The results were tragic. The cattle, unable by pawing through the snow to find enough of the scanty herbage to sustain life, drifted before the bitter winds across the barren prairies, or huddled together in ravines and died by thousands. In many localities nearly all of the Texas cattle died, while the loss among the native cattle was frightful.[57] For years following the winter of 1886–7 the streams of the northern range country were bordered by dead willows and other brushwood that the starving animals had peeled as high as they could reach in their struggle for existence.[58]

54 Proclamation of August 7, 1885. *24 Stats.,* p. 1024.

55 In 1886 the Commissioner of the General Land Office reported that up to that time 375 inclosures aggregating nearly six and a half million acres had been brought to his attention and that 130 miles of fence in one single case had been built. *Report of Commissioner of General Land Office,* 1886, p. 455.

56 Clay, pp. 177-178. The Continental Cattle Company drove 32,000 steers north in the summer of 1886, the Worsham Cattle Company, 5,000, Dickey Brothers, 6,000, and numerous others brought large herds.

57 *Ibid.,* pp. 180-181.

58 *Ibid.*

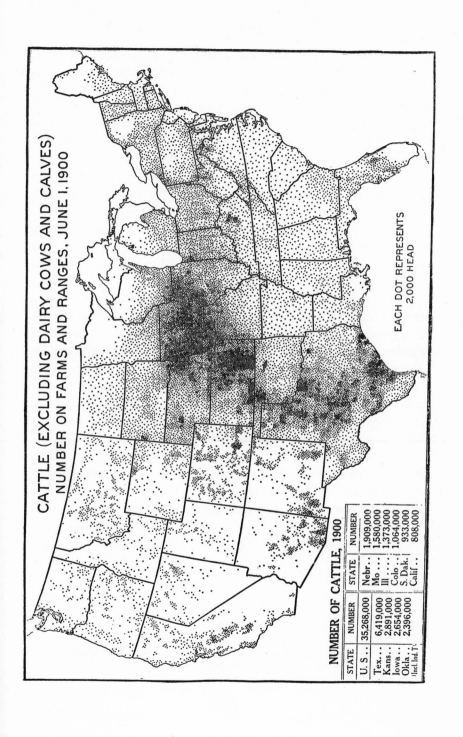

CATTLE (EXCLUDING DAIRY COWS AND CALVES)
NUMBER ON FARMS AND RANGES, JUNE 1, 1900

EACH DOT REPRESENTS
2,000 HEAD

NUMBER OF CATTLE, 1900

STATE	NUMBER	STATE	NUMBER
U. S...	35,268,000	Nebr...	1,909,000
		Mo....	1,580,000
Tex...	6,419,000	Ill....	1,373,000
Kans...	2,891,000	Colo..	1,064,000
Iowa..	2,654,000	S.Dak.	933,000
Okla..	2,396,000	Calif..	808,000
(Incl.Ind.T.)			

The winter of 1886–7 was a tragedy for most of the ranchmen in the plains area from southern Colorado to Canada. The Continental Cattle Company lost most of the 32,000 head of southern cattle brought to the northern ranges the preceding summer. One ranchman recovered but 100 out of 5,500 head of Texas cattle turned on the range in the fall of 1886.[59] Other men made no attempt to gather the few animals left from herds they had brought up from Texas the fall before.[60] Losses of forty to sixty per cent among southern cattle were common. In Montana 663,716 head of cattle were assessed for taxation in 1886 and only 471,171 in 1887 and the difference was said to be entirely due to the heavy loss in the winter.[61] Wyoming dropped from nearly 900,000 head assessed for taxes in 1886 to a little over 750,-000 in 1887.[62]

It was not until spring came that most men began to realize the extent of their losses. Then it soon became apparent that virtually every ranchman on the northern plains was facing bankruptcy. Men who from humblest beginnings had, at the expense of much toil and hardship, built up a good business found the work of years wiped out in a few months. An industry that but a short time before had been flourishing was prostrate. Not only had these vast numbers of cattle perished but prices were low and were destined to be much lower.

The disaster was so great that many of the British and numerous eastern men engaged in ranching were completely discouraged and sold their cattle and quit the business.[63] A few others, in company with many pioneer western ranchmen, set bravely to work to try to avoid complete financial ruin.

It was a difficult and, for not a few, an impossible task. Many men had borrowed heavily from western banks to buy cattle and

---

59 *Ibid.*, pp. 180-181.
60 *Ibid.*
61 *First Annual Report of the Montana Bureau of Agriculture, Labor and Industry*, 1893, p. 272.
62 *Wyoming Bulletin of Agricultural Statistics*, 1923, p. 40.
63 It was at this time that Theodore Roosevelt gave up ranching in Dakota on the Little Missouri. See Hagerdorn, *Roosevelt in the Bad Lands.*

pay operating expenses. The notes were due and the bankers were often not in a position to renew them, especially since the collateral was in many cases entirely insufficient owing to the heavy losses and reduced prices.

To meet the growing demands of their creditors, the western ranchmen began the shipment of cattle early and in ever increasing volume. Many of the animals were only half fat and, so, unfit for slaughter.[64] The summer of 1887 was extremely dry in the corn states. The corn crop was much damaged and the pastures in Illinois and other states of the Middle West dried up completely, forcing stock farmers to ship their cattle to Nebraska for pasturage.[65] Under such circumstances there was little or no demand for stockers and feeders and prices went lower and lower. By October from 5,000 to 7,500 range cattle were reaching the Chicago market every day and prices for fair to choice northwestern range steers were $2.50 to $3.25 a hundred weight, while Texans were $1.90 to $2.50.[66] Cows brought $1.25 to $2.75 and stockers $1.90 to $2.25.[67]

Such prices were ruinous, and yet shipments continued, since many men could obtain money in no other way. Failures that had begun early in the spring increased in number throughout the summer and autumn. Swan Brothers, the largest operators in Wyoming, failed as a result of the severe winter, and closed out their interests to a group of Scotch capitalists who formed the Swan Land and Cattle Company.[68] The largest banking house in Cheyenne failed, as did also the Niobrara Cattle Company of Nebraska which carried with it the leading bank of the St. Louis Stock Yards.[69] Minor failures were common, while throughout

64 *Breeder's Gazette,* Sept. 15, 1887, p. 434.

65 *Ibid.,* July 7, 1887, p. 2.

66 *Ibid.,* Oct. 6, 1887, p. 552-553.

67 *Ibid.,* Sept. 29, 1887, p. 514.

68 *Ibid.,* July 28, 1887, p. 117. The Scotch investors paid two and a half million dollars for the Swan interests. They later claimed that they had paid $800,000 too much since the price was based upon a much larger number of cattle than they actually received. It was stated that the price paid was based upon 89,167 head of cattle while the number was really only 60,000 and on 22,826 head of calves when the number amounted by actual count to only 1,600.

69 *Ibid.,* Oct. 27, 1887, p. 662.

the range area nearly every large operator was facing ruin and the small ones were in even worse condition.[70]

The year of 1887 marked the beginning of a change. Men realized for the first time that year around grazing in most areas of the northern plains was a myth.[71] The dangers of over-stocking the range and of the reckless policies formerly employed became all too apparent. Forced by the necessity of paying their debts, many large operators began a policy of retrenchment, made even more necessary by the shortage of range due to reduced carrying capacity of many large areas that had been for years over-stocked. Also the homesteaders were by this time advancing west in ever increasing numbers and taking up the best grass lands of the fertile valleys.[72] In addition to heavy shipments of cattle to market, large herds were removed from many of the closely cropped ranges of Wyoming to Montana and other newer ranges that did not yet show so clearly the results of over-stocking.[73] Above all, large operators began to reduce their herds and to change their methods. Hay was cut in summer and feeding done in winter and better care of the animals began to be practiced. Smaller numbers and better care meant a tendency to improve breeds and more and more thoroughbred and high grade cattle were purchased in the corn belt for that purpose.[74]

As the number of cattle was reduced the number of sheep increased. They were brought in large numbers to many ranges that had been so closely grazed in the past as to be no longer capable of supporting a large number of cattle. Wyoming, which in 1886 had according to the assessment rolls 898,121 head of cattle and 308,997 head of sheep, by 1894 had only 234,724 head of cattle and 881,695 head of sheep.[75] By 1900 the cattle numbered

[70] Clay, pp. 180-181.

[71] *Ibid.*

[72] *Annual Report of the Bureau of Animal Industry*, 1886, p. 105, or *Ibid.*, 1887-1888, p. 331.

[73] Cox, p. 19.

[74] The purchase of high grade cattle in the corn belt had been begun early but increased as the years went by. Swan Brothers are said to have paid $20,000 to one breeder in Illinois for thoroughbred bulls. See *Breeder's Gazette*, Feb. 28, 1882, and June 14, 1883.

359,069 while the number of sheep had risen to 2,624,689.[76] By 1907 the value of sheep in Wyoming exceeded that of cattle,[77] while by 1909 the number of sheep assessed for taxation had reached the enormous total of 4,580,433 while the number of cattle was 792,797.

The number of sheep began to decline after 1909. The number of cattle also declined each year for the next two years and then began to rise again, but not until the peak year of 1919 were there as many assessed for taxation as in 1886. By that time the number of sheep had fallen to 2,719,249 and the number of both cattle and sheep fell steadily annually for the next five years.[78]

In Montana the decline of cattle was not so noticeable in the years following 1886, but the increase in sheep was equally apparent. Montana in 1886 had, according to assessment rolls, 663,-716 cattle and 968,298 sheep.[79] In 1893 the number of cattle was 770,931 and sheep 2,254,527.[80] By 1900 the number of cattle had fallen to 678,508 and that of sheep had increased to 3,552,081.[81]

These changes did not take place without many difficulties between cattlemen and sheepmen, but space cannot be given to details. There were bloodshed and almost "range wars" in some localities, but eventually such troubles were adjusted and the two groups carried on their business in comparative peace, though smoldering fires of bad feeling would occasionally flare up and threaten a conflagration.[82]

Neither is it possible to give within reasonable space a de-

[75] See Wyoming Agricultural Statistics, 1923, pp. 39-40.

[76] *Ibid.*

[77] *Ibid.*

[78] *Ibid.*, 1923, pp. 39-40.

[79] *First Annual Report of Montana Bureau of Agriculture, Labor and Industry,* pp. 272-276.

[80] *Ibid.*

[81] *Seventh Annual Report of Montana Bureau of Agriculture, Labor and Industry,* p. 429.

[82] See *House Executive Doc.* No. 232, 50 Cong., 1 Sess., Vol. 28. The so called "Rustlers' War" in Wyoming which came about 1892-93 was brought on in part by the bad feeling between ranchmen and homesteaders. Troops were at one time called out to settle disturbances.

tailed account by years of the conditions of the cattle industry on the central and northern plains for the decade following 1887. It is extremely doubtful if such an account would, in any case, be profitable. The depression in the business during most of this time contributed to the growth of the tendency that began in 1887 to reduce the size of herds and ranches and to give better care to animals and improve the quality. It was accompanied by a growing tendency to finish animals for market younger than had been the case earlier. Soon after the Civil War steers were frequently kept until five or six years of age or even older. Later four-year-old beeves were the rule and still later three-year-olds and even younger. This was in part due to the growing scarcity of range which made it necessary to market animals as early as possible. Coupled with this was the growing tendency to improve the breed and give better care which made it possible to produce fat, merchantable cattle at a much earlier age than in the old days of wild Spanish steers reared entirely upon the open range. Perhaps the increasing demand of the public for "young beef" of high quality had its influence also.[83]

The opening of the great Indian reservations of Oklahoma to settlement in the years following 1889 reduced the "cow country" by an area nearly equal to that of Ohio.[84] The Cheyenne-Arapaho reservation, opened in 1892, had supported over 200,000 head of cattle,[85] and the Cherokee Outlet, settled in 1893, 300,000 head.[86] Forced off the Indian lands, these cattle must either be marketed or thrown upon the already over-stocked ranges of the North. The scarcity and increased cost of pasturage brought the ranchmen of the plains into still closer relationship with the corn belt.

[83] The demand for so called "baby beef" came somewhat later, but the tendency to market young cattle for slaughter began early.

[84] The state of Ohio has 40,740 square miles. Oklahoma Territory which was composed of the Indian reservations and some other lands west of the territory of the Five Civilized Tribes contained in 1900 about 36,000 square miles.

[85] See Sheridan's Report, *House Ex. Doc.* No. 1, 49 Cong., 1 Sess., Vol. II, Part II. Sheridan estimated the number of cattle removed from the reservation in 1885 was 210,000 head. These had all been removed by the early winter of 1885 but the following summer other cattle were brought to this reservation and later leases of Indian lands for grazing had been approved by the Department of the Interior.

[86] Memorial of the Cherokee Strip Live Stock Association.

Instead of attempting to mature and fatten animals for market upon the grass alone, they began more and more to ship young steers to the corn belt to be finished upon hay and corn. To a certain extent the corn states became a feeding and finishing ground for young steers from the central and northern plains in somewhat the same relation that the latter area had formerly been with respect to Texas.[87]

The early nineties was a hard time for the ranch cattle business, as well as for agriculture in general. Low prices continued which, coupled with increased cost of production, caused many men to quit the business and served to reduce the profits of those remaining. Yet, in some areas the number of cattle increased largely from 1890 to 1900 and careful operators at times secured fair profits. Toward the close of the decade came higher prices and renewed activity, but the days of extremely large scale production and enormous profits were gone forever. In the future ranching was to be carried on in a more sane and conservative fashion, in most cases by comparatively small operators who must use care and sound business methods in order to gain even a reasonable profit from the business.

[87] Paper of R. M. Allen. *Proceedings of National Stock Growers' Convention,* Denver, Colorado, 1889, pp. 101-102.

6.

TEXAS AND THE
SOUTHWEST

As the ranch cattle industry spread over the central and northern plains and developed to enormous proportions, it was also advancing rapidly in Texas and the Southwest. In addition to the outlet furnished for Texas cattle by the northern drive, shipments by sea were resumed almost as soon as the war had closed. Also a number of slaughtering establishments grew up along the Gulf and these purchased a considerable number of cattle. These were at first formed largely to slaughter old cows and other unmerchantable cattle for their hides and tallow,[1] but some of them soon began to buy beeves and pack the meat in cans for shipment to the East.[2] By 1870 it was stated that Texas was shipping five times as much tallow to New Orleans as ever before, owing to the number of beef packeries in the state.[3] Even as late as 1880 three establishments located at Fayette, Aransas, and Robertson slaughtered over 16,000 beeves annually, selling about eighty-five per cent of their output in the form of canned beef and the remainder either fresh or salted or cured.[4]

These small establishments, the shipments by sea and, above all, the northern drive furnished a market for enormous numbers of cattle. Prices soon began to rise and there came a renewed activity in the ranching industry.

As has been indicated hardly more than one third of Texas was occupied by any considerable population at the close of the

[1] James Cox, *op. cit.*
[2] McArthur Manuscript, p. 260.
[3] Texas *Almanac*, 1870, p. 182. Quoted in the McArthur Manuscript, p. 264.
[4] 10th Census, Vol. III, p. 977. The exact number given was 16,688.

Civil War (see map). To the west of the frontier line lay a vast unoccupied area which may be divided roughly into several regions according to topography and climate.

In the extreme northwest lay the "Panhandle" composed largely of high level plains covered with short mesquite or grama grass. It was an excellent grazing region except that much of it had little water. In the eastern portion of the Panhandle the high plains dropped abruptly for several hundred feet to a region of rolling prairies. This region along the foot of the plains was better watered than the plains themselves since numerous small streams had their sources there. Here also were ridges, ravines, and patches of low, sandy hills covered with scrub oaks and coarse bunch grass.

South of the Panhandle was an enormous region lying between the hundredth meridian and the Pecos, most of which was well adapted for grazing. The northern part of this was the so-called Southern Plains, quite as level as those of the Panhandle, and, in fact, part of the same region but lower and not so cold in winter.

Farther south were rougher areas with open forests of mesquite and in the extreme south much cactus and other desert plants.

West of the Pecos was a large region fairly well adapted to grazing, but so remote from the settlements to the east, and so exposed to Indian and Mexican marauders that its occupation by cattle did not come until comparatively late.[5]

West of the Nueces, and between that river and the Rio Grande, was an excellent grazing region including such counties as Nueces, Cameron, Hidalgo, and Starr. The climate was mild, the pasturage, generally speaking, good, and it was better watered than many other parts of Texas.[6]

East of the hundredth meridian and north of the Nueces was a large region extending north to Red River, most of it covered with excellent grass and fairly well watered.[7]

[5] *Ibid.*, p. 969.
[6] *Ibid.*, p. 970.
[7] *Ibid.*, p. 970.

[103]

Within a few years after the close of the war, the Texas ranch-men were pushing their herds westward into these unoccupied areas all along the western frontier, occupying new ranges and holding them in spite of frequent attacks by bands of hostile Indians.

Northwestern Texas for some distance south of Red River was, for several years, peculiarly open to Indian attacks. The Kio-was, Comanches, Cheyennes, Arapahoes, and other fierce plains tribes had been located in the western part of Indian Territory, and were presumably confined to their reservations and under the control of their agents. Nevertheless, they frequently organ-ized war parties for the purpose of raiding in Texas, where they drove off horses and cattle and murdered and scalped people.

In 1871 there were many depredations committed by these Indians and in fact almost every year thereafter until about 1875, by which time they had been pretty well reduced to submission.[8]

In spite of the danger of Indian attack the ranchmen were soon pushing their herds northwest into the region south of Red River, and even beyond into the Panhandle itself. In 1872 Ikard Brothers established a ranch on the Wichita River in what is now Wichita County, where they were frequently forced to defend themselves and their property against the Kiowas and Coman-ches.[9] A year or so later Daniel Waggoner brought a herd to the same region. Here also came Harrold Brothers with large herds and a few years later numerous others.[10]

As the range became crowded many men advanced farther west. Greer County between the 100th meridian and the two forks

8 In 1871 one ranching firm in Concho County is said to have lost 6,000 or 7,000 head of cattle by Indian attacks. The McArthur Manuscript, pp. 118-120. The Indian Territory was for years a source of trouble and danger to the people of northwest Texas since out of it there came not only bands of savages to raid and plunder but also white outlaws and renegades who had found the Indian country a convenient and fairly safe hiding place. The people of northwest Texas, no doubt, came to look upon the Indian Territory in somewhat the same fashion as the New England and New York border settlers of the seventeenth and early part of the eighteenth centuries regarded Canada. Both were the home land of savage marauders.

9 10th Census, Vol. III, p. 973. Also Richthofen, p. 47.

10 *Ibid.*, p. 972.

of Red River was early occupied, and about 1875 a few men had reached the Panhandle.

About 1877 Charles Goodnight brought a herd to the Panhandle from Colorado and established a range on the head of Red River along the Palo Duro Canyon.[11] His location was two hundred miles or more from a railroad and large numbers of buffalo were grazing about over the range, yet he remained and eventually developed one of the largest ranches in Texas.

As the ranchmen advanced into northwest Texas there came an equally rapid advance farther south. Virtually all of these earlier operators pastured their herds almost exclusively upon the public domain of the state and organized themselves into groups, as was the case on the northern plains, for mutual aid and protection. Several large regional associations were formed quite early. These set the time and made plans for the round-ups, appointed inspectors to watch the trails and markets for cattle belonging to members of the organization, sought to secure legislation helpful to the cattlemen, and tried in every way to advance the interests of the stock raising business.

The best known of all these was the Northwest Texas Cattle Raisers' Association, formed at Graham in 1877 by a comparatively small group of ranchmen.[12] The territory covered by its operations extended from the Colorado to Red River. This was divided into districts and members were appointed in each district to watch for stray animals and return them to their owners.[13] In 1883 brand inspectors were appointed to devote their entire time to the inspection of cattle driven from one region to another or shipped to market. A convention was held each year at which reports were given by officers and various committees, and plans made for the following year's work.

[11] Cox, pp. 479-480. Goodnight had gone from Texas to Colorado in 1868 where he settled near Pueblo. He established another ranch near Trinidad and was a large stockholder in the Stock Growers' Bank of Pueblo, but lost his fortune in the Panic of 1873 and formed a partnership with John G. Adair to engage in ranching in the Panhandle. The firm is said to have owned at one time 100,000 head of cattle. *Ibid.*

[12] *The Cattleman*, March, 1916, pp. 15–18.

[13] *Ibid.*, March, 1925, p. 30.

The influence of this organization upon legislation as well as in securing better freight rates and in protecting the property of its members was enormous. About 1895 a large body of ranchmen from southwestern Texas became members, and the name was changed to the Cattle Raisers' Association of Texas. Later it was changed to the Texas and Southwestern Cattle Raisers' Association when in 1921 the Panhandle and Southwestern Stockmen's Association was merged with it. Since its organization it has recovered 110,000 cattle, or their value, for its members, and its benefits in preventing heavier losses by theft are almost incalculable.

As the cattle industry grew in importance and competition for ranges grew keener due to the spread of cattle over the western plains, many ranchmen began to realize the importance of securing a more permanent tenure of ranges than could be acquired by mere occupation of the state's public domain with their herds. This was rendered comparatively easy by the liberal laws of the state. During the period of the Republic large grants of land had been made to endow the university, and 17,712 acres had been given to each county for public schools.[14] The state continued the liberal policies of the Republic in disposing of the public lands, and in 1858 passed a law providing that sixteen sections a mile should be granted in alternate sections to railroads constructing as much as twenty-five miles of track within the state.[15] A homestead of 160 acres was also provided for every head of a family, and grants were made to soldiers of the Texas War of Independence as well as to soldiers of the Civil War.[16]

In 1876 Texas made a new constitution which provided that the alternate sections of tracts granted to railways and one-half of the public domain should be set aside to form a permanent school fund.[17] Subsequent acts provided for the sale of these school lands, the maximum amount that could be purchased by one person being set first at 4,480 and later at 2,560 acres, while

14 Miller, *A Financial History of Texas*, p. 53.
15 *Ibid.*, p. 116.
16 Constitution of 1876, Art. VII, Sec. 6.
17 *Ibid.*, Art. VII, Sec. 2.

the price usually ranged from one to two dollars an acre.[18] Payments for school lands were at first distributed over a period of ten years which was later raised to thirty and at last to forty years.[19]

The low price of these lands and the liberal terms of payment prompted many ranchmen to secure permanent control of ranges by purchase, particularly as the competition for pasturage grew increasingly keen. Large tracts were bought by many men, the clause relating to the maximum amount purchasable by one person being persistently evaded by buying land in the names of employees or various members of the ranchman's family.[20]

Not only were these enormous areas of school land placed on the market, but large grants were also made to railroads under the law previously mentioned, usually with the provision that the railway must alienate these lands within a specified time. This too was often evaded by ostensible sales to land companies formed among the railway stockholders, yet the state sought earnestly to stop this practice and apparently met with some success.[21]

The period from 1870 to 1890 saw an enormous amount of railway construction in Texas due at first, no doubt, in part to land grants. The railway mileage within the state was at the close of the war but 335. By 1870 it had risen to 711; by 1880 to 3,293, and by 1890 to 8,709.[22]

In 1873 the Missouri, Kansas and Texas, building southwest from St. Louis, reached Denison on Red River. That at once became a great shipping point to which thousands of cattle were driven in the autumn of that year for shipment north.[23] The road was soon extended to Fort Worth and from there to Houston and Galveston, giving to Texas her first outlet by rail to the northern markets.

[18] Miller, pp. 332-340.

[19] *Ibid.* Land laws were changed so frequently that generalizations are difficult and never more than approximately correct.

[20] *Ibid.*, p. 331.

[21] Texas Constitution of 1876, Art. VII, Sec. 5.

[22] *Report of the Comptroller*, 1910, or *Texas Almanac*, 1910, p. 116. After 1890 construction was halted somewhat, though in 1900 there was 9,867 miles and in 1910 nearly 14,000 miles. *Ibid.*

[23] Cox, pp. 697-704.

By 1888 the Gulf Colorado and Santa Fe had been opened from Kansas City to Fort Worth and south to Galveston, and soon after came the Rock Island crossing the Indian Territory a little west of the Santa Fe. This gave Texas excellent railway facilities and shipments by rail gradually took the place of driving on the trail, which eventually ceased entirely.

These main lines running to the northern markets soon came to be crossed by other lines running east and west with the result that nearly every part of Texas was at last brought within comparatively easy reach of railroads. Prominent among these east and west lines were the Southern Pacific from Orange and Beaumont to El Paso, and the Texas Pacific reaching from Texarkana to El Paso through the heart of an excellent grazing region.[24] The Panhandle which had been quite remote from railroad was penetrated before 1890 by the Fort Worth and Denver, upon which construction was begun near Fort Worth in 1881. By the autumn of 1882 it had reached Wichita Falls, which remained the terminus until 1885. Construction was then resumed and in 1888 the line was opened to Denver.[25]

Grants of land were given to all of these roads except the Rock Island and the Fort Worth and Denver. Grants were also made to the Houston and Texas Central, the International and Great Northern, and the St. Louis Southwestern, as well as to one or two short lines and to some other internal improvement companies.[26] The entire area granted to railways amounted to 32,400,-000 acres with an additional 4,088,000 acres for other internal improvements, making a total of 36,488,000 acres.[27] Much of this railroad land was placed upon the market at about the same price as school land, and with liberal terms of payment.

No doubt the purchase of school and railway lands and the establishment of permanent and well improved ranches was considerably influenced by the invention and growing use of barb

[24] See map. The Texas Pacific was built through the range area about 1883, and had a great influence in that region.
[25] Cox, p. 696.
[26] Miller, p. 326.
[27] *Ibid.* Also *Report of Texas Land Office,* 1910.

wire. The first marketing of barb wire was in 1874, though a patent had been issued for one type as early as 1868.[28] In 1875 two salesmen for Joseph E. Glidden, the pioneer manufacturer of barb wire, appeared in Texas with samples of the new fencing material. Their experience was at first not encouraging. Most ranchmen feared that so many animals would injure themselves on the barb wire fences as to make the use of such fences entirely impracticable. Bills were even introduced in the legislature to prohibit their construction though none of these bills ever passed.[29]

A few spools were sold to local dealers, and at last a carload to a ranching firm. Within a year or two the demand had grown to considerable proportions, and the two salesmen established an agency for the state of Texas at Houston. Within a few years they were selling barb wire to the value of $750,000 annually.[30]

Barb wire almost revolutionized the cattle industry in Texas just as it did farther north. Great quantities were hauled to the western ranges and an era of fencing began, fostered by the increasing scarcity of range, and the growing prosperity of the ranching industry. The first cost of fencing was considerable, usually $100 to $200 a mile, depending upon the distance that wire and posts must be hauled. But once a range was inclosed operating expenses were greatly reduced. Not only was less labor required in caring for the cattle, but losses from straying and theft were much lessened. It also became possible to conserve the range and to give better care to young and poor animals in the winter.[31] Finally, fencing had an important influence in improving the quality of cattle.

When cattle must be pastured exclusively upon the open range, many men were reluctant to purchase purebred or high grade bulls, since they could not be sure of having exclusive use of them. This was made possible by fencing, and heavy purchases of high grade animals were made in the East, while not a few

28 Statement of American Steel and Wire Company, pp. 1 and 5.
29 Cox, pp. 501-502.
30 *Ibid.*
31 10th Census, Vol. III, p. 990.

ranches were established in Texas that were to be devoted entirely to raising breeding animals for market in the range cattle area.[32] As a result the quality of cattle in Texas steadily rose.

There can be little doubt that wire fencing also had a great influence upon the efforts of numerous ranchmen to open large, unwatered areas to grazing by providing an artificial water supply. In 1880 it was stated that nearly half of the Staked Plains were unwatered, and that a total of 29 million acres of land in Texas was entirely unavailable for grazing owing to lack of water.[33] Further extension of grazing, it was said, must be dependent upon discovering some means of watering large areas.[34] This was undoubtedly true as cattle will not ordinarily graze more than five to ten miles from water, and large areas in the Panhandle and other parts of western Texas were much farther than that from any permanent supply.[35]

As range became scarce more and more ranchmen began to purchase these unwatered lands, inclose them with wire fences, and provide water by drilling wells and erecting windmills. On the Southern Plains and in much of central and southern Texas, an abundant water supply was found comparatively shallow, but on the northern plains of the Panhandle, it was often necessary to drill from 300 to 800 feet in depth. This made the first cost of wells so great as to keep most homesteaders and men with small herds out of this region, and put the larger part of it into the hands of comparatively large operators.

In a later period, with comparatively good railway facilities for the hauling of drilling machinery and casing, the cost of a well from 50 to 500 feet in depth was usually from $1.25 to $2.00 a foot.[36] This meant that in most of the plains area a single well would cost, when complete with windmill, tower, tank and reservoir, about $1,000, and in some regions perhaps twice that

[32] Nimmo, p. 144.
[33] 10th Census, Vol. III, p. 967.
[34] *Ibid.*
[35] Barnes, "Stock Watering Places on Western Grazing Lands," *Farmer's Bulletin* 592, p. 4.
[36] *Ibid.*, p. 17.

much.[37] This cost was prohibitive for the ordinary homesteader or stock farmer, but the larger ranches drilled many such wells since one, if provided with a reservoir to furnish a surplus supply of water for days when there was insufficient wind to turn the windmill, would furnish water for from 350 to 500 head of cattle.[38]

The high prices of 1882 and the years immediately following caused a tremendous activity in the ranching industry of Texas and brought on an area of feverish speculation in cattle and lands. Cattle that sold on the Texas ranges in 1880 at $7.00 a head were $11.00 a head by 1881, $16.00 by 1882, and $25.00 a head by 1883.[39] Large numbers were sold in the last year named at $20.00 to $25.00 a head, and huge sums were borrowed at 1½ to 2 per cent a month for investment in cattle and lands.[40]

Most of this land was soon fenced and, in their eager desire to secure full control of more range, many men inclosed not only their own lands, but large areas of the state's public domain, and even private lands that were unoccupied by the owners. Homesteaders and men with small holdings of land and a few head of cattle frequently found themselves inclosed by the wire fences of the larger ranchmen, who in many cases left few gates and, so, subjected those inclosed to much inconvenience. The situation became so bad by 1883 as to bring on a series of fence cutting difficulties that threatened to assume the proportions of a "range war," and finally resulted in the calling of a special session of the legislature early in 1884.[41]

This special session sought to adjust these troubles. Laws were passed providing for the opening of roads through pastures, while fence cutting was made a penal offense, and fencing the public domain or herding cattle on it a misdemeanor.[42] Yet difficulties between the ranchmen and farmers continued, though with some-

37 *Ibid.*

38 *Ibid.*

39 *National Live Stock Journal,* July, 1883, p. 201.

40 Bentley, H. L., "Cattle Ranges of the Southwest," *Farmer's Bulletin,* No. 72, p. 9.

41 Miller, p. 335.

42 Laws of 1884, pp. 34 and 68.

what less violence, and the use of the state's public domain for grazing could not be entirely stopped. In 1887 it was stated that over three million acres were unlawfully fenced or used, and complaints of a similar nature were made as late as 1899 and perhaps even later.[43]

The matter of leasing school lands had been much discussed in Texas, but not until 1883 was a leasing act passed. This provided that school lands might be leased for a period of ten years at a minimum rental of four cents an acre.[44] When leasing began the State Land Board complained that it was a mere farce since the ranchmen out of custom or by agreement respected one another's ranges and refused to enter into competition.[45] Accordingly, the Land Board raised the price of leases to eight cents an acre for unwatered lands, and twenty cents an acre for watered lands, with the result that many ranchmen refused to lease at all. They openly defied the Land Board, used the land for grazing without paying anything, and when brought to trial escaped conviction because of sympathetic jurors.[46] These lease difficulties, perhaps, proved an influence in the calling of the special session of the legislature in 1884.[47]

The first leasing act was followed by others in 1887, and 1889, and still other changes were made in the sale and leasing of lands in 1901, 1905, and even later.[48] Some of these provided that lands were not subject to sale during the time of the lease, fixed a minimum price and awarded leases by competitive bidding.[49] By 1898 Texas awoke to the fact that the public domain was about all gone and the school fund had not received the one-half granted to it by the Constitution of 1876. Accordingly, the remainder of the state's unsurveyed and unappropriated lands amounting to nearly four and half million acres were transferred to the schools,

43 Miller, p. 336.
44 *Ibid.*, p. 334.
45 *Ibid.*, p. 335.
46 *Ibid.*
47 The act of the Land Board in raising the price of leases was later declared unconstitutional, in the case of Smissen *v.* the State of Texas.
48 Miller, pp. 338-342.
49 *Ibid.*, pp. 338-342.

together with nearly a million and a half acres more that had been recovered from railroads.[50] Most of this was eventually leased or sold, but difficulties still continued because purchasers endeavored to secure title to large areas by purchases made in the names of friends or members of their families.[51]

The depression following the boom of the early eighties was quite as apparent in Texas as on the northern plains, and the same tendencies for large operators to give place to smaller ones was apparent. Yet, because of the liberal land laws of Texas and the policy of leasing school lands, the ranches and scale of operations remained larger, broadly speaking, than in the North.[52]

The large ranches may be divided roughly into three groups. These were the establishments of the early citizens of Texas, mostly in the South who in many cases had as a nucleus for their ranges land grants made by Mexico or the Republic of Texas. Many of these ranches had been founded long before the Civil War, and had literally grown up with the business. Another group was composed of the ranches of men who had come in since the Civil War, or who had begun ranching since the beginning of the northern drive and had gradually secured large holdings of land by purchase or lease. Still a third class was made up of the establishments of eastern or foreign corporations, many of the latter being Scotch or English that came in during the boom period and that in some cases controlled enormous areas on which were pastured tens of thousands of cattle.[53]

One Texas ranch deserves special mention because it was said

50 *Ibid.,* p. 340.

51 *Ibid.,* p. 342.

52 It should be noted that Texas, unlike the United States, made an attempt to grade and classify her public lands as agricultural and grazing lands, or as watered and unwatered lands, and made provisions for sale or lease on the basis of classification. Larger areas of grazing and unwatered lands could be acquired than of agricultural or watered lands, and at a lower price.

53 Belonging to the first type were men like Col. Richard King, who acquired the Santa Gertrudes Ranch in 1853, and laid the foundations of the famous "King Ranch" of Texas. Others of the same type were Captain Kennedy of the Kennedy Ranch of Nueces County, O'Connor of the O'Connor Ranch and numerous others. Belonging to the second group were firms like, Ikard Brothers, Harrold Brothers, or such men as Dan Waggoner, S. B. Burnett, and Charles Goodnight operating largely in northern Texas.

to be for years the largest ranching enterprise in the world. This was the Capitol Freehold Ranch, sometimes known as the Capitol Syndicate Ranch, or X I T. In 1879 the Texas legislature had appropriated 3,050,000 acres of land for the construction of a state capitol.[54] Apparently the legislature expected that these lands would be sold in comparatively small tracts, and that the funds received would be used in the construction of a suitable building. A syndicate was formed, however, controlled largely by a group of Chicago capitalists that offered to construct a capitol building of the type desired, and to take in payment three million acres of land previously appropriated. A contract was accordingly drawn, and it was provided that certain amounts of the land should be delivered from time to time as work on the building progressed.[55] In order that the contractors might have immediate possession of the land, the entire area was leased to them at an annual rental of six cents an acre which was to be remitted in case the capitol was completed according to specifications and within the time agreed upon.[56]

The lands were located in the Texas Panhandle, and included part of nine counties. Cattle were purchased to stock the entire area, which was divided into two parts and a manager placed over each.[57] A reorganization was effected, however, in 1887; a new manager was appointed for the entire ranch which was divided into seven divisions with a foreman over each, and more than a million dollars were spent in improvements. Three hundred wells were drilled, the entire ranch was fenced and cross-fenced into pastures of convenient size, and ample buildings and corrals were provided.[58]

[54] See J. Evetts Haley, *The X I T Ranch of Texas,* for complete and scholarly account of this great ranching enterprise.

[55] Manuscript copy of the Capitol Contract, Files of Texas Library, Austin, Texas.

[56] *Ibid.*

[57] Cox, p. 495. The new manager was A. G. Boyce.

[58] *Ibid.,* p. 495. The divisions were, 1. Buffalo Springs; 2. Middle Water; 3. Ojo Bravo; 4. Rita Blanca; 5. Escarbada; 6. Spring Lake; 7. Yellow House. Each had its own headquarters while there was a general headquarters for the entire ranch. J. E. Moore, Log Book and Diary. (Manuscript.)

The ranch had at one time 160,000 head of cattle, but the number was eventually somewhat reduced.[59] The calf brand was about 35,000 a year and every effort was made to improve the quality by the use of Hereford and Polled Angus bulls.[60] A large range was secured in Montana and for several years about 12,500 young steers were driven to this northern range each summer.[61] The pay roll of the entire ranch amounted to from $7,000 to $8,000 a month. Efficient business methods were employed and the X I T ranch presented an excellent example of well-organized ranching on a very large scale.[62]

A great Texas ranch which is typical of the ranching enterprises established with foreign capital is the Matador. The Matador Land and Cattle Company Limited, was formed in December, 1882, by a group of Scotch investors with a capital of $2,500,000. Its first ranch, the original Matador, was established by the purchase of several properties in the counties of Motley, Cottle, Dickens and Floyd, with its headquarters a hundred miles from railroad. At the end of the first year the company had about 375,000 acres of land and over 75,000 head of cattle. By perseverance and stern determination the Matador weathered the storms of the latter half of the eighties, and in 1891 had increased its holdings to 540,000 acres of deeded land and about 200,000 more leased from the state.

So much of this leased land was taken up by settlers that the company purchased a new ranch of 227,000 acres in Oldham County known as the Alamocitas ranch. To this, 120,000 acres more were added and the entire area was utilized as a breeding ranch. Large ranges were also leased in Montana and Dakota, and to these were sent the two-year-old steers from the Texas ranches to be matured.

59 *Ibid.*

60 *Ibid.* Also Moore, Log Book and Diary.

61 *Ibid.*

62 The high price of land and reduced prices for cattle eventually caused the owners of the Capitol Syndicate ranch to dispose of their cattle and begin to sell out the land in small tracts to actual settlers. However, in 1922 they still owned about a million acres which they leased to cattlemen. Moore, Log Book and Diary.

The Matador company owned in 1925 about 830,000 acres of land and had under lease about 700,000 more in South Dakota and Montana. It maintained a herd of about 70,000 head of cattle and marketed about 10,000 head annually. The ranches were fenced and cross-fenced into numerous pastures, wells had been drilled to provide watering facilities and careful attention to breeding had made its herd one of the finest in the world. The company keeps a small breeding herd of pure bred Herefords to produce bulls, and also buys a number of pure bred bulls each year, so that it has on its two ranches more than a thousand head of pure bred sires.[63]

As the cattle industry spread west and northwest over the Texas plains, there was a tendency for the Panhandle and much of northwestern Texas to become a feeding ground for the maturing of young steers purchased in the eastern and southern portions of the state. This, added to the demand for young steers for the northern drive, led to a considerable movement of cattle into Texas from the cotton states farther east. Buyers visited Arkansas, Louisiana and the southern states east of the Mississippi, and purchased large numbers of "milk pen calves" to be driven to the Texas ranges. This led to some interesting results. The calves were shipped or driven to Texas, held for a year or two upon the range and were then driven up the trail to the northern plains to be matured. From there they were shipped to the corn belt for feeding, and thence to the packing centers for slaughter. As local meat and provision dealers came to depend more and more upon the great packing houses for their supply of fresh meat, the beef was shipped to the cotton states and no

[63] Statement of Murdo MacKenzie, manager of the Matador Land and Cattle Company ranches since 1891. Of the numerous large Scotch companies incorporated during the boom period for ranching on the plains, but two, the Matador and the Swan Land and Cattle Company in Wyoming, remain. The Swan, however, is devoting much attention to sheep, so the Matador may be said to be the only one of these early Scotch companies exclusively in the business of producing cattle. A study of its operations since its formation in 1882 together with those of the "X I T" would reveal much of the history of ranching in Texas during the past four or five decades since these two are entirely typical of the large and successful ranching enterprises of the state.

doubt sold in many cases to the very men who had originally produced the animal supplying it.

The opening of a direct railway communication with the eastern markets not only checked greatly the northern drive, but also led to the development of cattle feeding in Texas, especially in the cotton growing sections of the state. Animals were at first fed largely upon raw cotton seed, but as oil mills were built the superior qualities of cotton seed meal and cake were soon discovered. Feeding yards were established at many places in central, eastern and southern Texas and large shipments of steers, fattened on these products, were made to the packing centers of Kansas City, St. Louis and Chicago.

It was early felt that packing establishments should be built up in Texas and, as has been indicated, numerous small ones were developed soon after the Civil War. The high prices of the early eighties caused most of these to suspend operations, but as prices began to decline in the years following the boom period others were formed. Small packing plants were established at Houston, Waco, San Antonio, Dallas, and numerous other points; but Fort Worth, because of its central location and superior railway connections, soon became the chief packing center of the state. It was not until the establishment of the Armour and Swift plants at that city, however, that Fort Worth began to assume a position of national importance in the meat packing industry. By 1910 it was the fifth cattle market of the country and in 1917 its annual receipts of cattle had risen to over 1,960,000 head.[64]

The great depression in the ranching industry and the consequent distress of most men engaged in it after 1885 was almost, if not entirely, as apparent in Texas as on the northern plains. In both regions no small part of the cattlemen's troubles was due to the reckless policy of overstocking the range during the prosperous years of the earlier period. This heavy over-stocking was no doubt in part due to the failure of the ranchmen to realize, as they advanced westward into dryer areas, how much less was the carrying capacity of the ranges there than farther east in regions

[64] See table.

[117]

of more abundant rainfall. Also as more and more homesteaders came upon the ranges settling and fencing small tracts of choice lands, there can be little doubt that many ranchmen failed to understand that the carrying capacity of large areas was thereby reduced out of all proportion to the actual percentage of lands so inclosed. There can be no doubt, however, that the chief reasons for over-stocking were the eager desire to make money quickly and the added fact that the tenure of lands was in many cases precarious and of a temporary character. Keen competition existed for ranges, and most men pasturing herds on the public domain of the state realized that they could not hope to be permitted to remain long, and in consequence pastured their ranges so heavily in many cases as to destroy the grass almost entirely. Other men with leases also over-stocked their pastures very much, particularly as the period of the lease drew to a close, seeking to get the greatest possible return from the pasturage in the short time that remained to them.

Lack of water and the expense of creating a supply by artificial means were also responsible for much damage to the range. The watering places were often so few and far apart that large numbers of cattle remained near them for several hours each day tramping out the grass until the ground for some distance in every direction was entirely bare, while other areas remote from the watering places were not pastured enough.[65] Within a few years the carrying capacity of large areas was reduced more than half.[66] Ranges that formerly would require not more than five acres to the head for year around grazing were so damaged that they would not support more than fifty head to the section (640 acres).[67] Weeds took the place of grass, the cattle did not fatten, and when dry summers came, followed by cold winters, the loss was frightful.

After 1890 the number of cattle steadily decreased for many

[65] See H. L. Bentley, "Cattle Ranges of the Southwest," *Farmer's Bulletin 72* (1898), for a detailed account of how much Texas ranges were damaged by over-stocking.

[66] *Ibid.*, pp. 8-9.

[67] *Ibid.*

years. In that year the census showed 8,543,635 head on farms and ranges as compared with 3,990,158 on farms in 1870, and 4,894,-698 on farms and ranges in 1880. In 1890, 7,378,203 head of cattle were assessed for taxation in Texas, and by 1895 this number had fallen to 4,873,898.[68] Toward the close of the century there came an era of higher prices and a consequent renewed activity in ranching, and the number of cattle listed for taxation in 1900 was 6,308,254 head, while the census that year gave the state 7,279,935, exclusive of calves less than one year old.[69] This had fallen to 7,139,400 by 1910.[70]

While many of the large ranches were broken up into smaller ones or into farms the effects of the Texas land policy are still shown in the number of large holdings maintained down to the present time. As late as 1923 there were seventy-nine individual holdings in Texas of more than fifty thousand acres each and at least forty of over 100,000 acres each.[71] Most of these were in the western regions still given over largely to grazing. Although some of them will doubtless be reduced within the next few years, the tendency to break up large ranches into smaller ones so prevalent a decade or two ago seems to have been checked now that the best agricultural lands have already been converted into farms, and there is some indication that many large ranches may be maintained indefinitely, and may even be increased in size.[72]

The development of the cattle ranching industry in New Mexico presents nothing new in the history of that business and may be dismissed with a very brief sketch. While cattle ranching became very important there, New Mexico's pre-eminence early lay in sheep raising. In this industry its importance was almost equal to that of Texas in the cattle business, since from the New Mex-

[68] *Reports of Texas Comptroller,* 1890 and 1895.

[69] 12th Census, Vol. V, p. 480.

[70] 13th Census, Vol. VII, p. 623.

[71] Of these seventy-nine holdings of over 50,000 acres thirty-nine were between 50,000 and 100,000 acres, twenty-nine were from 100,000 to 200,000, five were of 200,000 to 300,000, four 300,000 to 500,000 and two above 500,000 acres. *Report of Texas Department of Agriculture,* 1924, pp. 34-37.

[72] The well known "King Ranch" has recently been considerably extended by purchases of additional land.

ican ranges were drawn millions of sheep to stock the northern plains and large areas in the Rocky Mountains, as well as in Texas and the Pacific Coast states.[73]

While cattle were doubtless raised in New Mexico by the early Spanish inhabitants, cattle raising did not assume any considerable proportions there until after the Civil War. About 1865 there was a large number of troops, together with about 10,000 Navajo Indians, gathered at Fort Staunton, and many herds of cattle were brought from Texas to supply them with beef.[74] As more were brought than were needed, some of the surplus animals were driven to Colorado and others were placed on ranges in northeastern New Mexico.[75] The Indians of the Texas Panhandle were at first a source of great annoyance, but their raids were finally checked by expeditions of the New Mexico ranchmen, and the cattle industry steadily grew.[76]

Many herds were brought in from Texas over the old Goodnight Trail and pastured on the public domain of northeastern New Mexico, the ranchmen seeking to control the water supply by means of homesteads along the streams or by the purchase of railroad lands and territorial school lands. Much of the plains area and nearly all of the southern portion of the territory remained unoccupied until several years later owing to the lack of water supply and the depredations of Indian and Mexican marauders.[77]

As the Panhandle of Texas was occupied by ranchmen, some of them crossed over into New Mexico and established ranches. By 1880 it was stated that some of the northeastern counties were over-stocked, and that the range was by no means so good as it had been five years before.[78]

With the coming of barb wire many men began to inclose ranges, not only fencing the lands they had purchased and held

[73] 10th Census, Vol. III, pp. 986-994.
[74] *Ibid.*, pp. 988-989.
[75] *Ibid.*
[76] *Ibid.*
[77] *Ibid.*, p. 986.
[78] *Ibid.*

as homesteads, but large areas of the public domain as well.[79] Difficulties came between cattlemen and sheepmen, and at times between ranchmen and homesteaders, and controversies arose at times among the cattlemen themselves with respect to ranges.[80] Extravagant stories were told of the profits to be made in ranching.[81] The business eventually was spread over the entire plains area by drilling wells and erecting windmills throughout the unwatered regions. The building of the Southern Pacific and the Atchison, Topeka, and Santa Fe Railways gave New Mexico good shipping facilities and did much to promote the ranching industry. As in other parts of the plains area, the quality of stock was greatly improved by the bringing in of fine bulls from the East. In 1870 New Mexico had, according to the census, 57,534 head of cattle which had risen to 347,936 head in 1880, to 1,631,533 head by 1890, and had dropped to 803,097 head by 1900.

The lack of rainfall in New Mexico prevented the great influx of homesteaders that came to so many of the states formerly largely given over to grazing, and while some small areas were made very productive through irrigation, a large part of the state seems to be a permanent grazing region.

[79] Thorp to Secretary of Interior, Dec. 15, 1884. *House Ex. Doc. 232, 50 Cong., 1 Sess., Vol. 28,* pp. 11-12.

[80] Light to Commissioner of General Land Office, July 26, 1887. *Ibid.,* pp. 18-19.

[81] Ritch, *New Mexico, Its History, Resources and Attractions,* pp. 58-59. The author who writes in 1885 estimates a profit of 62 per cent a year in a ranching enterprise extending over a period of five years.

7.

THE RANGE CATTLE
INDUSTRY IN
OKLAHOMA

To the north of Texas between the breeding grounds of that state and the feeding grounds of the northern plains, lay the Indian Territory, later to become the state of Oklahoma. Its area was greater than that of all New England, or about equal to the combined areas of Indiana and Ohio, and much of it was almost ideal for grazing. It was well watered, the climate mild, and the pasturage in most cases excellent.

The development of ranching in this region presents a curious and interesting study. Here, as throughout the "cow country," the industry came into existence very quickly, but in the Indian Territory it declined even more rapidly than elsewhere, owing to the opening of the great Indian reservations to white settlement.

At first such settlement of the Indian Territory was forbidden, with the result that as the pioneer farmers moved westward in the years following the close of the Civil War and spread themselves over the eastern portion of the Great Plains, they were halted at the border of the Indian country by government decree. It was as though a dike, or wall, had been built about this region, a wall impervious to the waves of civilization that beat against it. Yet this barrier was not entirely proof against the ranch cattle business. An industry more fluid in its character than is agriculture, in the ordinary sense of the term, soon began to penetrate it and to spread itself over the rich pasture lands within.

As has been previously indicated, the Five Civilized Tribes of Indians were compelled in 1866 to cede a large part of their western lands as a home for friendly Indians, and as a result the Indian Territory became divided into two distinct parts: the eastern half occupied by the Five Civilized Tribes, and the western half composed of numerous reservations of western Indians, together with several large areas entirely unoccupied. Later this western region became the Territory of Oklahoma, after which the term "Indian Territory" was applied only to the area occupied by the Five Civilized Tribes. Much of this eastern part of the Indian country was wooded, and hilly, or mountainous. While a certain amount of ranching was carried on there, largely by mixed blood Indians or white men who had married Indian wives, it was only upon the wide prairie plains of the western part that the business came to assume such proportions as to have a far reaching influence upon the progress of the range cattle industry as a whole.

Among the chief Indian reservations of this region were those of the Kiowa-Comanche and of the Cheyenne-Arapaho, with some three and a half and four and a half million acres respectively, upon each of which lived less than four thousand Indians. Others less important were those of the Osage, Sac and Fox, Ponca, Otoe and Missouri, Kaw, Iowa, Pawnee, Shawnee, and Tonkawa.[1] There were three large areas entirely unoccupied. One of these was Greer County, a region some ninety miles long by seventy miles wide lying between the two Red Rivers and the hundredth meridian. It was claimed by both Texas and the Indian Territory, but the former early took possession of it and eventually organized it as a county. In the very center of the Indian Territory lay a tract of about two and a half million acres known as the "Oklahoma Lands." It had been ceded as a home for friendly Indians by the Creeks and Seminoles, but no Indians were ever located there. Farther north was the unoccupied portion of the Cherokee Outlet embracing some six million acres. It belonged to the Cherokee, who in 1866 had given the United States the right to locate friendly Indians there.

Soon after the close of the Civil War a number of herds of

1 See map, p. 125

[123]

cattle were driven to western Indian Territory by contractors who supplied beef to the Indians.[2] These were held on the reservations near the agencies and some of the beef contractors began to consider the possibility of bringing in other cattle than those intended for the Indians, to be pastured there.[3] Also, all the trails from Texas to shipping points in Kansas led across the Indian Territory. Trail drivers frequently turned aside and lingered for days and weeks in order to rest and recuperate tired and footsore animals and even drove their herds considerable distances from the trail in search of better pasturage.[4]

As the cattle industry of western Texas spread and range began to grow scarce, some of the men who had driven trail herds across the Indian Territory began to think of a permanent occupation of that region for grazing. However, when requests were made to the Department of the Interior for permission to graze herds in Greer County, the Oklahoma lands, or upon Indian reservations, they were always refused with the statement that that department had no right to grant such permission.[5]

Such occupation began, however, in spite of this attitude of the Department of the Interior. Cattle belonging to men with ranges just south of Red River or in the Panhandle of Texas came swarming across the border or, in some cases, were driven across by their owners. In the summer of 1881 Ikard and Harrold brought herds into Greer County and by 1882 had sixty thousand head there.[6] Other ranchmen brought large herds to this region, and by 1882 cattle were crossing the North Fork of Red River in large numbers and grazing on the lands of the Kiowa-Comanche.[7] Early in that year there were 50,000 head grazing on this reserva-

2 In 1882, 4,500,000 pounds of beef were required for the Indians of the Cheyenne-Arapaho agency, and 3,000,000 for the Kiowa-Comanche. See *Senate Doc.* 200, 48 Cong., 1 Sess., Vol. VII, pp. 4-5.

3 Hunter to Randall, June 23, 1880. *Senate Ex. Doc.* 54, 48 Cong., 1 Sess., Vol. IV, pp. 2-3.

4 Pope to Williams, June 12, 1882. *Ibid.*, p. 66.

5 Lewis to Price, Oct. 20, 1881. *Ibid.*, pp. 2-3 and Price to Lewis, *Ibid.*

6 Harrold to Price, Jan. 13, 1883. *Ibid.*, p. 57.

7 *Ibid.*

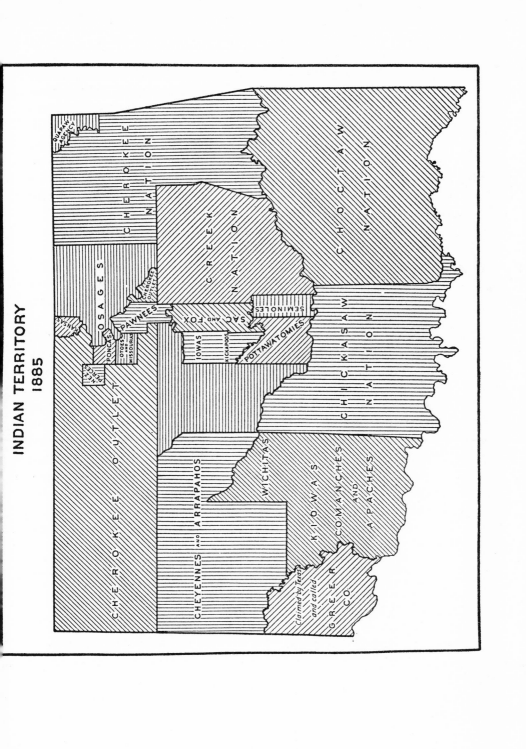

INDIAN TERRITORY
1885

tion,[8] and the Department of the Interior called upon the Secretary of War for troops to remove them.[9]

When the order of the War Department to remove these cattle was transmitted to the officers in the field, they protested that the task assigned them was an impossible one. When removed they came back immediately or were driven back by the owners.[10] It was also asserted that it was impossible to distinguish between the herds of trespassers and herds moving northward on the trail, and that in addition there were large numbers of cattle pastured on the Cherokee Outlet in consideration of the payment of a grazing fee to the Cherokee Indians. It was urged that the only solution of the problem lay either in forbidding cattle to be placed in the Territory under any circumstances—and forcing the trail drivers to go around that region with their herds—or in allowing grazing upon Indian lands upon the payment of a reasonable price for that privilege.[11]

Nevertheless, a detachment of troops was placed in the field and some effort made to remove cattle from the Kiowa-Comanche reservation, but the officer in command asserted that it was impossible. Cattle driven out one day returned the next. The ranges south of Red River were almost bare of herbage due to overstocking while the grass on the Indian Territory side was green and rank. The animals chose for themselves the better pasturage, even though their owners really tried to keep them off the Indian lands.[12] He declared that taxing ranchmen for the use of these lands for grazing was the only satisfactory way of dealing with the matter.[13]

In the meantime cattle were also trespassing upon the lands

[8] Henry to Pope, March 1, 1882, *Ibid.*, p. 60.
[9] Kirkwood to Secretary of War, Feb. 1, 1882. It was decided not to disturb the cattle in Greer County since Texas held a claim upon that area. See Kirkwood to Commissioner of Indian Affairs, Feb. 1, 1882. *Ibid.*, p. 58.
[10] Henry to Pope, *Ibid.*, p. 60.
[11] Sheridan to Lincoln, March 9, 1882. *Ibid.* Also Pope to Williams, June 12, 1882. *Ibid.*, p. 66.
[12] Henry to Pope, March 1, 1882, and Henry to Assistant Adjutant General of the Department of the Missouri, Aug. 26, 1882. *Ibid.*, pp. 60 and 78.
[13] *Ibid.*

of the Cheyenne-Arapaho Indians. Several men had driven herds to that reservation and held them there under an arrangement made with some small bands of Indians whose good will the ranchmen retained by more or less regular gifts of beef and money.[14] In the summer of 1882 the supply of beef issued by the government of the United States to the Indians of this agency was reduced, with the result that they were often hungry and became sullen and threatening in their attitude. A group of cattlemen appeared before the agent, John D. Miles, with an offer to supply sufficient beef to make good the deficiency, in consideration of being given permits to pasture cattle for a time upon the reservation. However, this offer when referred to the Commissioner of Indian Affairs was promptly rejected.[15]

Nevertheless, the ranchmen were extremely eager to secure the privilege of grazing these lands for a term of years, and apparently enlisted the sympathy and support of Agent Miles. In December, 1882, a council of Cheyenne and Arapaho chiefs assembled and filed with the agent a request to be permitted to lease a large part of their lands for grazing.[16] This request was forwarded to the Commissioner of Indian Affairs, but without awaiting a reply from that official a second council met early in January, 1883, and authorized the agent to lease all or any part of the lands mentioned in the preceding request.[17]

Agreements were immediately entered into with seven ranchmen who were to receive a total of 3,117,880 acres for a term of ten years in consideration of an annual rental of two cents an acre payable semi-annually in advance.[18] They were to be allowed to fence the land and to cut timber from the reservation for that purpose, but this fencing and all other improvements were to become the property of the Indians when the lease should expire. The Indians and the Indian Bureau were to see that the lessees

14 Dickey Brothers to Commissioner of Indian Affairs, July 30, 1883. *Ibid.*, pp. 110–11.
15 Price to Miles, Aug. 26, 1882. *Ibid.*, pp. 73-74.
16 *Sen. Ex. Doc.* 17, 48 Cong., 2 Sess., Vol. I, pp. 23-24.
17 *Ibid.*, p. 21.
18 *Ibid.*, pp. 21-22.

had exclusive use of the land during this ten-year term.[19] Copies of the leases were at once given to one of the ranchmen to be carried to Washington and presented to the Department of Interior.[20]

The action of Agent Miles brought forth a storm of protest from cattlemen who were pasturing herds on the Cheyenne-Arapaho lands or who wished to do so but had not been included in the negotiations.[21] It also brought the matter of grazing in the Indian Territory to an issue and elicited from the Secretary of the Interior a statement of policy in regard to pasturing Indian lands. This was given in a letter to Edward Fenlon, one of the lessees, who had gone to Washington and from that city had addressed a letter to Secretary Teller in which he stated that numerous trespassing ranchmen were still upon the reservation, and asked that the agent be instructed to remove these men and place him in possession of his lease.[22]

Secretary Teller replied that it was not the policy of the Department to recognize affirmatively any leases or agreements of the character mentioned, but that he saw no objection to allowing the Indians to grant permission to graze cattle upon their reservations upon fair and reasonable terms and subject to such supervision as the Department thought necessary. Teller's letter closed with the following statement of policy:

"While the Department will not recognize the agreement or lease you mention nor any other of like character to the extent of approving the same, nor to the extent of assuming to settle controversies that may arise between the different parties holding such agreements, yet the Department will endeavor to see that parties having no agreement are not allowed to interfere with those who have. Whenever there shall be just cause for dissatisfaction on the part of the Indians, or when it shall

19 *Ibid.*

20 Miles to Commissioner of Indian Affairs, April 6, 1883. *Senate Ex. Doc.* 54, 48 Cong., 1 Sess., Vol. IV, pp. 92-93.

21 Campbell to Logan, April 17, 1883. *Ibid.*, p. 96, and Campbell to Price, April 7, 1883. *Ibid.*, pp. 101-102.

22 Fenlon to Secretary of Interior, April 4, 1883. *Ibid.*, p. 98.

Drag End of the Trail Herd

The Trail Herd Reaches Water

Erwin E. Smith photograph
Library of Congress

appear that improper persons under the cover of such lease or agreement are allowed in the Territory by the parties holding such agreement, or for any reason the Department shall consider it desirable for the public interest to do so, it will exercise its right of supervision to the extent of removing all occupants from the Territory without reference to such lease or agreement, on such notice as shall be right and proper under the circumstances under which the parties have entered the Territory and have complied with the terms of the agreement and instructions of the Department. All parties accepting such agreements should accept the same subject to any future action of Congress and this Department in relation to occupants of such Territory. Instructions will be issued to the agents in accordance with this letter."[23]

It seems that anyone at all familiar with conditions in the Indian Territory should have realized that such a policy could result only in endless trouble and confusion, but in defense of Secretary Teller it must be stated that he evidently considered he had no authority to approve leases or permits for grazing on Indian lands. No opinion to that effect had been handed down by the attorney general, but such an opinion was given two years later by Attorney General Garland to whom the question was referred by the Department of the Interior.[24]

Copies of the letter to Fenlon were sent to the various Indian agents for their guidance in the matter of grazing.[25] The lessees of the Cheyenne-Arapaho reservation at once began fencing and stocking their ranges, but troubles came thick and fast.

The cattlemen on the reservation who had no agreements refused to remove their herds and small bands of Indians to whom they had been making presents of beef and money backed them up in this refusal, declaring that they had not signed the leases and did not approve of them. These Indians began to commit

23 Teller to Fenlon, April 4, 1883. *Ibid.*, p. 99.

24 July 21, 1885, 18 *Opinions*, pp. 253-258.

25 Price to Hunt, May 7, 1883, *Senate Ex. Doc.* 54, 48 Cong., 1 Sess., Vol. IV, p. 101.

depredations upon the herds of the lessees and to make trouble in many ways.[26]

To make matters worse the boundary between the Cheyenne-Arapaho and Kiowa-Comanche reservations was in dispute and the Kiowa complained that the lessees in fencing ranges had inclosed lands belonging to them. Accordingly, they proceeded to cut the wire fences, burn the grass and kill the cattle of the offending ranchmen.[27] The military was called upon for troops to restrain the Indians and protect the property of the cattlemen, but refused to furnish them on the ground that these leases had not been approved by the Department of the Interior.[28]

Under such circumstances disorder increased. The lessees formed an organization for mutual aid and protection, while trespassers and men with agreements made with isolated bands of Indians also formed groups among themselves. Factions grew up among the Indians. Some favored the lessees, others favored individual ranchmen who had been friendly to them. When hungry they killed cattle, usually avoiding animals belonging to their friends if others could be conveniently found. The ranchmen and their employees armed themselves and used every effort to protect their property, though not always with entire success.[29]

The question of grazing upon Indian lands had been referred by the Department of the Interior to Congress when that body met in December, 1883. During the next few months inquiries relative to leases or grazing of Indian Territory lands were answered by the Department of Interior with the statement that the matter had been referred to Congress and pending such reference it was deemed inexpedient to express any opinion which might embarrass the action of Congress in the matter.[30]

26 Miles to the Commissioner of Indian Affairs, July 30, 1883. *Ibid.*, p. 110-111. Also same to same, Aug. 28, 1883, pp. 117-118.

27 Cheyenne-Arapaho Live Stock Association to Price, April 10, 1884. *Senate Ex. Doc.* 17, 48 Cong., 2 Sess., Vol. I, p. 117.

28 Augur to Adjutant General of the Army, April 7, 1884, and Miles to De-Wees, March 30, 1884. *Ibid.*, p. 97.

29 *Report of the Commissioner of Indian Affairs*, 1884.

30 Price to Fyon, Dec. 15, 1883, and Price to Frew, April 5, 1884. *Senate Ex. Doc.* 17, 48 Cong., 2 Sess., Vol. I, p. 99.

$2336 25/100 — THE STOCK EXCHANGE BANK 5118 CALDWELL, KAS.

Caldwell, Kansas, March 14, 1884

On the fifteenth day of March 1888

We promise to pay to the order of S. Tuttle, Trustee, the sum of

Twenty three hundred and thirty six x 25/100 — Dollars

at the — Stock Exchange — Bank, Caldwell, Kansas

with interest after maturity at the rate of twelve per cent, per annum, until paid. Without defalcation, value received.

This note is given, as evidence of indebtedness under a lease and agreement, entered into between the undersigned and E.M.Hewins, A.J.Day, et al., Trustees, whereby certain lands in the unoccupied Cherokee Country, Indian Territory, were leased, and is to be governed as to its maturity, and payment by the terms of the lease and agreement aforesaid, on file at the office of the payee, at Caldwell, Kansas, but payment is enforceable in any court of the United States, or elsewhere.

Gregory Eldred & Co

No. 140

GRAZIER'S LICENSE.

CHEROKEE NATION

OFFICE NATIONAL TREASURER

Caldwell Kans., July 12th 1883

By virtue of authority given me by an act of the National Council, approved December 1st, 1880, to supervise the collection of the Revenue of the Nation derivable from that portion of the country not included within the Nation as organized by law, but remaining in the possession of the Cherokee Nation for the profits accruing from such possession, until sold and occupied in accordance with the provisions of the 16th Article of the Cherokee Treaty of 1866, I hereby acknowledge to have this day received, for the Treasury of the Cherokee Nation, the sum of — Three Hundred — Dollars, from — Gregory Eldred & Co — citizen of the United States, the said sum being paid by said party, and received by me, as payment made to said Nation, for grazing Cattle — upon the lands designated to the number of — 2000 — head, and no more, for the period of time included within — First — day of — May — 1883, and the — 30th — day of — Sept — 1883

Ranch located — On Salt Fork and Cimarron Rivers —

and branded —

REMARKS

D. W. Lipe

Authorized Agt. for Treasurer Cherokee Nation

Treasurer Cherokee Nation

Above—Lease Indenture; Below—Grazier's License

Many ranchmen apparently interpreted the failure of the Interior Department to prohibit their entering Indian Territory as a tacit permission to do so, and when cattle were set in motion in the spring of 1884, large numbers came pouring in. By June there were 75,000 head on the Kiowa-Comanche lands alone.[31] Also the Oklahoma lands were occupied and large areas there inclosed by wire fences.[32] The smaller reservations became covered with cattle and all vacant ranges in Greer County were occupied. A special agent sent to the Kiowa-Comanche reservation reported that a group of ranchmen there had organized themselves and were seeking to gain control of the entire region by leases or agreements.[33]

In the meantime conditions on the Cheyenne-Arapaho reservations grew steadily worse. The Indians were relieved somewhat from dependence upon the bounty of the agent by the payments of lease money, gifts from individual ranchmen, and the ease with which food could be obtained by depredations upon the herds on their lands. In consequence they became insolent and threatening in their attitude. D. B. Dyer, who had succeeded Agent Miles about April 1, 1884, became frightened and in a panic sent request after request for troops. All of his pleas were entirely disregarded.[34]

Late in 1884 the Secretary of the Interior called upon the Secretary of War for troops to control these Indians, asking that not less than three thousand be sent.[35] However, a Congressional investigation of grazing in the Indian Territory was begun in December, 1884. This perhaps tended to delay action and further delay was caused by the change of administration the following March, so it was not until July, 1885, that General Sheridan was sent to the Cheyenne-Arapaho reservation with orders to take

---

31 Benedict's Report, June 28, 1884. *Ibid.*, p. 32.

32 *Senate Report* 1278, 49 Cong., 1 Sess., Vol. VIII.

33 Report of Special Agent Folsom, Dec. 16, 1884. *Ibid.*, pp. 136-144.

34 Six such requests were sent out by Dyer between May 1 and the latter part of August, 1884. They bear the dates of May 6, May 20, May 28, July 22, Aug. 12, and Aug. 21. *Senate Ex. Doc.* 16, 48 Cong., 2 Sess., Vol. I, pp. 6, 10, 12, 13, 14, and 15.

35 Teller to Secretary of War, Dec. 26, 1884. *Ibid.*, p. 24.

charge of the situation.[36] However, before Sheridan was able to make a report, President Cleveland issued a proclamation declaring all leases on this reservation void and ordering all persons there to remove with their cattle, horses, and other property within forty days.[37]

Appalling as was this order to the ranchmen they had no choice but to comply with it, though few of them were able to remove their herds within the time specified. There were 210,000 head of cattle on the reservation. What to do with them was a problem;[38] the season was too far advanced to attempt a drive to ranges in the North, while most of the animals were not in condition for shipment to market for slaughter. As a result most of these cattle, together with many thousands of head removed from the Kiowa-Comanche and other reservations, were thrown, at the beginning of winter, upon the already over-stocked ranges of the adjoining states.

By December the reservation was entirely clear of cattle.[39] Altogether perhaps 300,000 head were removed from the Cheyenne-Arapaho and nearby reservations and distributed over nearby ranges largely in Texas or Kansas. The winter of 1885–6 was very severe in the Southwest, and cattle died by thousands. Ranchmen later asserted that Cleveland's order removing all cattle from the Cheyenne-Arapaho reservation was "an act by which every head of cattle in America on farms or ranges was depressed in price," and that it "struck the cattle interests of the country a blow from which they never recovered."[40] While this was probably an exaggeration, yet it seems certain that this order did have far reaching influences. Many of the cattle forced out of the Indian Territory in the autumn of 1885, if they survived the rigors of the ensuing winter, were sent up the trail to northern ranges in

[36] Sheridan's Report, July 24, 1885. *House Ex. Doc.* 1, 49 Cong., 1 Sess., Vol. II, Part II, pp. 69-70.

[37] Proclamation of July 23, 1885. 24 *Stats.*, p. 1023.

[38] Sheridan's Report. *Op. cit.*

[39] *Report of the Commissioner of Indian Affairs*, 1886, p. 114.

[40] Memorial of the Cherokee Strip Live Stock Association to the President of the United States, Nov. 27, 1889.

the summr of 1886—thus still further over-stocking the already crowded pasture lands of that region and contributing not a little to the causes of the disastrous losses of the winter of 1886–7.

Moreover, two weeks after the proclamation removing the ranchmen from the Cheyenne-Arapaho reservation, President Cleveland issued a second proclamation ordering the removal of all fences from the public lands and calling upon the United States officials everywhere to assist in the execution of this order.[41] This was done under authority given him by an act of Congress passed the preceding February which had declared inclosures of public lands unlawful and authorized the President to take whatever means necessary for the removal or destruction of any such inclosures as might be found there.[42]

As has been indicated this proved a source of great embarrassment to numerous ranchmen on the plains, since many of them had fenced large pastures on the public domain as a convenience in holding their cattle. The removal of these fences meant not only the loss of most of the money invested in them but greatly increased the expenses of operating, since additional labor had to be employed and camps erected on the boundaries of the range, while the loss from theft and straying was much increased.

Altogether it seems certain that the beginning of the decline in the prosperity of the ranch cattle industry can be quite definitely placed at the summer and autumn of 1885, though it was not until 1887 that conditions had become so bad as to show almost universal distress throughout the entire cow country.

Cattle came drifting back upon the Cheyenne-Arapaho reservation within a year or two. A considerable number were pastured there, part of the time at least, until that area was opened to settlement in April, 1892. Cattle were also brought to the Kiowa-Comanche reservation in considerable numbers and a system of leasing later provided for was put into operation in that

41 Proclamation of Aug. 7, 1885. 24 *Stats.*, pp. 1024-1025.
42 23 *Stats.*, p. 321.

region. However, none of these things helped the ranchmen who had been forced to remove in 1885. Whether or not it was true, as was later asserted, that this forced removal did an irreparable injury to the ranching industry of the West, it is quite certain that it was disastrous to the individuals affected by it, many of whom sustained financial losses from which they never recovered.

While these events were taking place on the Cheyenne-Arapaho and Kiowa-Comanche reservations, the Cherokee Outlet lying farther north had also been occupied with cattle. The status of this region was peculiar. The territory had been given to the Cherokee and they had received a fee simple title to it,[43] but in 1866 they had agreed to allow the United States to locate friendly Indians there and several tribes had been so located.[44] The residue upon which no Indians had been placed embraced an area of over six million acres, most of it excellent for grazing. Although it belonged to the Cherokee, they could not settle there owing to this right held by the United States, to locate other Indians.[45] Nor could they well use the territory for grazing since it was separated from their home lands by several large Indian reservations.[46] Thus the Cherokee Outlet was valuable property that might eventually by lease or sale yield the Cherokee a large sum of money, but for fifteen years after the Civil War it brought them virtually no revenue or other benefit.

The first cattle to enter this region were the trail herds driven from Texas to the shipping points of Kansas. As has been indicated, some of these herds moved slowly, the drovers stopping or turning aside for weeks in order to rest and fatten their cattle. Also, some men who reached the cow towns and found it necessary to wait for a buyer no doubt drove their herds back to this

[43] Holden *v.* Joy, 17 Wall., p. 211.

[44] See map. The Cherokee title to the lands of the Outlet was the same as their title to the Cherokee lands proper subject only to the right of the United States to locate friendly Indians there. See U. S. *v.* Ben Rees 5, Dillon, p. 405, and U. S. *v.* Rogers, 23, *Federal Reporter*, 695.

[45] Opinion of Attorney General Devens, Feb. 25, 1880, 16 *Opinions*, p. 470.

[46] See map.

region in order to find more abundant pasturage, while cattle belonging to the ranchmen located in southern Kansas strayed across the line or were driven across by their owners. By 1871 numerous cattle were grazing in the Cherokee Outlet and many others were brought there during the next few years.[47]

As there were no fences at first, herds could not be kept entirely separate. Also cattle of the more or less permanent occupants mingled with "drift cattle" from Kansas or with trail herds of "pilgrim cattle" from Texas. Moreover, range boundaries were not clearly defined and difficulties were often experiencd in determining the rights of each individual. In consequence of all these things a meeting of all ranchmen pasturing cattle on the Cherokee Outlet was held at Caldwell, Kansas, in the spring of 1880, and a crude association formed to make plans for the roundups and to look after one another's interests.[48]

In the meantime, the officials of the Cherokee Nation had decided to try to secure some revenue from grazing on these lands and began to send out officials to collect a grazing tax from men pasturing herds there.[49]

The rate was forty cents a head annually for grown cattle and twenty-five cents a head for all animals less than two years of age.[50] A receipt was given in the form of a grazier's license, which was a permit to pasture a certain number of head for a specified time.[51]

In spite of their best efforts the authorities of the Cherokee Nation were not able to secure payment from anything like all of the men pasturing cattle on these lands. Some avoided it on the plea that they were merely passing through the territory, while men with ranches in Kansas drove their cattle into the Outlet to avoid the payment of a property tax on them in that state, and

47 Memorial of the Cherokee Strip Live Stock Association to the President of the United States, Nov. 27, 1889, p. 1.

48 Testimony of Ben. S. Miller, *Senate Report* 1278, 49 Cong., 1 Sess., Vol. VIII, p. 79.

49 Memorial of the Cherokee Strip Live Stock Association, Nov. 27, 1889, pp. 4-5.

50 Testimony of Andrew Drumm, Jan. 8, 1885. *Sen. Rept.* 1278, 49 Cong., 1 Sess., Vol. VIII, pp. 76-79.

51 See cut, p. 143.

then drove them back to Kansas to avoid the payment of a grazing tax to the Cherokee.[52]

In the meantime, numerous inquiries had been received by the Department of the Interior relative to securing permits for grazing cattle on these lands. Such inquirers were referred to the authorities of the Cherokee Nation with the explanation that the lands in question were in the possession and under the jurisdiction of that tribe of Indians, and sometimes with the added information that these Indians granted permits for grazing cattle there.[53] However, to a question as to whether or not the Department of the Interior would recognize a lease made with these Indians and protect the lessees, an answer was returned in the negative.[54]

Nevertheless, the ranchmen with herds in the Outlet were so encouraged by the regular issuance of grazing permits by the Cherokee that they began to construct wire fences to inclose their ranges. Late in 1882 the inclosure of some small ranges by one of the larger operators led to difficulties which resulted in the matter of fencing being brought to the attention of the Department of the Interior.[55] That Department declared that the fencing of these lands was illegal and ordered the agent for the Five Civilized Tribes to notify all ranchmen who had constructed such fences to remove them within twenty days and that at the end of that time any remaining would be removed or destroyed by the military.[56] Fortunately for the cattlemen the War Department was reluctant to furnish soldiers for this purpose, and re-

[52] Testimony of Ben. S. Miller. *Ibid.*, p. 79. The total amounts collected by the Cherokee were as follows:

1879	$ 1,100.00	1882	$41,233.81
1880	7,620.00	1883	10,742.25
1881	21,555.64		

This last amount given is the sum paid to the Cherokee before the lease of the entire Outlet made in 1883 went into operation. *Cherokee Advocate*, Feb. 6, 1885.

[53] Acting Commissioner Stevens to Alvord and Woodruff, May 6, 1881, and same to Holt, May 20, 1882. *Senate Ex. Doc.* 54, 48 Cong., 1 Sess., Vol. IV, p. 128.

[54] Price to Strong, Oct. 11, 1881. *Ibid.*

[55] Price to Secretary of Interior, Dec. 28, 1882. *Ibid.*, p. 131.

[56] Price to Tufts, Dec. 30, 1882. *Ibid.*, pp. 130-131.

[137]

plied to a request for them by asking what provisions of law would protect officers and troops in removing or destroying the improvements mentioned.[57]

This caused delay, and in the meantime so many protests against the order were made that the Department of the Interior decided to hold it in suspension for a time pending a complete investigation of the question.[58] This investigation revealed the fact that nearly one thousand miles of fencing had been constructed on the lands of the Outlet. This had been erected by some nineteen ranching firms who had built from thirty-four to eighty-seven miles each.[59] It appeared that the lands had been occupied and ranges fenced with the knowledge and tacit approval of the Cherokee authorities, although no formal arrangement had been made with the tribe as a whole. The Department of the Interior accordingly agreed to hold the order for the removal of wire fences in suspension for a few weeks longer in order to give the ranchmen an opportunity to make some definite arrangements with the Cherokee Nation to occupy these lands for grazing, and in the event of their failure to do this the original order was to be carried out.[60]

In the meantime the ranchmen grazing cattle on the Outlet had met at Caldwell, Kansas, early in March, 1883, and formed an organization which was incorporated under the laws of Kansas as the "Cherokee Strip Live Stock Association."[61] Its purpose as stated in the charter was the "improvement of the breed of domestic animals by the importation, grazing, breeding, sale, barter, and exchange thereof." The term for which it was to exist was forty years, the number of directors nine, the principal place of business was Caldwell, Kansas.[62] A board of arbitration was pro-

---

[57] Lincoln to Secretary of Interior, Dec. 28, 1882. *Ibid.*

[58] See Campbell to Secretary of Interior, Jan. 2, 1883. *Ibid.*, pp. 131-134. Also Price to Tufts, Jan. 16, 1883. *Ibid.*, p. 142.

[59] Tufts to Commissioner of Indian Affairs, March 1, 1883. *Ibid.*, pp. 148-149. The total extent of fencing was 959 miles.

[60] Teller to Price, March 16, 1883. *Ibid.*, p. 152.

[61] *Senate Report* 1278, 49 Cong., 1 Sess., Vol. VIII, p. 683.

[62] Charter and By Laws of the Cherokee Strip Live Stock Association. *Ibid.*, p. 683. This is also found in *Senate Ex. Doc.* 17, 48 Cong., 2 Sess., Vol. I, pp. 149-150.

vided for that should settle all disputes between members of the association though an appeal might be taken to the board of directors, whose decision was to be final.[63]

With the organization thus effected the ranchmen were in a position to carry out the plan previously agreed upon, which was to secure from the Cherokee a lease of the entire Outlet.

Early in May the principal chief of the Cherokee Nation called a special session of the National Council of that tribe to consider the matter of grazing on lands of the Outlet.[64] Representatives of the Cherokee Strip Live Stock Association hastened to the Cherokee capital to act as lobbyists. An act was eventually passed authorizing the chief to execute a lease of the entire Outlet to the association for a period of five years at an annual rental of $100,000, payable semi-annually in advance.[65]

A lease was at once prepared and signed by the chief and directors of the association, and that organization assumed charge of the Outlet lands. Surveyors were appointed to determine the boundaries of each man's range, while the board of arbitration settled all difficulties. The Outlet was divided into a little over one hundred ranges, each held by an individual, firm, or corporation, so that some four or five hundred men were included in the organization as a whole. If to these be added the stockholders in the various companies, it is certain that not less than two thousand people were financially interested in the Cherokee Strip Live Stock Association.[66]

Each member was given a lease of his range by the association for the entire period of five years, and gave in payment a series of promissory notes maturing fifteen days before the semi-annual payment must be made to the Cherokee. The price fixed was one and a fourth cents an acre every six months. Each member fenced his own range, but wide trails were left for the passage of trail herds from Texas. Quarantine grounds were also provided just

63 *Ibid.*

64 Lyons to Eldred, March 24, 1883. Charles Eldred Papers.

65 *Senate Ex. Doc.* 17, 48 Cong., 2 Sess., Vol. I, pp. 151-152.

66 Memorial of the Cherokee Strip Live Stock Association to the President of the United States, p. 14.

south of the Kansas border, on which herds might be held while awaiting inspection.[67] Within a few months all difficulties within the organization had been settled and its affairs were running smoothly.[68]

Yet there were difficulties outside the organization that could not be so easily adjusted. The farmers along the border complained because the ranchmen were permitted to occupy these lands while they themselves were excluded, and their complaints were echoed by the press. There was also a general feeling that the Indians had not been paid the full value of the land for grazing purposes, and it was persistently asserted that the association had resorted to bribery in securing the lease. Late in 1884 came the beginning of the Congressional investigation of grazing in the Indian Territory previously mentioned.[69] Numerous witnesses were summoned to Washington, and a long and painstaking investigation was made of the allegations with respect to bribery, but the charges remained unproved.[70]

Alarmed by the removal of the lessees from the Cheyenne-Arapaho reservation in 1885, the Cherokee Strip Live Stock Association made an effort in 1886 to have their lease renewed for a period of five years. This failed and the only result was to create further rumors of bribery and corruption.[71] Late in 1888, however, the Cherokee Council passed an act which was approved by the chief giving the association a new lease of the Outlet for five years at an annual rental of $200,000 a year.[72]

In the meantime public opinion in favor of opening the

[67] Testimony of J. A. Blair. *Senate Report* 1278, 49 Cong., 1 Sess., Vol. VIII, pp. 180-181 and 235-240.

[68] Miller to Bushyhead, April 14, 1884. *Senate Ex. Doc.* 17, 48 Cong., 2 Sess., Vol. I, p. 158.

[69] *Congressional Record*, Dec. 2 and 3, 1884, Vol. 16, pp. 11 and 33.

[70] *Senate Report* 1278, 49 Cong., 1 Sess., Vol. VIII. There is ample reason to believe that the Senate investigating committee did not arrive at the whole truth and that a large sum was really expended in bribing members of the Cherokee National Council to vote for this lease.

[71] Owen to Atkins, April 29, 1887. *Senate Ex. Doc.* 136, 50 Cong., 2 Sess., Vol. IV, pp. 2-4.

[72] Lyons to Eldred, Dec. 8, 1888. Charles Eldred Papers.

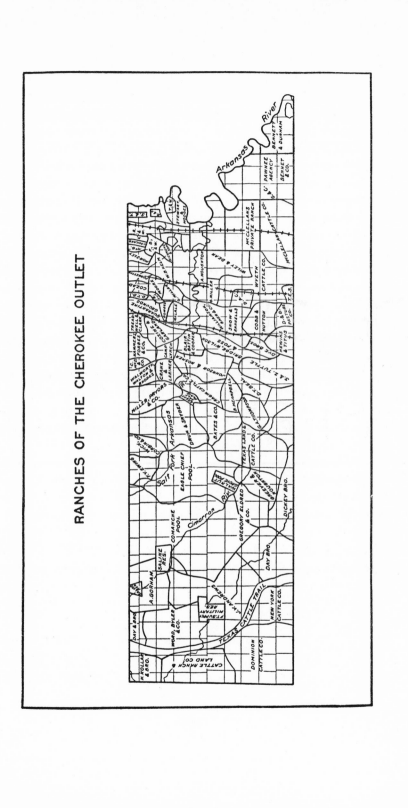

RANCHES OF THE CHEROKEE OUTLET

"Oklahoma Lands" and other portions of western Indian Territory to white settlement had been steadily growing. In January, 1889, an agreement was signed with the Creeks, and a little later with the Seminoles, by which these tribes surrendered all claim to the Oklahoma Lands, and the following April they were opened to white settlement by a proclamation of the president.[73]

Early in March, 1889, an act of Congress provided for the appointment of a commission to negotiate with the Cherokee relative to the cession of the Outlet and with other tribes in western Indian Territory for the cession of their surplus lands. This act provided that the Cherokee should be offered $1.25 an acre for the lands of the Outlet, and that in the event of their acceptance these lands should be opened to white settlement.[74]

Late in 1888, however, a syndicate of ranchmen had offered to purchase the entire Outlet from the Cherokee at a price of three dollars an acre provided the latter could get the consent of the United States government to sell.[75] This would have been a total of over eighteen million dollars for the entire area while the offer of the government was only a little over seven and a half million dollars. Naturally the Cherokee refused to accept the governmental offer, and the Cherokee Commission found itself at a loss as to how to proceed.

The matter was complicated by the question of title to the Outlet lands. Secretary of the Interior Noble asserted that the Cherokee title was only an "easement" which had probably been forfeited by the failure to use the lands and that the United States had the right to take them over if necessary.[76] On the other hand the Commissioner of Indian Affairs urged that the Cherokee title to the Outlet was perfect except for the right of the United States to locate friendly Indians there, and that to take these lands over by an act of Congress would be for the government of the United

73 *25 Stats.*, p. 757.

74 *Ibid.*, p. 1005. This commission known as the Cherokee Commission was continued by subsequent acts of Congress. 26 *Stats.*, p. 1008, and 27 *Stats.*, p. 138

75 *Senate Misc. Doc.* 80, 50 Cong., 2 Sess., p. 20.

76 Noble to Struble, Feb. 13, 1891. *Senate Ex. Doc.* 63, 51 Cong., 2 Sess., Vol. V, pp. 1-8.

States "to violate its faith and disregard its solemn obligations."[77]

Late in October, 1889, Secretary Noble wrote a letter to Chairman Fairchild of the Cherokee Commission in which he asserted that the cattlemen were largely responsible for the refusal of the Indians to sell these lands. He reviewed the history of grazing upon the Outlet, stated that the leases of Indian lands for grazing were void, and that the President had the right to declare them so, and to remove the ranchmen and their property by force. He also said that the offer of $1.25 an acre for the land was under the circumstances munificent, while the title of the Cherokees even to the use of the land was extremely precarious and likely to be defeated entirely. He criticized the "cattle syndicate" for its attempts "to rival and defeat the government," and said it was acting in defiance of law and against public interest. He said it was now deemed best to lay hands upon these pretended lessees and remove them and their property by force not later than June 1, 1890. He declared that if the United States found its own title to these lands good it would not hesitate to take them over if circumstances of the American people should require it. He closed by instructing Fairchild to make such use of his letter as he saw fit, and to report to the department whatever action he might take.[78]

The letter of Secretary Noble was at once a warning and a threat. The Cherokees had refused to sell the Outlet lands at the price fixed by Congress, and in consequence were warned that they would be deprived of any use or benefit from them until such a time as they should be willing to accept the terms offered. At the same time a threat was made to take the lands by force if the United States found that it had the superior title. This would, of course, be determined by the United States itself, and the Cherokee knew by bitter experience not to expect too much if the matter were pushed to an issue.

In the meantime the ranchmen were the victims. The Indians,

[77] Morgan to Secretary of Interior, Jan. 26, 1892. *Ibid.,* pp. 9-28. The question of Cherokee title to the Outlet is discussed in this document and in *Senate Ex. Doc.* 56 of the same volume and in *House Report* 3768, 51 Cong., 2 Sess., Vol. IV.

[78] Noble to Fairchild, Oct. 26, 1889. *House Report* 3768, 51 Cong., 2 Sess., Vol. IV, pp. 9-16.

as long as they received revenues from these lands, would not sell them for seven and a half million dollars when private parties were offering eighteen million. In order to compel a cession the ranchmen were to be removed and all revenue stopped until such a time as the Cherokee should be willing to yield. Worst of all, the men whose business was thus threatened had no recourse. No court could give them redress or protection, or even order that they be allowed time in which to arrange their affairs.[79]

Realizing the seriousness of the situation, the Cherokee Strip Live Stock Association prepared a memorial addressed to the President of the United States in which they set forth very ably their side of the controversy, but nothing could help the ranchmen at this time. The Department of the Interior, urged on by popular clamor, had determined that these lands should be opened to white settlement. The most that the ranchmen could hope for was a reasonable delay to give them time to adjust their affairs and market their herds.[80]

Fortunately President Harrison was more lenient in his attitude than was Secretary Noble. Having secured from the Attorney General an opinion that the lease of the Outlet lands was without legal force,[81] the President, about the middle of February, 1890, issued a proclamation forbidding all grazing on the lands of the Cherokee Outlet and ordering all cattle to be removed from them by October 1, 1890.[82] When we consider that the lands were not actually opened to settlement until September, 1893, the question may well be raised as to whether the object sought was not to force the Cherokee to cede this area rather than in order to prepare the land for settlement.

The Cherokee were too wise to push the matter too far. When the House Committee on Territories reported favorably on a bill to take over the Outlet lands at a price to be fixed by Congress,

[79] See Dale, "The Cherokee Strip Live Stock Association," *Proceedings of the Fifth Annual Convention of the Southwestern Political Science Association* for a more detailed account of this matter.

[80] Memorial of the Cherokee Strip Live Stock Association to the President.

[81] Opinion of Attorney General Miller, 19 *Opinions,* p. 499.

[82] 26 *Stats.,* p. 1557.

Zack Miller (at extreme right) of the 101 Ranch and Cowboys
Wait at the Chuck Wagon

Rest Period During the Round Up

these Indians decided to accept the inevitable, and late in 1891 signed an agreement with the Commission to sell these lands in consideration of a payment of about eight and a half million dollars, or a little over $1.40 an acre.[83]

The issuance of the Presidential proclamation had in the meantime destroyed the last hope of the Cherokee Strip Live Stock Association. A brief extension of sixty days was secured, but December 1, 1890, was set as the final date for the removal of all cattle from the Outlet. Nothing remained for the ranchmen to do but to market such cattle as they could and remove the remainder to other ranges.

No doubt the removal of this 300,000 head of cattle from the Cherokee Outlet had a considerable influence upon market prices in the autumn of 1891, and also resulted in further over-stocking many ranges and an increased price for pasturage in many places. In 1893 the Cherokee Outlet, together with the reservations of the Tonkawa and the Pawnee Indians, were opened to white settlement, a great block of lands formerly used for grazing thus being given over to the production of crops.

The Cheyenne-Arapaho reservation had been opened the preceding year, while a number of smaller reservations had been settled in 1891.[84] Greer County was added to Oklahoma by a decision of the Supreme Court in 1896, and the Kiowa-Comanche and Wichita reservations were the only considerable purely grazing areas left in Oklahoma. A leasing law had been enacted by this time and the lands of these reservations were leased to ranchmen until 1901, when they too were opened to white settlement.

Even with the settlement of these lands the ranchmen were able to retain a small corner into which they might drive such cattle as could not be marketed. By the agreement in which these Indians ceded their surplus lands, it was provided that each individual Indian should retain an allotment of 160 acres and that the tribes as a whole should retain an area of 480,000 acres in two or three large tracts as pasture lands for their surplus live stock.

[83] *Senate Ex. Doc.* 56, 52 Cong., 2 Sess., Vol. V, pp. 14-15.
[84] The Sac and Fox, Iowa, Shawnee and Potawatomi.

As a matter of fact the Indians had no surplus live stock and had evidently been encouraged by ranchmen pasturing herds upon their reservations to insist upon this clause in the agreement. At any rate these pasture lands were immediately leased to cattlemen and herds were pastured there until 1906 when the Indians were induced to surrender their title, and the land was sold at auction to actual settlers.

With the opening of these "Big Pasture Lands" in 1906 ranching in Oklahoma upon Indian lands may be said to have come to an end. True there was for some years a certain amount of grazing upon Indian allotments and the lands belonging to members of the Five Civilized Tribes or the Osage. And some live stock raising is still carried on there, but this is exactly the same as is grazing in any other agricultural state. It was of comparatively little importance and was carried on only as an adjunct to the chief business of the people of that region, which was the raising of crops.

Oklahoma was one of the last of the agricultural states to contain large areas devoted exclusively to grazing. Moreover, it presents perhaps the best example in our history of the changing of considerable regions from one form of agriculture to another by governmental action. When the great Indian reservations were opened to settlement it is popularly believed that the land was taken from the Indian and given to the white man. As a matter of fact the Indian did not use the land and so as an economic factor in the history of the region is negligible. The man who really used these lands was the ranchman, and what really happened in the opening of large Indian reservations to settlement was that the land was taken from the cattleman and given to the farmer, or its use changed by governmental action from grazing stock to the growing of crops. Even after the last Indian lands had been settled there was a considerable production of beef cattle in Oklahoma, but this was by stock farmers rather than ranching, and the passing of the Indian reservation meant, largely speaking, the passing of the ranch cattle industry.

8.

THE RANGE
AND THE CORN BELT

During the period of the settle- ment of the corn belt states and the bringing of their rich agricultural lands into cultivation, that region became a combined breeding, grazing and fattening ground for cattle. For some years after settlement had begun there were large areas of prairie lands in the western part of these states that were very thinly peopled. Farmers of the more densely populated eastern portion would send small herds of cattle to these western prairies each summer under the care of a responsible herder who established a camp for himself and built a corral into which the cattle were driven at night, while during the day they were herded upon the open prairies.[1] In the autumn the cattle were returned to the farm of the owner, and mature steers were fattened on corn during the winter and eventually driven or shipped to market.[2]

As settlers continued to come in, these western prairie lands were at last all occupied. In the meantime, as it became increasingly apparent that soil and climate were remarkably suited to the production of corn, the acreage devoted to that crop constantly grew, and to a corresponding degree the area of grazing land was diminished.

[1] *Annual Report of the Patent Office,* 1853, p. 6. Also Hopkins, *Beef Production in Iowa,* p. 164.

[2] Early feeders used what was sometimes called the "Kentucky method" of fattening cattle for market. The corn was cut and shocked in the field and was later hauled directly from the shock to the feed lots and distributed to the cattle. The fodder furnished the necessary "roughness" while hogs were kept with the cattle to consume the waste grain. It was estimated that about fifteen bushels a month was fed to each steer, worth in 1853 about $3.00 in Illinois at the farm. See *Report of Patent Office,* 1853, p. 6.

With the extension of the range cattle business over the Great Plains in the years following the Civil War, and the establishment of relations between that region and the corn belt, the latter entered upon a period of transition. Slowly but steadily it changed from a cattle raising area to one devoted to the feeding of steers and the rearing of a comparatively small number of pure bred animals, to be marketed for breeding purposes.

It is necessary therefore to consider two aspects of the relations between the range cattle area and the corn belt, since both are of great importance and far reaching influence. The first of these is the sending of large numbers of breeding animals from the corn states to the western plains to improve the quality of the cattle in that region, while the second is the supplying of feeders from the western ranges to consume the surplus grain and hay of the corn belt. The two movements were contemporaneous and each dependent somewhat upon the other. So long as the cattle on the western ranges were largely of the wild, long horned, Texas type, they were not very desirable or profitable as corn belt feeders. Also, while there was abundance of open range on the plains and conditions there with respect to raising live stock were quite primitive, the ranchmen found it profitable to raise common or scrub animals and to market them directly from the ranges for slaughter as grass fed beef.

As time went on, however, land grew increasingly high in the grain growing section, and the farmers there began to find it no longer profitable to pasture a sufficient number of breeding animals to supply themselves with feeders, or to rear calves to an age suitable for feeding. At the same time the growing scarcity of range prompted the ranchmen to improve the quality of their live stock and to sell the animals earlier, not for slaughter, but to be finished for market by several months of feeding on corn. Thus the corn belt farmers sought to conserve their high priced lands by avoiding keeping breeding animals and potential feeders during the earlier or growing period of their lives, while the ranchmen sought to conserve their ranges by marketing animals early, thus avoiding pasturing them in the later or maturing and fattening period. A division of labor grew up. It became the function of one region to rear cattle and of the other to fatten them for market. In both the importance of good blood quickly became apparent. In the one in order that the animals might grow larger and reach maturity in a shorter time than did the common Texas cattle, and in the other in order that they might take on fat readily and so utilize to the best advantage the grain and hay upon which they were fed.

Even before the Civil War some attempt had been made to improve Texas cattle by bringing in high grade bulls from states farther east, but the number of animals thus brought in was so small as to have little effect.[3] Generally speaking, the animals making up the great herds of cattle that were driven north from Texas in the years following the war were wild, long horned Texans, angular, lean, narrow flanked creatures, comparatively light in weight, that furnished, when slaughtered, beef by no means high in quality.

As these cattle were spread over the western plains many men began to realize the importance of improving the breed, with the result that they began almost immediately the purchase of breeding animals from the corn belt. This movement of breeding stock from the corn states to western ranges steadily increased in volume until the ranching industry on the plains reached its peak of prosperity about 1885. After this the depressed condition of the ranching interests caused it to decline somewhat. By this time the quality of cattle on western ranges had been vastly improved and eventually averaged higher than in many of the farming states farther east.[4] Then too, a number of breeding ranches in the Great Plains area had begun to devote their entire attention to producing pure bred or high grade cattle for breeding purposes,[5] while not a few large operators had developed small breeding

3 *A Six Year Resident, Texas, the Australia of America*, pp. 65-66.

4 *Proceedings of National Stock Growers' Convention*, Denver, Colorado, 1899, p. 103.

5 Nimmo, p. 144.

herds from which animals were drawn to improve the quality of the beef cattle upon their ranges.[6]

As the cattle business spread over the Great Plains, the ranchmen found themselves facing some difficult and intricate problems. Confronted by the necessity either of continuing the breeding of cattle adapted to the hard conditions of the open range or of so changing those conditions as to make them suited to the production of well bred cattle, they eventually struck a compromise between two extremes. Through the use of pure bred, or high grade sires, and Texas cows, a type of animal was produced that was of high quality and yet, because of the strong strain of Texas blood, was hardy and able to endure the cold of winter and the heat of summer, and to thrive in spite of the hardships incident to life on the open range.[7] At the same time they eventually began to improve the conditions under which the cattle must live by making provision for feeding in winter by the construction of additional watering places, the fencing of pastures, and the better utilization of summer and winter ranges. By such means hardships were reduced and conditions made more suitable for well bred animals.[8]

The first pure bred or high grade bulls sent from the corn belt to the range area were in most cases Shorthorns but later the hardy qualities of the Hereford made them the favorite breed, and eventually many of the larger ranchmen, in particular, began to use Herefords almost exclusively, though a strain of Shorthorn blood was usually retained.[9]

By the early seventies the corn belt was sending numerous high grade bulls to the range cattle area. Many of these were Shorthorns though there were also other breeds.[10] The task of improving the breed of the vast numbers of Texas cattle on the west-

[6] Statement of Murdo MacKenzie, general manager of the ranches of the Matador Land and Cattle Company.

[7] McCoy, p. 376.

[8] Nimmo, p. 23.

[9] Clay, p. 328. Also Thompson Manuscript, Ch. XIII, p. 19.

[10] McCoy, pp. 237-238, and page 355. In Colorado a law had been passed by 1874 prohibiting allowing a Texas or scrub bull to run at large.

ern plains was an enormous one, and so heavy was the demand for high grade bulls by the ranchmen of the West as to give a great impetus to the production of such animals in the corn belt. Pure bred bulls from the corn states were sent to every part of the cow country, including large numbers to Texas. Many animals brought to that state died of Texas fever, but the ranchmen seemed to accept this as merely one of the natural hazards of the business and did not allow these losses to discourage them from making additional purchases.[11]

Yet this was an added difficulty to improvement of breeds, and parts of southern Texas did not advance the quality of cattle as rapidly as did other portions of the cow country.[12] During the decade from 1870 to 1880 the demand of the range cattle region for pure bred bulls steadily increased. By 1882 it was stated that a single ranching firm in Wyoming had purchased $20,000 worth of pure bred bulls from one breeder in Illinois.[13] At this time it was said that hundreds of ranchmen in Texas used only pure bred bulls while the quality of the cattle throughout the entire Great Plains area had been vastly improved.[14] In the decade from 1873 to 1883 the average weight of all cattle slaughtered for beef in various parts of the cow country had risen as follows: Wyoming from 700 to 880 pounds, Colorado 675 to 825 pounds, Dakota 650 to 875 pounds, New Mexico 600 to 700 pounds, Texas 750 to 789 pounds.[15]

In the corn states this decade also showed a considerable advance in the weights of animals slaughtered. This rose between 1873 and 1883 in Kansas from 1,035 to 1,090 pounds, Nebraska 1,042 to 1,100, Indiana 1,018 to 1,112, Iowa 1,060 to 1,121, Mis-

11 Statement of Mrs. Marvin Ikard Smith, April 25, 1925. It seems that few if any Herefords were brought to Texas before about 1876.

12 *Proceedings of National Stock Growers' Convention*, Denver, Colorado, 1899, pp. 101-103.

13 *Breeder's Gazette*, Feb. 28, 1882.

14 Nimmo, p. 144. In 1900 the average value of bulls in the western states was higher than in any other section of the country, $42.12 as compared with $34.19 for the country as a whole and only $15.26 for the South. Georgia was lowest with an average value of $9.25.

15 *Report of the Commissioner of Agriculture*, 1883, p. 282.

souri 1,006 to 1,026 and Kentucky 996 to 1,062 pounds. Certain districts of Illinois reported that well matured animals weighed three hundred pounds more than had been the case ten years before.[16] This increased size of animals was due largely to improvement of blood and is the more remarkable when it is considered that the average age at which most cattle were slaughtered was considerably less in 1883 than it had been ten years before.[17]

It is quite clear that while producing breeding stock to be sent west for improving the quality of cattle in the range area the corn states were also improving their own cattle very rapidly. Naturally this improvement is hardly so noticeable as on the western ranges since the quality of cattle in the corn states in the years immediately following the war was far above that of the great herds brought up from Texas to stock the plains. Yet the advancement was so great as to cause the Department of Agriculture to report in 1883 that the value of the cattle of the country as a whole had been more than doubled by improvement of breeds.[18] In 1884 it is stated that the cattle of Ohio and Kentucky were 40 per cent half-breeds or above and of Illinois and Indiana 35 and 33 per cent respectively.[19] Iowa and Missouri each had 21 per cent improvement while New Mexico and Arizona were lowest with only 5 per cent.[20]

The desire to improve the quality of cattle in the corn states was due in part to the great competition offered in beef production by the Great Plains regions. Within a few years after the close of the war a great volume of Texas and western grass fed cattle was pouring into the markets each summer and autumn for slaughter. It soon became evident to the stock growers of the corn belt that they could not compete with Texas and the remainder of the cow country in the production of cheap, coarse beef, and that in the future they must grow cattle of superior quality and

16 *Ibid.*
17 *Ibid.*
18 *Ibid.*, pp. 280-281.
19 *Ibid.*, 1884, p. 447.
20 *Ibid.*

cater to that portion of the public which demanded high grade beef even at a considerable advance in price.[21]

The tendency to produce better bred animals was also increased by the steady rise in land values throughout the corn belt. Higher priced lands not only made it unprofitable to grow scrub cattle but also made it imperative that animals be marketed at an earlier age than formerly. The same tendencies manifested themselves on the range where the growing scarcity of pasturage proved a great incentive to better breeding and earlier marketing. Before the Civil War and for a few years after it, steers five, six, or even seven years old and older were common enough. Later they were marketed at the age of four years, and still later at three and even younger, until eventually there came the demand for very young beef" which resulted in the slaughter of many two-year-olds or even long yearlings."[22]

The feeding of cattle for market began in the corn states soon after the first settlements had been established as a means of utilizing the surplus grain and hay which could not be sold at a profit owing to distance from market and poor transportation facilities. At this time most men raised their own feeder cattle or purchased animals from their neighbors though there were a few head brought from Texas to the corn belt for feeding even before the Civil War.[23]

With the close of that struggle and the movement of cattle northward from Texas large herds of cattle from that state were brought to Illinois, Iowa, Missouri and other corn states for feeding. This was the first considerable movement of feeder cattle from the range area to the corn belt, but the experience of men feeding Texas cattle was far from encouraging.[24] The cattle were wild and unmanageable. They ate heavily, but did not put on

[21] *National Live Stock Journal,* Nov. 1870, Vol. I, p. 76.

[22] See S. H. Day, "Production of Baby Beef," *Farmer's Bulletin No.* 811, or *Iowa Homestead,* Jan. 3, 1901, for discussion of methods of preparing young animals for slaughter.

[23] 10th Census, Vol. III, p. 965.

[24] *Country Gentleman,* March 10, 1870, p. 156. John T. Alexander of Champaign County, Illinois, fed as many as 7,000 Texas cattle in a single year. He reported them "uncertain, unsatisfactory and unprofitable." *Ibid.*

[153]

weight.[25] When shipped to market the returns were disappointing. The cattle were light and butchers and packers did not want them.[26] As a result they brought very low prices as compared with the native cattle, and feeding them in most cases proved unprofitable. Worst of all they brought, as we have seen, Texas fever among the native cattle, which caused heavy losses and resulted in a strong public opinion against Texas cattle and the passing of laws by most states prohibiting bringing them in except at certain seasons of the year.[27] By 1870 or a little later, most Illinois and Iowa feeders had ceased to purchase Texas cattle for feeding.[28] Yet, discouraging as had been the experience of most men in feeding them, the long horned Texas animals had been to a certain extent path breakers between the western ranges and the corn belt and formed a picturesque advance guard of the great volume of well bred feeders that came later.

They were not long delayed. Numerous forces were operating to hasten their coming. By 1870 large areas of the northern plains had been occupied by cattle from Texas and the industry of ranching was spreading rapidly. Into this region railways were extending from various points along the western edge of the corn belt making it easy to send breeding animals westward and feeders and fat cattle east. Numerous large ranches were growing up in this northern region far above the danger line of Texas fever.[29] Their owners, quick to perceive the importance of good blood, were improving their herds rapidly.[30] They were not only raising large numbers of calves but were also purchasing herds of young Texas steers driven northward on the trail. These after a winter spent in the North could not by any possibility transmit Texas

25 Hopkins, p. 61.

26 *Country Gentleman*, Sept. 30, 1869, p. 254.

27 See Chap. III, pp. 43-54.

28 *Country Gentleman*, Sept. 30, 1869, p. 254, or March 10, 1870, p. 156.

29 The same tendency of the range area for small operators to give place to large ones was manifested in feeding operations in the corn belt. Large feeders grew up who purchased and fed thousands of head each year. However, just as was the case among the ranchmen changing conditions and a series of unprofitable years eventually caused a shift back to somewhat smaller operations again.

30 McCoy, pp. 237-240.

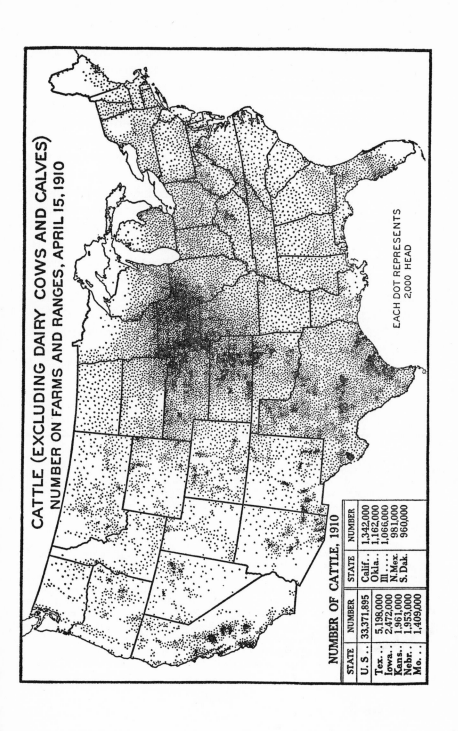

CATTLE (EXCLUDING DAIRY COWS AND CALVES)
NUMBER ON FARMS AND RANGES, APRIL 15, 1910

EACH DOT REPRESENTS
2,000 HEAD

NUMBER OF CATTLE, 1910

STATE	NUMBER	STATE	NUMBER
U. S.	33,371,895		
Tex.	5,198,000	Calif.	1,342,000
Iowa.	2,472,000	Okla.	1,162,000
Kans.	1,961,000	Ill.	1,066,000
Nebr.	1,953,000	N. Mex.	981,000
Mo.	1,409,000	S. Dak.	960,000

fever. Late in 1875 came the first shipments of dressed beef to Europe and the trade grew enormously within two or three years, and was accompanied by heavy shipments of live cattle.[31]

The export trade demanded beef and live animals of the highest quality and so was a powerful incentive to better breeding and feeding.[32] Within a few years many ranges were over-stocked. Pasturage began to grow scarce. The cattle no longer grew as fat on the grass as formerly while the public demand for beef of higher quality steadily grew. Shortage of pasture made most men eager to market animals as young as possible in order to make room for the latest "calf crop." At the same time corn crops of the corn producing states were very heavy and the price low. This low price of grain and high freight rates to the seaboard seemed to leave no choice but feeding cattle.[33] In the meantime the Corn Belt states were rapidly increasing in population and the price of lands steadily rising. Land values in Iowa, Illinois, Indiana, Missouri, Kansas and Nebraska increased enormously in the two decades from 1880

[31] The shipments of dressed beef to Europe were as follows during the first eighteen months after the trade was begun:

1875	POUNDS		
October	36,000	July	1,170,000
November	36,000	August	1,365,000
December	134,000	September	2,451,550
1876	POUNDS	October	2,569,075
January	162,000	November	2,974,480
February	292,000	December	3,036,980
March	302,000	1877	POUNDS
April	1,256,000	January	1,796,000
May	1,012,000	February	3,605,610
June	1,140,000	March	6,262,355

Annual Report of Commissioner of Agriculture, 1876, p. 320.

[32] The *Annual Report of the Commissioner of Agriculture* for 1876 contains this significant bit of advice:

"Let the vast areas of pasture in the border states and territories be employed for breeding and feeding the cattle until they are two years old and then let them be sent forward to the older sections to be fed a year on corn and rounded up to the proportions of the foreign demand." p. 319.

It is quite evident that the Commissioner foresaw, even at this time, the need of a closer relationship between the range area and the corn belt though many years elapsed before the conditions which he urged were really created.

[33] Hopkins, pp. 43-44.

to 1900 while from 1900 to 1910 the value per acre in most of these states doubled and from 1910 to 1920 doubled again.[34]

By 1877 farm lands were selling in Iowa at $20 to $25 an acre and the price was steadily rising.[35] From 1876 to 1880 the corn crop each year throughout the corn belt was extremely large.[36] Five good corn crops in succession meant heavy feeding of cattle and large numbers of feeders were brought in from the West. The cattle on western ranges had been much improved by this time and were very different from the wild Texas steers that had been brought in ten years earlier.

Also by this time railway connections between the corn belt and the range region as well as between both of these areas and the principal markets were excellent.[37] Kansas City, Omaha, St. Paul, Sioux City, and St. Joseph grew up as markets located not far from the border line between the range and the corn growing areas, and vied with Chicago for shipments from both regions.[38] Cattle feeders soon found that it was more profitable to buy most of the animals to be fed than it was to rear them on high priced lands that might better be devoted to growing corn.[39] They also began to find it more convenient to go to one of the large markets and there purchase a few carloads of young steers from western ranges than it was to gather them up among the farmers of their own community.[40] The freight charges from the market center were usually no more than was the cost of buying animals one or two in a place and bringing them together at the feeding pens.[41] Also the cattle from the West were likely to be more uniform in age, size, and condition while the time came when the quality was quite as good or even better. This was due to the fact that the great

[34] See 13th Census, Vol. V, p. 82, or Abstract of 14th Census, p. 605.
[35] Hopkins, pp. 43-44.
[36] Thompson Manuscript, Chap. XIII, p. 2.
[37] See railroad map, p. 39.
[38] Hopkins, p. 256.
[39] Some men combined the raising of pure bred breeding stock for market with feeding steers. No doubt these men sold breeding animals to western ranchmen and in many cases purchased the descendants of these animals as feeders bringing them for fattening to the same farm upon which their sires had been reared.
[40] *Wallace's Farmer,* Sept. 14, 1902.
[41] Ordinarily it cost about $1.00 a head to buy calves from the farmers.

ranchmen with thousands of head could well afford to purchase the best bulls obtainable, particularly after wire fencing began to be used extensively. On the other hand the farmer whose chief business was producing crops could not afford to buy as valuable bulls since he had but a few cows. As a result the calves were frequently inferior to those produced on the open ranges of the West.

The drought throughout the corn belt in the summer of 1887 greatly lessened the demand for feeder cattle at a time when the ranchmen who had suffered such disastrous losses the preceding winter were most eager to sell.[42] Also the depressed conditions of the period of the early nineties affected the cattle industry much, both in the production and the feeding phases of the business. Yet while cattle and beef were low corn was usually low too, and the volume of cattle sent from the plains to the corn states for feeding was very great.

There were many factors affecting this heavy shipment of cattle from the range area. The financial difficulties of the ranchmen in the years following the severe winters of '86–87 and '88–89 caused many of them to market their herds and quit the business completely.[43] Numerous others reduced their herds owing to the decreased carrying capacity of the ranges due to over-stocking and to the lessening of the area available for grazing cattle because of the coming in of homesteaders and sheepmen.[44] Also the opening of the great Indian reservations of Oklahoma to white settlement in the period of 1889 to 1901 transformed a great block of the cow country into a crop growing region.

About the close of the century increased prices and the ease with which money could be obtained gave a considerable impetus both to the range cattle business and to feeding. This was but temporary, however, with respect to range production and within a few years depression set in again.

It would be both tedious and unprofitable to attempt to give details as to feeding in the corn states year by year after 1900. It

[42] *Breeder's Gazette*, July 21, 1887.
[43] *Report of the Bureau of Animal Industry*, 1889-90, p. 268.
[44] *Ibid.*

is perhaps sufficient to say that the westward advance of the home-steaders rapidly reduced the area in the range cattle region that could be utilized for grazing, while the growing scarcity of free land contributed to the rapid increase in the price of farm lands in the corn belt. Steadily the relations between the two areas grew closer. More and more the tendency grew for each of the two regions to devote itself to one particular phase of the cattle business—the range area to rearing animals and the corn belt to fattening them for slaughter. There still remained some tendency for the Great Plains region to separate itself into two parts, and for Texas and the southern plains to raise calves and for the northern plains to mature them to an age suitable for feeding, but this tendency was gradually growing less. Numerous feeders were shipped directly from Texas to the corn states while the number of breeding herds on the central and northern plains increased.[45]

While it may not be practicable or profitable to attempt a description of the operations of ranchmen and feeders year by year the tables of figures showing market receipts and shipments, the price of farm lands and of corn, the number of homesteads taken, the number of sheep in certain states, and the volume of exports of cattle and beef, tell an eloquent story.[46]

By 1909 the lands left available for homestead entry consisted mainly of areas so dry and barren in character that the homestead unit was raised from 160 to 320 acres. This resulted in a great rush to enter homesteads which is reflected in the large number of final entries made four or five years later. In 1916 an act of Congress was approved providing for "stock raising homesteads" of 640 acres.[47] This brought many more people into the range states and resulted in the passing of large areas of the public domain

[45] Texas also fed many cattle on cotton seed or cotton seed products. Raw cotton seed was first used but with the rapid development of oil mills it soon became apparent that cotton seed meal or cake was much better, and large numbers were fed on this in many parts of the Southwest.

[46] See these various tables.

[47] 39 *Stats.*, p. 862. The proposal to provide for "stock raising homesteads" resulted in a bitter controversy between the ranchmen and the farmers farther east.

into private hands.[48] More and more the ranchmen were compelled either to purchase lands for grazing or to retire into the rougher and more arid regions or into the remaining Indian reservations. The cost of pasturage steadily rose, increasing operating expenses and making it still more important to produce animals of high quality and to market them at as early an age as possible to cattle feeders in the corn belt.

Both feeding operations and the production of cattle on ranges required large amounts of capital, and in time a machinery grew up for supplying this.[49] Men engaged in the business of feeding cattle in the earlier stages of the business usually themselves reared the animals to an age suitable for feeding, or in some cases purchased them from their neighbors, giving in payment notes due in about six months, or at about the time they expected the cattle to be ready for market. The seller held this note until maturity, or if in need of money discounted it at one of the local banks.[50] In time as these banks grew stronger, they began to make direct loans for the purchase of feeder cattle to men who had a large supply of corn and hay which it seemed more profitable to feed than to sell in the market. These cattle feeders gave their notes, sometimes indorsed by one or two of their neighbors, but at first it was not customary to give a chattel mortgage on the cattle.[51] Interest rates were high for many years, fifteen per cent being common in the seventies and early eighties, while in some cases they were even higher.[52] Eventually rates began to decline somewhat and soon after 1900 reached 8 per cent in most parts of the corn belt, remaining at this figure for several years.[53]

As the demand for money to buy feeder cattle increased, it became the custom for the borrower to secure the notes given by a chattel mortgage on the cattle purchased. Banks, finding that the

[48] From the time of the approval of the Stock Raising Homestead Act in 1916 to June 30, 1924, 98,048 entries have been made for a total of 38,478,606 acres. *Report of Commissioner of the General Land Office*, 1924, p. 9.

[49] Hopkins, pp. 260-261.

[50] *Ibid.*

[51] *Ibid.*, pp. 260-261.

[52] *Ibid.*

[53] *Ibid.*

demand for money for the feeding business continued to grow, began to rediscount in the larger cities some of the notes received, so that credit channels were established from the local banks to credit sources in the East.[54]

In the meantime the western range industry was demanding credit facilities, and a machinery was gradually developing to supply them. As has been indicated the earliest ranchmen of Texas had little need of any considerable amount of capital. They merely acquired a few breeding animals and allowed them to run at large on the unoccupied lands until they had increased in many cases to a large herd.

As the cattle industry extended itself over the central and northern plains, however, and the economy of large scale production became apparent the demand for capital greatly increased. Men establishing themselves on large ranges found that they could not hold them, under "cow custom" and the rules of the stock associations, unless fully stocked and so sought eagerly to borrow money at ruinously high rates of interest for the purchase of additional cattle.[55] Mention has already been made of British and other foreign syndicates formed for the launching of ranching enterprises or to lend money for carrying on the cattle business.[56] The volume of capital supplied by them was large and had a great influence upon the industry as a whole.

As markets and packing establishments grew up there were formed in all important market centers large "stock yards banks" whose chief business was lending money to cattle raisers or feeders. Commission firms also grew up to handle shipments of live stock and there in time began to lend money on cattle. The personal relations between commission men and shippers were frequently very close and it is probable that loans began by commission merchants introducing to a banker ranchmen or feeder

---

[54] *Ibid.*

[55] See Chas. S. Cole, "Cattle Loans and their Value to Investors," *Year Book of Department of Agriculture*, 1918, or G. L. Clemen, *American Live Stock and Meat Industry*, Chap. 23, for excellent brief accounts of methods of financing the cattle industry.

[56] See Chap. V, p. 82.

[161]

friends in need of funds to buy cattle or for operating expenses, and in some cases indorsing their notes or even lending them money from personal funds.[57] However, the importance of maintaining these close relations with shippers and of extending the circle of their customers eventually caused them to combine the lending of money on live stock as a regular business with their ordinary functions as commission merchants. Some loans were made to feeders but the tendency of the commission firms was to lend money to producers, leaving feeder loans largely to the local banks.[58]

Soon after 1890, when the cattle industry had begun to recover somewhat from the disastrous depression of the late eighties, there came the formation of numerous cattle loan companies. Some of these were organized by packer interests or stock yards banks with the object of promoting the cattle business by extending credit to producers and feeders.[59] Many of them were affiliated with some large bank and their officials were frequently the same as those of the bank, though a separate organization was maintained in order to avoid those clauses of the banking laws limiting the size of single loans made by banks.[60] These laws often prevented the banks from handling the larger ranch loans which were, in most cases, the most profitable ones.

Both commission firms and cattle loan companies obtained funds for carrying on their business by rediscounting cattle paper. Commission men usually loaned money directly to the borrower, while cattle loan companies sometimes made direct loans and sometimes acted as brokers and took paper on loans made by commission firms or other credit agencies.[61] Thus before the close of the century three avenues had been developed through which ranchmen and feeders might obtain funds: banks, commission companies, and cattle loan companies.[62]

57 Hopkins, pp. 267-268.
58 *Ibid.*, p. 267.
59 *Ibid.*, p. 265. Also Cole, *op. cit.*, p. 101.
60 Clemen, p. 504.
61 *Ibid.*, p. 308. Also Hopkins, p. 264.
62 *Ibid.*

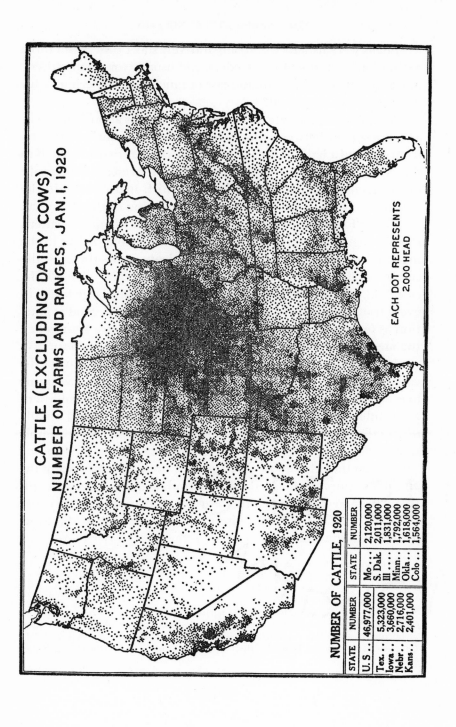

CATTLE (EXCLUDING DAIRY COWS)
NUMBER ON FARMS AND RANGES, JAN. 1, 1920

EACH DOT REPRESENTS
2,000 HEAD

NUMBER OF CATTLE, 1920

STATE	NUMBER	STATE	NUMBER
U. S.	46,977,000	Mo.	2,120,000
		S. Dak.	2,011,000
Tex.	5,323,000	Ill.	1,831,000
Iowa	3,660,000	Minn.	1,792,000
Nebr.	2,716,000	Okla.	1,618,000
Kans.	2,401,000	Colo.	1,564,000

Loans were usually for a comparatively short time, from three to six months in the case of feeders, and usually for six months or more—rarely for eight—in the case of ranchmen, sometimes with the promise of a renewal.[63]

As indicated, the rate of interest by 1900 was about 8 per cent and the spread between the interest and rediscounting rate was from one and a half to three per cent with two or two and a half to three per cent as about the average.[64] This represented the profit of the agency making the loan out of which had to be paid the expenses of operation, including the inspecting of the collateral.

Cattle loans were usually rediscounted in financial centers, the loan agencies establishing relations with strong banks in the market for commercial paper.[65] Such loans were theoretically carefully safeguarded and inquiries made into every phase of the risk.[66] At the same time the personal element was a large factor in every transaction. Men of undoubted integrity and good reputation as feeders or ranchmen could frequently secure loans when the men of questionable honesty or ability could not do so.[67]

It was customary to lend from one-half to the full value of the collateral since it was asserted that 20 to 25 per cent was ample margin for safety. Feeders of good reputation who had sufficient corn and hay to finish a few cars of cattle for market could usually obtain the money with which to buy them. Ranchmen with ample range and water often borrowed large sums with which to buy cattle even though they could offer little or no security except the animals so purchased. On the other hand men whose facilities for pasturing and caring for cattle were regarded as inadequate could in many cases not borrow more than fifty per cent of the value of the collateral offered.

63 Cole, *op. cit.,* p. 102.
64 *Ibid.,* p. 105.
65 *Ibid.*
66 *Ibid.,* pp. 105-106.
67 *Ibid.,* pp. 1-4-106. Most loaning agencies are members of the various state cattle raisers' associations and through such connections are able to know more of borrowers and their reputation as well as to utilize the protection afforded by the association against losses by theft of animals upon which they have loaned money.

These methods of financing the cattle business have continued, largely speaking, down to the present time. Cattle paper eventually became quite popular as an investment. It was short time paper, and the buyer in normal times enjoyed an ever increasing margin of safety as the cattle matured and fattened, or in the case of breeding herds, increased in numbers. Moreover it was easily liquidated, in fact was in many cases "self-liquidating." Cattle on feed must be marketed when fat, steers on the range must be sold when mature. Also the paper when rediscounted was guaranteed by the agency making the loan and had its resources back of it as well as the collateral named in the loan.[68]

Even so, there were sometimes heavy losses in times of depression and these served to lessen the confidence in cattle paper as an investment. The interdependence of cattle loans and other credit has always been very close. When money was plentiful cattle loan companies were frequently tempted by the ease with which the paper could be re-discounted to expand their business to dangerous proportions. Fifteen or twenty times the amount of their capital stock, or even more, was loaned upon range cattle sometimes without sufficient care in inspecting the collateral offered.[69] The ranchman finding money easy to obtain was frequently tempted to expand his business at the very time when conditions of the industry demanded retrenchment. Then came cold winters, resulting in heavy losses, a shrinkage of range due to the inroads of homesteaders, drought, low prices and disaster. Individual loans were large and the failure of a single important ranchman might easily ruin the financial agency that had loaned him money, whose failure might in turn seriously embarrass the bank, or individual investor, holding the paper.[70] On the other hand when money was close even the ranchman who had in the past been fairly conservative in borrowing money found it diffi-

[68] Clemen, p. 526.

[69] *Ibid.*, p. 527.

[70] Losses on cattle paper were very heavy for three or four years during the period of depression following the war but in most cases these losses fell upon the agency originally making the loan. In only comparatively few instances were they borne by the investor.

[165]

cult to obtain funds and was sometimes forced to market cattle at ruinously low prices to pay operating expenses and retire such loans as were most pressing.

Feeder loans were much safer but there were some losses even on this paper. In times when money was abundant and cattle high, feeders borrowed large sums and hastened to market and bid against one another for cattle with the result that they obtained them at a price which doomed the enterprise to failure before feeding actually began.[71]

The speculative element in feeding is always great and cannot be avoided. The gain in weight and the spread in price between feeders and fat cattle can be estimated quite closely, but what cannot be foreseen are market fluctuations in the price of fat cattle, which are often so great as to bring about heavy losses or gains.

When money was scarce feeders could not obtain loans and as a result there was little market for grain. Ranchmen found a reduced demand for feeder cattle and stagnation ensued.

It is certain that the use of the same credit channels served to draw the range area and the corn belt more closely together. Ranchmen and feeders of cattle both borrowed money from the same cattle loan companies or stock yards banks, they consigned shipments to the same commission houses, met at the stock yards or hotels in the market centers and so became personally acquainted.[72] Large feeders sometimes visited the range area and purchased feeders to be shipped directly to them. Corn belt banks with surplus funds often bought from commission or cattle loan companies cattle paper secured by loans on range cattle.

[71] Hopkins, p. 276.

[72] In 1922 an interesting experiment was undertaken for the development of a method of co-operation between producers and feeders of cattle. Apparently at the request of the War Finance Corporation, the Iowa Farm Credit Corporation made an arrangement for the shipment of 4,000 head of feeder cattle from New Mexico to Iowa farmers for feeding. It was provided that the feeder should have all the added weight plus two cents a pound as his payment for feeding. Des Moines *Register*, Nov. 8, 1922. (Quoted by Hopkins, p. 291). This amounted to the cattle raisers retaining all risk and at the same time financing the feeders. Apparently the experiment was not an unqualified success any more than had been others of a similar nature tried out before.

With the outbreak of the European war exports of fresh beef, which had fallen quite low, began to rise rapidly. Then came the entrance of the United States into the war, with a great advance in the price of cattle and beef, in common with all other food products.

There is no doubt but that the "meatless days" inaugurated by the government and the active campaign for food conservation and the use of meat substitutes kept prices from going as high as they otherwise would have done. Yet they rose enormously and a record price was established on December 11, 1918, when native beef steers sold at $20.50 a hundred on the Chicago market, while the average price for that year was $14.65.[73] Pure bred animals also sold about this time at the highest prices ever known. Corn rose from 76 cents in January, 1916, to $2.09 in September, 1917.[74]

Then came the close of the war and the great lowering of prices. In the fall of 1919 the government launched an attack on the high cost of living by beginning the sale of surplus war supplies. The public, urged during the war to substitute other food for a part of the meat ordinarily eaten, continued to do so after peace had come. The price of beef steadily declined, going from $15.30 for fat steers in October, 1920, to $8.80 the following February.[75]

When we consider that the cattle loan business had grown to a point where hundreds of millions of dollars were loaned on cattle each year,[76] the extent of the disaster brought about by this enormous shrinkage in values must be apparent. For a time it was almost as though nearly half the collateral for all cattle paper had been wiped out. Financial depression set in, and there came a great shrinkage in the deposits of most western banks, forcing them to collect loans when possible to do so. Heavy losses occurred. Cattle paper, regarded in normal times as an excellent

73 See Table of prices. Figures from Chicago *Daily Drover's Year Book of Figures.*
74 See Table of Prices. Prices from Annual Reports of Chicago Board of Trade.
75 See Table of Prices.
76 Cole, *op. cit.,* p. 108.

investment, was unsalable. A large volume of the range loans had to be renewed again and again with hardly more than an even chance at best that they could ever be paid in full.

Under such circumstances the old machinery for financing the cattle industry broke down. It had been dependent upon rediscounting loans in financial centers and when that was no longer possible it ceased to function.

Some financial reorganization was absolutely necessary since it was clear that most live stock loans could not be liquidated without still further loss and increased demoralization. Out of this condition grew the Stock Growers' Finance Corporation with headquarters at Chicago. A pool of fifty million dollars was formed by a group of New York and Chicago bankers to extend credit to men engaged in the live stock industry.[77] No direct loans were made by this corporation but live stock paper was rediscounted from banks, trust companies, and cattle loan companies who guaranteed payment.[78]

Altogether this corporation bought about twenty million dollars worth of cattle paper, mostly from banks in the Southwest. It dealt largely in range loans since the feeder loans could usually be cared for by the credit machinery already in operation.

The United States government recognized the need of the live stock industry for more adequate financing and in 1921 an amendment was made to the War Finance Corporation Act providing that loans could be made to banks, bankers, trust companies and cattle loan companies for the benefit of farmers and live stock growers.

Still further assistance was given in the Farm Credits Act approved in March, 1923, by which intermediate credit banks were established with power to make properly secured loans or advances to co-operative associations formed by individuals engaged in producing or marketing live stock or staple farm products. They were also given power to discount or purchase paper, the proceeds of which had been advanced for agricultural purposes,

[77] See Clemen, pp. 529-530 for a brief sketch of its work.
[78] Ibid.

or to raise and fatten live stock. Other provisions of the act authorized the formation of privately financed agricultural credit corporations each with a capital stock of not less than $250,000 and
national agricultural credit corporations of not less than $1,000,-
000 capitalization. A later amendment to the act provided that
the intermediate credit banks might rediscount the paper of such
an organization as the agricultural credit corporation up to ten
times the amount of the latter's capital stock.

This new credit machinery did a great service and probably
saved the cattle industry from almost complete collapse. Even so,
conditions were bad enough. By 1923 every branch of the business
was in the depths of depression. Feeders had lost money, ranchmen in the range area were nearly all in distress. Pasturage was
scarce and high when it was to be leased, while if the land was
purchased outright the investment was so heavy as to make it almost impossible to operate at a profit, since labor, taxes, and
freight rates were all high.

The fairly good prices of 1920 had resulted in a large amount
of feeding in 1921. Many feeders lost money which not a few tried
to regain in 1922, but with little success. The result was a great
reduction in the shipment of feeders from Chicago to the corn
belt in 1923 and 1924 and ranchmen found the demand for feeder
cattle comparatively light and prices low, when the cost of operating expenses was considered.[79]

Bad as conditions had been, there were hopeful signs by 1925
that perhaps the worst was over. Prices rose somewhat though still
subject to considerable fluctuations. Conditions seemed to be
more stable. Most men who were unable to weather the storm had
by this time sold their cattle and retired from the business. Others,
more fortunate of more efficient managers, had so arranged their
affairs as to make it possible to continue until the dawning of a
better day should again make the business profitable.

The tremendous advance in the price of farm lands throughout the corn states during the war period made it even less profitable to combine raising and feeding cattle than ever before, while

[79] See tables.

[169]

the range area became more clearly defined than formerly. It seems that most of the public domain suitable for growing crops has already been taken by homesteaders and the remaining portion, together with forest reserves and the Indian reservations that are still left, will in the future be used as a permanent grazing area for rearing cattle to an age suitable for feeding. These will then be marketed in the corn belt, or the regions not too remote from cotton seed oil mills, for feeding on corn and cotton seed products. Altogether it seems probable that the relations of the range cattle area and the corn belt may in the future be even closer than they have been in the past.

9.

THE DAWN OF A
NEW DAY

Even the most cursory study of the history of the range cattle industry on the Great Plains must reveal the fact that the business was characterized by a number of peculiar and very significant features. It rose very quickly to enormous proportions, shifting from small to large scale individual operations in the process; and then declined with equal rapidity, reverting again to comparatively small type producers. It was spread over a vast area and, considering the volume of production, had comparatively few persons engaged in it. The activities of some of these individuals extended from Mexico to Canada and from the financial centers of the East to the Pacific Ocean.

Accustomed at first to think of the range cattle region as a self sufficing area, and of themselves as a class apart from all others, the ranchmen eventually formed close relationships with sections and industries farther east. These were established by the purchase of breeding animals to improve the quality of their herds, by the sale of large numbers of feeder cattle to consume the surplus grain and hay of the corn belt, and by the opening up of credit channels reaching to the financial centers of the East through which flowed capital for the financing of the industry. Carried on largely upon the public domain and Indian reservations, it was also inevitable that the men engaged in the range cattle industry should soon become involved in political controversies relative to the disposal of public lands and with respect to the leasing of Indian lands or the opening of them to settlement.

It is doubtful if any great industry or group of men engaged

[171]

in it has ever been less understood or subjected to more bitter criticism by the public at large than have the ranchmen and the ranch cattle business.

In 1889 a large group of the most important ranchmen in the Southwest addressed a memorial to the President of the United States containing this statement:

"Though bitterly attacked by the hostile part of the press and some members of Congress, the nature of our pursuit and the character of the men engaged in it have prevented us from responding to defamations and calumnies that seem to have well nigh convinced the public mind that the man who has, or has had, an interest in cattle on the range is little better than a highwayman, and a bandit worthy of penal reprobation."[1]

Exaggerated as this statement must be, there can be no doubt that it contains a large element of truth. Through his occupation of the public domain the ranchman was brought into conflict with the homesteaders and through his large scale production of beef came into competition with the stock farmers farther east. It mattered little that he laid no claim to the land itself or that he insisted that he was merely utilizing it for grazing until it should be needed or wanted for the production of crops. He was using and deriving benefit from lands that belonged to the people as a whole and the people as a whole resented it to a greater or less degree depending upon their personal interest. Nor did the fact that he had established a huge productive industry and had greatly reduced the price of beef for millions of people serve to lessen the criticism against him. In some cases this fact merely served to increase it. The attitude of many people is well expressed in this statement made about 1887 by one of the Inspectors of the Bureau of Animal Industry:

"A matter of special importance to the cattle interest as it is represented on Kansas farms is the raising and feeding of

[1] Memorial of the Cherokee Strip Live Stock Association to the President of the United States, November 28, 1889, p. 6.

[172]

large numbers of cattle on Indian lands and on the public lands belonging to the government. To raise cattle that way costs little for there is no rental charge on the lands and no taxes are assessed against the occupants. It is free cattle raising and the animals are sold in the open market in competition with others produced by farmers on their own individual lands at great expense. It is an outrage on the rights of men who buy their own lands and pay taxes on them. This practice ought to be suppressed at once and without any ceremony."[2]

Writing further upon this subject the same author sums up the feeling of numerous stock farmers in the following language:

"Feeders who raise cattle in southern Kansas feel unable to compete with the cattlemen on the Cherokee Strip and in the Indian nations who practically have free range, and urge that the government should charge for pasturing on its lands, or what would be much better, prohibit it altogether in the interest of legitimate cattle raising."[3]

It is a little difficult to see at this time why the grazing of animals upon public or Indian lands should be regarded as any less "legitimate cattle raising" than was grazing and feeding them upon farms farther east. Certainly it ought not to have been expected that the herbage covering the enormous area of the Great Plains and capable of furnishing food for millions of cattle should be entirely unutilized and allowed to rot or be destroyed by prairie fires. Yet there was just cause for objecting to "free grazing" and the failure to assess for taxation many of the cattle on Indian reservations and the public domain.

It now seems clear that a fair and reasonable charge should have been made for grazing but since this was not done the criticism should have been directed against Congress for its failure to provide for this rather than against the ranchmen for taking

2 Report of Inspector H. A. Heath, *Report of the Bureau of Animal Industry,* 1889-90, pp. 407-409.

3 *Ibid.,* p. 415.

advantage of the opportunity offered to them. This however was not the case. It was the ranching industry that received most of the criticism and it was even urged in some quarters that congressional action was much influenced by ranchmen who objected to paying for grazing privileges. Largely speaking, this is evidently untrue since there is ample evidence that most ranchmen even quite early were strongly in favor of a policy of leasing both Indian lands and the public domain for grazing purposes.

There can be no doubt, however, that the acts of a few ranchmen, who bullied home seekers, sought to prevent the opening of Indian reservations to settlement, and maintained a group of rough and lawless employees about them, helped to bring the entire business into bad repute. These were only a small minority and yet they served to lower the whole industry in public esteem. The many were compelled to suffer for the actions of the few.

Whatever may have been the ranchmen's faults, they were in many areas advance agents of civilization and their contribution toward the upbuilding of the West has been enormous. Regarded by some as a "favored class," it is certain that any favors received were earned at the expense of infinite toil and hardship. Many men of wealth and culture journeyed to the Great Plains of the West where they risked death at the hands of hostile Indians, lived under most primitive conditions, and endured heat and cold and all the vicissitudes of life on the extreme frontier. If at times they made large profits in many other cases they met great losses and if their competition was destructive to the interests of some of the stock farmers farther east, they also gave a powerful impetus to breeding and feeding in the corn belt, and furnished cheap beef to untold thousands of people. If in some cases they sought to discourage the advance of home seekers or in rare instances to drive them off their ranges, they were more often pathbreakers who pointed the way to men who wished to till the soil. And by purchasing feed, drilling wells, and furnishing the settlers with cows to milk, the ranchmen enabled many men to remain upon their prairie claims who otherwise would have been forced to abandon them. Yet it was inevitable that the ranchmen should receive criticism. They were fighting a losing battle. Their interests were necessarily opposed to those of the men who cultivated the soil, and no group in America has ever been able to succeed in a fight waged openly against the farming population of the country.

Historical tradition has had a great influence upon the range cattle industry. Carried on since colonial times as a frontier pursuit and giving way to ordinary farming as settlement advanced westward, ranching inevitably came to be regarded as a temporary and transitory business to be pursued in any area only until the lands it occupied were needed for cultivation.

When the range cattle industry reached the comparatively dry region of the Great Plains the ranchmen confidently asserted that they were at last in an area that must always be devoted to grazing since the rainfall was not sufficient for the production of crops. An eager throng of homesteaders was unconvinced. They advanced rapidly into the "cow country," pushing the cattle raisers steadily farther and farther west. Again and again the ranchmen declared that the western limit of crop production had been reached by the settlers, and again and again the latter proved them mistaken. Even when grazing lands had been reduced to extremely dry and barren areas, the belief was current that much further reduction would come as soon as there was a greater need for farming lands. The ranchman had been wrong so often in asserting that it was impossible to grow crops on the ranges occupied by his cattle that many people refused to believe him when he was at last right.

It seems that Congress fully shared this popular view. Attempts to secure laws for leasing the public domain for grazing always failed and the same was true with respect to laws providing for the sale of public lands in tracts of a size suitable for ranching purposes. Even acts for the leasing of Indian lands were long delayed and in the meantime the tenure of ranchmen on both Indian reservations and the public domain was most precarious.

This general feeling that the business of ranching was temporary in character, together with the uncertain tenure of nearly all lands occupied for pasturage, was productive of many ills. It resulted in a great over-stocking of many ranges which eventually proved disastrous, not only to individual ranchmen but to the entire industry, since large areas that had formerly furnished excellent pasturage were converted into barren wastes incapable of supporting one fourth as many animals as they had formerly done. Cattle raisers, fearing that they would within a few years be compelled to remove, resolved to get the most possible from the range while it was in their possession, and exploited it shamefully without any thought of the future. Such a short sighted policy brought its own punishment. In the regions so heavily over-stocked the time came when the animals did not fatten and the pasturage was so closely grazed as to leave little food for winter. Cold weather with deep snows came, and cattle died by thousands leaving their owners facing bankruptcy.

Another evil of the temporary and precarious tenure of grazing lands was that the industry was kept in a more or less wild and primitive condition. It was impossible to erect permanent improvements upon public or Indian lands. Camps occupied by ranchmen and their employees and corrals for use in caring for the animals were of the most flimsy and temporary character. Under such circumstances homes and family life were virtually impossible. As a result the range area developed as a "man's country" where women and children were seldom seen. Another tradition grew up that ranching is necessarily a rough and lawless occupation entirely removed from the refining influences of home and civilization.

Still a third result of the temporary character of the ranchman's occupation of grazing lands, was that it tended to discourage any scientific study of the business itself. It was impossible to look forward and make definite plans for future years. Experiments designed to reveal the carrying capacity of certain ranges, or in methods of range restoration, could not well be made. Nor was it possible to make a scientific study of watering facilities, summer and winter range, or the proper proportion of breeding animals, young steers, and older animals on a general ranch. Experiments could not be made to determine the best type of corrals, branding chutes, vats, or shelter for winter; nor was it possible to make definite plans for financing a business over a long term of years, or to obtain adequate credit facilities under the conditions that existed.

Because his business was carried on largely upon lands under the control of the federal government, the ranchman often came into contact with governmental agencies in a fashion by no means pleasing to either party. Finding that any notice the government might take of his business was likely to assume the form of Presidential proclamations, or departmental orders that restricted his operations or interfered with his business—in the interest of more intensive forms of agriculture—it was quite natural that the ranchman should cling closely to the old idea that "a government governs best which governs least," and should even at the present time be somewhat chary of governmental efforts to help the range cattle interests even though the beneficent effects of its aid to other forms of agriculture seem apparent to all.

As has been indicated, the live stock industry was soon after the close of the World War in a most depressed condition, but there were indications that the depression was only temporary and that the business would soon be on an upward trend. While the question as to whether the federal government was right or wrong in the past in its refusal to lease or sell the public domain in tracts of a size suitable for ranches is an academic one that may well be left for each individual to answer for himself, it seems certain that the time has now come when grazing on public lands should be put upon a more firm and permanent basis. Contrary to a large popular opinion the ranching industry is by no means a thing of the past, nor is the public domain entirely gone. In 1924 there were more than 186,000,000 acres of vacant, unreserved and unappropriated public lands in the United States.[4] Most of this was either used or capable of use for pasturage. While Texas has little unappropriated land, more than 123,000,000 acres of land in that state, or over 73 per cent of the total area, were utilized

4 *Report of the Commissioner of the General Land Office,* 1924, p. 86

for grazing in 1922.[5] Of course, the area of lands in private hands outside of Texas that are devoted to grazing is enormous, while the forest reserves also furnish pasturage for millions of sheep and cattle each year.

It seems clear then that the raising of large numbers of cattle largely upon native pasturage will be continued indefinitely in the United States. It also seems certain that but little of the remaining public lands can ever be profitably cultivated. Some areas will doubtless be brought under irrigation but these are likely to be so small as to be almost negligible in considering policies for the future administration of the public domain as a whole. If the recent recommendations of the Commissioner of the General Land Office should be taken, and the remaining public lands leased for grazing in tracts of convenient size, or if they should be sold in tracts of suitable size for "family ranches" upon liberal terms of payment, it would go a long way toward stabilizing the ranching industry in many large areas.[6] An incentive would then be offered for the proper conservation of ranges and a consistent policy could be entered upon for the restoration of those ranges that have been sadly depleted through constant overstocking. That such damaged ranges can be restored has been shown in the case of certain areas rendered almost bare and worthless by excessive grazing that have since been included in forest reserves. Through the wise and efficient managment of the Forest Service many of these have been brought back almost if not quite to their original value for pasturage.[7] Adequate provisions could be made for a water supply and facilities provided for handling and caring for cattle.

Best of all, real homes would grow up; temporary camps and cabins would doubtless be replaced by comfortable, well built houses occupied by families, and the rough and primitive conditions still prevailing in certain areas would disappear. By means

5 Youngblood and Cox, *An Economic Study of Ranching on the Edwards Plateau*, p. 32.

6 *Report of Commissioner of General Land Office*, 1924.

7 *Proceedings of Fourteenth Annual Convention of American National Live Stock Association*, pp. 27 and 61.

of wells and windmills a small area might be irrigated on each ranch to furnish fruit and vegetables, and large areas now undeveloped and unoccupied except by a few men to look after cattle might, except for a sparse population, become very similar to any prosperous farming region. Nor would life in a comparatively thinly peopled ranching community be likely to prove unattractive. Cheap automobiles, telephone and radio would do much to reduce the feeling of isolation that formerly would have been a serious objection to living in a region where the land holdings of a single family were so large.

Historical tradition is still strong and there is yet some feeling that public lands ought not to be leased for grazing or sold in comparatively large tracts for ranches. It seems important to realize, however, that most of the public domain still remaining is useful only for grazing, that ranching can no longer be regarded as a temporary business but is located in certain areas to stay, and that these facts should be considered in formulating policies for the disposal of the remaining public lands.

Certainly no one would be willing to see the interests of the homeseeker made to suffer in order to benefit the ranchman. However, most of these lands have been subject to settlement for many years and have never been occupied, while some that were occupied at one time have since been abandoned because it was found they could not be made to yield a living when planted to crops, except under irrigation. Also the question may be raised as to whether the man who goes west with his family expecting to secure sufficient land to support them through grazing live stock upon native pasturage is not quite as much a "homeseeker" as is the homesteader who expects to grow crops. The important thing in working out a policy for the disposal of these lands is to determine what is the smallest area that will pasture a sufficient number of cattle to support an ordinary family according to American standards of living. This will, of course, vary widely in different localities, but approximations could be made for various regions.

Not only has the feeling that much of the land on the Great Plains now used for grazing will eventually be devoted to farming greatly affected ranching on the public domain, but it has also resulted in the placing of fictitious values upon much land in private hands now utilized for grazing, land that likely will never be used for any other purpose. Such lands are frequently valued far too high both when offered for sale and when assessed for taxation.

Important as it is that ranching be placed upon a more firm and permanent basis with respect to the lands now utilized for grazing, it is even more important that it be placed upon a more scientific basis with respect to the industry as a whole. Little scientific study has ever been given to grazing, either by governmental agencies or by the great majority of the men engaged in it. As a result there has been little improvement made in the business of growing cattle largely upon pasturage. While other forms of agriculture have advanced enormously in the last few decades, the grazing industry, except for improvement of breeds and the construction of better fences, is virtually where it was many hundreds of years ago. In the past many men have secured as much pasturage as possible, purchased as many cattle as they could obtain money to buy, and turned them loose upon the open range staking the lives of the animals and their own fortunes upon the uncertain hazard of a mild winter. There has been in many cases but little thought of the morrow and apparently all too little learned from the experience of yesterday.

The time has clearly come when inefficient and haphazard business methods in the ranching industry can no longer hope to succeed. Careful, scientific study should be given to utilization, conservation and restoration of ranges. Such study should reveal the carrying capacity of pasture lands in terms of the various types of animals, the proper proportion of summer and winter range, and the best methods of restoring to their former value areas damaged by over-stocking. In certain instances it might disclose the fact that some cattlemen should discard their prejudices against sheep and goats and graze a certain number of these animals with their cattle in order to utilize their pasturage to the best advantage. Experiments should be made in re-seeding bare spots, in methods of eliminating noxious weeds and poisonous plants, and in removing all animals from certain areas at times in order to give the grass seeds an opportunity to mature and ripen.

Better watering facilities should be provided, and scientific investigations made as to the proper size of a "one family ranch" in various regions, and the correct percentage of breeding animals, young stock, and more mature cattle, soon to be finished for beef, that should be kept on a ranch devoted to producing and maturing cattle for market. A study should be made of marketing and some attention given to determining what should be the relative size of the investments in land, in cattle, and in buildings and improvements, in establishing or in conducting a ranching enterprise.

The financing of the cattle industry has in the past been most unscientific, and no phase of the business is in more urgent need of investigation and reform. There has been too much of speculation on the part of both borrower and lender. Ranchmen have borrowed money recklessly, hoping that a rise in prices would enable them to pay their loans and at the same time make a fair profit. Money lenders have loaned money equally recklessly after hasty and careless inspection of the collateral offered, and have sought to justify and protect themselves by shortening the term and increasing the interest rate of the loan. The results have been disastrous to all parties concerned. It seems clear that some adequate system of long term loans should be evolved for men raising cattle. While six months is usually a sufficient time for feeder loans, it is entirely too short to be of any great value to the man who raises and matures cattle for market. If means could be provided for such men to obtain, upon adequate security, loans extending over a period of several years with the first payment on the principal to be made at the end of two or three years, it would furnish a powerful incentive to many men of small capital to engage in cattle raising.

As has been pointed out, the relations between the range area and the corn belt are very close and there are indications that they

[181]

may become even closer. Under such circumstances some experiments with respect to such relations may be worthy of consideration. It has often been urged that under present methods of operation too large a percentage of the value of the fat steer marketed for slaughter has been paid out for freight. The calf is often shipped from Texas to ranges farther north, matured there to an age suitable for feeding, and then shipped to one of the markets. Here he is purchased by a cattle feeder from the corn belt and shipped to the latter's farm, and when fat is again returned to market for slaughter.

During the boom period of the grazing industry, we have seen that many men owned breeding ranches in Texas where animals were raised and other ranges in the North where they were matured and fattened on grass. Since this proved quite profitable the question might be raised as to whether it might not be profitable for a single operator to own a ranch in the range area upon which cattle should be raised and matured to the age of feeders and also a tract of farm land in the corn belt to be used for the production of corn and hay and to which these animals might be shipped directly for feeding. This would avoid at least one shipment of the animals and would result in a considerable saving in freight, yardage, feed, commissions, and possibly scalper profits, and would mean a return to the older system under which the individual cattle raiser reared the animals to maturity and also fattened them for market. It would also in all probability mean a return to larger scale operation, though this could perhaps be justified on the ground of greater efficiency. Some experiments in such methods of producing beef seem worth while.

Some further study might also be made along the lines tried out in Iowa in 1922 relative to shifting the speculative risk of feeding by inducing ranchmen to supply corn belt feeders with cattle. Since the plan tried merely meant the partial financing of the feeder by the ranchman and the assumption of all speculative risks by the latter, it seems unlikely that it will ever prove popular. At the same time some investigations might be made to determine whether some system might not be evolved under which the speculative risk of feeding would be distributed between the cattle raiser and the feeder. Perhaps the ranchman might furnish the feeder with cattle under a contract providing that each should receive a certain percentage of the increased gain in the weight and price of the animals due to feeding.

Doubtless many other phases of the grazing and feeding industry might be suggested as proper subjects for scientific experimental research by governmental agencies and the men engaged in the business. The work of the Texas Experiment Station with respect to the study of a typical ranching area on the Edwards Plateau and the experiments of the Department of Agriculture in range restoration in certain areas of the Southwest have been admirable, but are only a beginning.

It is imperative that steps be taken to place grazing upon the same scientific basis that has been attained by other forms of agriculture. Ranching permits the utilization of a larger amount of capital for each person engaged in it than does any other branch of agriculture. Such being the case it seems most important that the operations of every individual growing cattle on the range should be brought to the highest possible point of efficiency.

An effort should be made to correct the popular impression that ranching is inherently a wild and lawless occupation carried on in regions that have no home life, or the comforts of civilization. If this has been to a certain extent true in a more or less remote past, it has been due to the precarious tenure of much of the grazing land of the country rather than to the nature of the industry itself.[8] While the comparatively large land holdings necessary in ranching give to the business some peculiar features, there is no reason to think that the production of beef upon native pasturage is any more rough or lawless an occupation than is the production of corn or potatoes or any other agricultural commodity.

The time has come when the lax business practices and short

8 See *The Nation*, Vol. XLI, p. 173 for a discussion of this subject.

sighted policies that have been all too characteristic of ranching in the past must give place to efficient and progressive methods of operation based upon the results of long and careful scientific study.

The federal and state governments can and no doubt will, through experimental research, do much to put the grazing industry upon a more scientific basis, but every ranchman should give systematic study to the details of every phase of his business. Instead of making plans for but a year or two in advance, he should look forward over a long period of time and not only work out consistent plans for an increased measure of success from year to year with respect to his own affairs, but should do his part toward the steady advancement of the industry as a whole.

While looking forward it might be well worth while at times to give an occasional glance backward. The experience of the past may be of great value in studying the conditions of the present, or in considering the possibilities of the future. Any general history of the ranching industry of the West must necessarily be brief and more or less incomplete, since it deals with many regions varying widely in topography, soil, vegetation and climate. Competent persons should make careful, detailed studies of the history of the grazing industry in a number of typical ranching areas. Such studies would serve to disclose the earlier conditions under which the business was carried on in that particular locality. They would give a detailed account of operations from year to year, show the early carrying capacity of ranges, the facilities provided for watering, the percentage of winter losses, and of calves dropped over a long period of years, and the changes made in methods pursued. They would show something of profits and losses in the past and would, no doubt, serve to explain why some men succeeded while others failed.

In many ways the industry lends itself to such study in admirable fashion. Its beginning in various regions are quite definite and the period of time it has been in existence is not so great but that it could be treated year by year in such a way as to show quite clearly just what took place. Moreover, the number of men engaged in the business within a region of considerable size was not large.

If it were possible to place in the hands of the intelligent and progressive ranchman an authentic and detailed record of the ranching industry in his particular community or region, there can be little doubt that he would find it most helpful. A knowledge of the past could hardly fail to lead him to a better understanding of present conditions and prove of benefit in making plans for the future. A careful study of the experiences and business methods of earlier operators might well furnish both a basis and an incentive for a more intensive study of his own business and teach him to avoid some of the disastrous mistakes made by others.

Finally, the early history of the grazing industry in any part of the Great Plains region is a story of men who met hardship and danger and financial reverses in a fashion that must prove an inspiration to those who have succeeded them. It is doubtful if any man now engaged in ranching can read a full account of the grazing industry in his particular locality since earliest times without gaining thereby an increased devotion to his chosen business and an added determination to do everything possible for the advancement of an industry that has back of it so remarkable a history.

BIBLIOGRAPHY

The author regrets that he did not have the opportunity to use the great manuscript collections at Cheyenne of the Wyoming Stock Growers' Association. Some compensation for this serious omission has been found, however, in the study of the personal papers of Frank Canton, who was successively ranchman in Wyoming, live stock inspector for this association, four years sheriff of Johnson County, and an active participant in the difficulty known as the "Rustlers War."

Other material used in this and previous work on the range cattle industry include the great collections of the library of Harvard University, the Boston Public Library, the Library of Congress, the library and files of the United States Department of Agriculture, the War Department, the Department of the Interior, especially the files of the Bureau of Indian Affairs, the library and manuscript collections of the University of Oklahoma, the University of Texas, the Oklahoma Historical Society, the Kansas Historical Society, the files of the Texas and Southwestern Cattle Raisers' Association at Fort Worth, and of the Old Trail Drivers' Association at San Antonio. Visits have also been paid to such cities as Chicago, Kansas City, St. Louis, and Wichita where much information has been gleaned from the stock yards banks and live stock commission firms. Correspondence has also been carried on with the managers of some of the more important ranching enterprises now in operation, including the Matador, King Ranch, the S. M. S., the J. A., and numerous others.

Before beginning work on this volume the author's experience with the subject of the range cattle industry had included not only five years work as a ranchman in western Oklahoma, but also the preparation of numerous monographs and magazine articles dealing with the cattle business, including a doctor's dissertation at Harvard and a number of magazine articles and sketches. Since much of the material collected in this earlier work has been used in the present volume, it has not seemed practicable to attempt to give an exhaustive bibliography, but to list only those things that have proved most useful. Since he has had considerable personal experience in ranching the author feels that the chief value of his bibliography may lie in the fact that it has been carefully selected and only those things given that have been most useful. The volume of material included in Reports of the Bureau of Animal Industry, Bureau of Agricultural Economics, Bureau of Forestry, Reports of the Commissioner of the General Land Office, and Reports of the Agricultural Experiment Stations of the various states, to say nothing of books, newspapers, and periodical literature, is so enormous as to make the task of listing even the most important of it seem a well nigh hopeless one.

SOURCE MATERIAL

1. MANUSCRIPTS

Archives of the Cherokee Nation, 1866–1906.—About 60,000 documents in the manuscript collections of the University of Oklahoma contain much valuable material on the Cherokee Outlet and southern Kansas. Uncatalogued as yet and, so, difficult to work.

Archives of the Choctaw Nation.—Some 2,000 documents dealing chiefly with the legislative branch of the Choctaw government. Valuable for a part of Indian Territory and northern Texas. In the University of Oklahoma manuscript collections.

Canton Manuscripts.—Several hundred papers of the late General Frank M. Canton of Edmond, Oklahoma. Canton drove cattle on the trail in the late sixties and early seventies, was an inspector for the Wyoming Stock Growers' Association, four years sheriff of Johnson County, Wyoming, and later took part in the so called "Rustlers War." These papers now in the manuscript collection of the University of Oklahoma, contain, besides many letters, the manuscript story of Canton's life written by himself.

Cherokee Letters.—About 2,000 letters written by citizens of the Cherokee Nation from 1830 to 1895. Include many letters of General Stand Watie, J. M. Bell, E. C. Boudinot, W. P. Adair and others. Valuable for the Cherokee Outlet and a part of Indian Territory. In the University of Oklahoma manuscript collections.

Eldred Papers.—Nearly 300 letters and documents dealing with ranching in the Cherokee Outlet. Most of the letters are addressed to Charles Eldred who was vice-president of the Cherokee Strip Live Stock Association and one of the directors of that organization. Many of them are of a confidential nature and are invaluable in supplying the deficiencies of public documents with respect to the leasing of the Cherokee Outlet to cattlemen. This collection was stored at the University of Oklahoma for two years, but was then returned to Mrs. Charles Eldred of Alva, Oklahoma. Copies of all the more valuable papers were made and may be found in the University of Oklahoma manuscript collections.

Proceedings of the Meetings of the Texas and Southwestern Cattle Raisers' Association.—The minutes and proceedings of the meetings of this association from 1877 to 1892 have never been published, but the original manuscripts are on file in the association's offices at Fort Worth.

Texas State Library Manuscript Collections.—Contain much valuable material including the manuscript copy of the contract for building the Texas State Capitol by the founders of the Capitol Syndicate Ranch.

University of Texas Manuscript Collection.—This is an extremely valuable collection containing among other priceless items the manuscript records of C. H. Marselus, an inspector of trail herds at Trail City in 1886, the Diary and Log Book of J. E. Moore, trail boss for the X I T in 1892, and the Journal of Ignatius Erskine of a trip to California in 1854.

II. FEDERAL DOCUMENTS

Annual Reports of the Secretary of Agriculture, 1870–1918; the Bureau of Animal Industry, 1886–1890; Board of Indian Commissioners, 1869–1880; the Commissioner of the General Land Office, 1868–1924; the Commissioner of Indian Affairs, 1860–1908; the Patent Office, 1850–1853.

Census, Eighth to the Fourteenth, 1860–1920.

Congressional Record.

Farmers' Bulletin No. 72, Department of Agriculture, Bently, H. L., Cattle Ranges of the Southwest; No. 592, Barnes, W. C., Stock Watering Places on Western Grazing Lands; No. 811, Day, S. H., Production of Baby Beef.

Forestry Service Report No. 72, Barnes, W. C., and Jardine, J. T., Live Stock Production in Eleven Western Range States.

Indian Laws and Treaties (3 Vols.). Compiled by Charles J. Kappler.

Messages and Papers of the President (10 Vols.). Compiled by James Richardson.

Monthly Reports of the Department of Agriculture, 1866–1867.

Opinions of the Attorney General, Nos. 16, 18, and 19.

United States Geological Survey, Bulletin No. 611.

United States Statutes at Large.

House Executive Document 286, 24th Congress, 1st Session, Vol. 7, Serial 292.—The memorial and protest of the Cherokee against removal from Georgia (167 pages).

Senate Miscellaneous Document 143, 41st Congress, 2nd Session, Serial 1408.—A memorial to the Creek, Cherokee and Choctaw delegates protesting against the erection of a territorial government in Indian Territory (12 pages).

Senate Report 336, 41st Congress, 3rd Session. Serial 1443.—Report giving a description of Indian Territory (11 pages).

Senate Miscellaneous Documents 34, 66, 71, and 72, 43rd Congress, 2nd Session, Volume VII, Serial 1630.—These various documents are protests or memorials of the citizens of the Cherokee, Creek, Chickasaw, and Osage tribes against the erection of a territorial government over them in the Indian Territory. They aggregate about 27 pages.

House Report 105, 43rd Congress, 2nd Session, Volume II, Serial 1657.—A report of the transportation of cattle (14 pages).

Senate Executive Document 74, 45th Congress, 2nd Session, Volume II, Serial 1781.—On the subject of the right of the Indians to impose taxes on cattle crossing their lands or pastured there (55 pages).

Senate Miscellaneous Document 52, 45th Congress, 3rd Session, Volume I, Serial 1833.—Memorial of the Principal Chief of the Choctaw against a territorial government for Indian Territory (13 pages).

Senate Executive Document 30, 46th Congress, 1st Session, Volume I, Serial 1869.—On the subject of the occupation, or attempted occupation, of Indian Territory by white settlers (34 pages).

House Miscellaneous Document 13, 46th Congress, 1st Session, Volume I, Serial 1876.—A protest of the Indian delegates against territorial government (7 pages).

Senate Executive Document 6, 46th Congress, 2nd Session, Volume I, Serial 1882.—Tells of the removal of certain Cherokee citizens from the Outlet (7 pages).

Senate Executive Document 111, 47th Congress, 1st Session, Volume V, Serial 1990.—On attempts to settle in Indian Territory (4 pages).

House Executive Document 145, 47th Congress, 1st Session, Volume XXII, Serial 2030.—On the trespass of whites upon Indian land (3 pages).

Senate Executive Document 54, 48th Congress, 1st Session, Volume IV, Serial 2165.—This contains correspondence in relation to pasturing cattle upon lands of the Indian Territory. It covers the period from May, 1880, to October, 1883, and is very valuable used in conjunction with other materials (160 pages).

Senate Executive Document 200, 48th Congress, 1st Session, Volume VIII, Serial 2168.—On the subject of contracts to supply beef cattle to the Indians (120 pages).

Senate Report 64, 48th Congress, 1st Session, Volume I, Serial 2173 (2 pages).

House Executive Document 17, 48th Congress, 1st Session, Volume XIII, Serial 2193.—Trespass upon Indian lands (5 pages).

Senate Executive Document 16, 48th Congress, 2nd Session, Volume I, Serial 2261.—A document dealing entirely with the disorder growing out of pasturing cattle upon the lands of the Cheyenne-Arapaho reservation (26 pages).

Senate Executive Document 17, 48th Congress, 2nd Session, Volume I, Serial 2261.—This gives correspondence and documents relative to grazing upon lands of the Indian Territory. Most of the correspondence is for the period beginning about October, 1883, and closing about December, 1884 (220 pages).

Senate Executive Document 19, 48th Congress, 2nd Session, Volume I, Serial 2261.—In regard to the money paid by the United States for the lands of the Outlet (2 pages).

Senate Executive Document 50, 48th Congress, 2nd Session, Volume II, Serial 2263.—The status of certain lands in the Indian Territory and in regard to trespass upon them (71 pages).

Senate Executive Document 54, 48th Congress, 2nd Session, Volume II, Serial 2263.—The status of "Oklahoma" lands (7 pages).

Senate Executive Document 14, 49th Congress, 1st Session, Volume I, Serial 2333.—Trespass upon Indian lands (6 pages).

Senate Report 1278, 49th Congress, 1st Session, Volume VIII, Serial 2362.—This report contains testimony, correspondence, and documents relating to leases of grazing lands in the Indian Territory. Some of the material given in documents 54 and 17 mentioned above is reprinted here, but there is also a very large amount of valuable new material (768 pages).

House Miscellaneous Document 127, 49th Congress, 1st Session, Volume X, Serial 2415.—On the subject of Texas fever (8 pages).

Senate Executive Document 41, 50th Congress, 1st Session, Volume I, Serial 2504.—Trespass upon Indian lands (8 pages).

House Executive Document 232, 50th Congress, 1st Session, Volume XXVIII, Serial 2560.—This relates to grazing upon public lands (23 pages).

Senate Executive Document 98, 50th Congress, 2nd Session, Volume III, Serial 2612.—Creek lands and the price to be paid for them (8 pages).

Senate Executive Document 122, 50th Congress, 2nd Session, Volume III, Serial 2612.—A brief document in relation to Seminole lands (5 pages).

Senate Executive Document 136, 50th Congress, 2nd Session, Volume IV, Serial 2613.—On the subject of the alleged bribery of the Cherokee National Council by certain members of the Cherokee Strip Live Stock Association (6 pages).

Senate Executive Document 72, 51st Congress, 1st Session, Volume IX, Serial 2686.—Deals with the opening of "Oklahoma" to settlement (61 pages).

House Report 3768, 51st Congress, 2nd Session, Volume IV, Serial 2888.—Deals almost entirely with the question of the Cherokee title to the lands of the Outlet (27 pages).

Senate Executive Document 56, 52nd Congress, 1st Session, Volume V, Serial 2900.—Relates to the negotiations with the Cherokee in regard to opening the Outlet to white settlement (39 pages).

Senate Executive Document 63, 52nd Congress, 1st Session, Volume V, Serial 2900.—The Cherokee title to the lands of the Outlet (28 pages).

III. STATE DOCUMENTS AND RECORDS

Annual Reports of Missouri State Board of Agriculture.

Annual Reports of Montana Bureau of Agriculture, Labor and Industry.

Annual Reports of Nebraska State Board of Agriculture, 1873–1874.

Annual Report of Texas Comptroller, 1890–1895.

Annual Reports of Texas Land Office, 1910–1911.

Annual Report of Texas Department of Agriculture, 1924.

Wyoming Bulletin of Agriculture Statistics, 1923.

Wyoming Board of Immigration Publication, 1874.

Cases Cited

1. Holden *v.* Joy, 17 Wallace, 211.
2. United States *v.* George Cook, 19 Wallace, 591.
3. United States *v.* Hunter, 21 Federal Reporter, 615.
4. United States *v.* Ben Rees, 5 Dillon, 405.
5. United States *v.* Rogers, 23 Federal Reporter, 659.
6. United States *v.* Texas, 162 United States, 1.

BIBLIOGRAPHY

Newspapers

In addition to these listed, the New York Times and other large metropolitan dailies have been consulted for prices of cattle and beef and other specific information.

The Vinita Indian Chieftain, 1880–1888.—Complete files covering this period are to be found in the Kansas State Historical Society and the Oklahoma State Historical Society.

The Cherokee Advocate, 1880–1889.—Files are to be found in the Oklahoma Historical Society and the Kansas Historical Society.

Fort Gibson Indian Arrow.—Incomplete files are to be found in the Oklahoma Historical Society.

Caldwell Post.—Incomplete files are in the Kansas Historical Society.

Caldwell Journal.—Incomplete files are in the Kansas Historical Society.

Topeka Daily Capital, 1883–1885.

St. Louis Globe Democrat, 1883–1889.

Kansas City Star. Various files.

Kansas City Gazette, 1890.

Wallace's Farmers, 1902.

Iowa, Homestead, 1901.

National Live Stock Journal, 1870–1883.

Prairie Farmer, 1866, and following years.

Oklahoma War Chief.—Several copies are in the Kansas Historical Society.

Buckskin Joe's Emigrant's Guide.—A number of copies are in the Oklahoma Historical Society's collection.

SECONDARY MATERIAL

Abbott, Luther J.—History of Oklahoma (Boston, 1910).

Adair, James.—History of the American Indians (London, 1775).

Adams, Andy.—
1. The Log of a Cowboy (Boston and New York, 1903);
2. Reed Anthony, Cowman (Boston and New York, 1907);
3. The Outlet (Boston and New York, 1905);
4. Cattle Brands (Boston and New York, 1906);
5. Wells Brothers (Boston and New York, 1911);
6. The Ranch on the Beaver (Boston and New York, 1927).

Abel, Annie Heloise.—
1. The American Indian as a Slaveholder and a Secessionist (Cleveland, 1919);

[193]

2. The American Indian as a Participant in the Civil War (Cleveland, 1919);
3. The American Indian Under Reconstruction (Cleveland, 1925);
4. A History of Events Resulting in Indian Consolidation West of the Mississippi, Annual Report of the American Historical Association, 1906, Volume I.

Aldridge, Reginald.—Life on a Ranch (London, 1884).

Allen, L. A.—Our Cattle Industry Past and Present (Pamphlet; no place or date).

Bechdolt, Frederick R.—Tales of the Old Timers (New York, 1924).

Branch, Douglas.—The Cowboy and His Interpreters (New York, 1920).

Brisbin, James S.—The Beef Bonanza (Philadelphia, 1881).—An interesting contemporary account of the ranch cattle industry giving figures to show profits made in the business.

Britton, Wiley.—The Civil War on the Border (New York and London, 1899 and 1904, 2 volumes).

Buck, Solon J.—The Settlement of Oklahoma, Vol. XV, Part II of the Transactions of the Wisconsin Academy of Science, Arts and Letters (Madison, 1907).

Burton, Harley T.—A History of the J. A. Ranch (Austin, 1927).

Cattle Industry of Texas, no author (St. Louis, 1875).

Clay, John.—My Life on the Range (Chicago, 1924, privately printed). —One of the best books ever published on the cattle industry in the West.

Collins, Hubert.—War Path and Cattle Trail (New York, 1928).

Cook, John R.—The Border and the Buffalo (Topeka, Kansas, 1907).— An interesting and picturesque account of conditions on the plains at the time of the spread of ranching. Of no great historical value.

Dale, Edward Everett.—
1. The Cherokee Strip Live Stock Association.—Fifth Annual Proceedings of the Southwestern Political Science Association (Austin, 1924);
2. The History of the Ranch Cattle Industry in Oklahoma.— Annual Report of the American Historical Association, 1920.

Dobie, J. Frank.—A Vaquero of the Brush Country (Dallas, 1929).

Dyer, Mrs. D. B.—Fort Reno (New York, 1896).—The story of life at a frontier army post and of difficulties with the Indians resulting from the leasing of their lands to ranchmen.

Drake, Samuel G.—Book of the Indians (Boston, 1841).

Forsyth, George Alexander.—The Story of the Soldier (New York, 1900).

Gideon, D. C.—Indian Territory (New York and Chicago, 1901).

Goodnight, Charles and others.—Pioneer Days in the Southwest, 1850–1879 (Guthrie, Oklahoma, 1909).

Grohman, W. Baillie.—Camp Fires in the Rockies (New York, 1882).

Hagerdorn, Herman.—Roosevelt in the Bad Lands (Boston, 1921).

Haley, J. Evetts.—The X I T Ranch (Chicago, 1929).

Hill, J. L.—The End of the Cattle Trail (Long Beach, California, 1923).

Hill, Luther B.—History of the State of Oklahoma (Chicago and New York, 1909, 2 volumes.—The ordinary type of "subscription history," but perhaps better than most of them. The first volume contains a considerable amount of valuable material.

Hough, Emerson.—The Story of the Cowboy (New York, 1897).

Hunter, J. Marvin, (Editor).—The Trail Drivers of Texas (Nashville, 1925).—Experiences of cowboys on the trail.

Inman, Henry.—The Old Santa Fe Trail (Topeka, Kansas, 1899).

Jackson, A. P., and Cole, E. C.—Oklahoma (Kansas City, 1885).—A small volume prepared especially for the purpose of advertising the lands known as "Oklahoma" and to urge their opening to settlement. Interesting and valuable as a contemporary account of conditions in the Indian Territory and along the border but must be used with care because of its frankly controversial character.

King, Edward.—The Southern States of North America (London, 1875).

Macdonald, James.—Food from the Far West (New York, 1878).—Valuable for a study of the ranch cattle industry as a whole or the development of the plains region.

Macy, Jesse.—Institutional Beginnings of a Western State (Baltimore, 1884).

Majors, Alexander.—Seventy Years on the Frontier (New York, 1893).

McCoy, Isaac.—History of the Baptist Indian Missions (Washington and New York, 1840).—Gives an interesting and valuable account of conditions among the Five Civilized Tribes during the first few years after their removal to Indian Territory.

McCoy, Joseph G.—Historic Sketches of the Cattle Trade and Southwest (Kansas City, Missouri, 1874).—One of the most valuable accounts of the cattle trade and the beginning of the so-called "northern drive." The author of this monograph has talked with many friends and former companions of McCoy, and they all speak highly of him and of his work in the cattle trade.

Miles, Nelson A.—Serving the Republic: Memoirs of the Civil and

[195]

Military Life of Nelson A. Miles, (New York and London, 1911).
—General Miles gives an interesting account of his work on the
Cheyenne and Arapaho reservation where he went with General
Sheridan in 1885 to assist in removing the cattlemen.

Nimmo, Joseph.—The Range and Ranch Cattle Business of the
United States (Washington, 1885).—Published as House Ex. Doc.
7, Part III, 48 Cong., 2nd Session, but also published separately.

O'Beirne, H. F.—Leaders and Leading Men of the Indian Territory
(Chicago, 1891).

Osgood, E. S.—The Day of the Cattleman (Minneapolis, 1929).

Parrish, Randall.—The Great Plains (Chicago, 1907).—Interesting
but popular in its nature.

Puckett, J. L. and Ellen.—History of Oklahoma and Indian Territory (Vinita, Oklahoma, 1906).—Of some value as giving the viewpoint of the author who was an inter-married citizen of the Cherokee tribe.

Paxson, Frederic Logan.—The Last American Frontier (New York,
1910).

Richthofen, Baron Walter von.—Cattle Raising on the Plains of
North America (New York, 1885).—An interesting contemporary
account of ranching by a European who was engaged in the
industry for some years on the American plains.

Rister, C. C.—The Southwestern Frontier (Cleveland, 1928).—Excellent on Texas and the Southwest.

Rollins, Philip Ashton.—The Cowboy (New York, 1922).

Royce, Charles C.—The Cherokee Nation of Indians.—In Annual Report of the Bureau of American Ethnology, No. 5 (Washington,
1887).

Russell, Charles M.—Trails Plowed Under (Garden City and New
York, 1928).

Schoolcraft, Henry R.—Indian Tribes of the United States (Philadelphia, 1851–1855, 5 volumes).

Shambaugh, Benjamin Franklin.—Frontier Land Clubs, or Claim
Associations (No place or date).

Sheridan, Philip Henry.—Personal Memoirs (New York, 1888, 2 volumes).

Shinn, Charles Howard.—Mining Camps; A Study in American Frontier Government (New York, 1885).—Interesting as showing simi-
larities between laws of the mining camps and "cow custom" or
laws of the range.

Siringo, Charles.—Riata and Spurs (Boston and New York, 1912).

Thoburn, Joseph B.—History of Oklahoma (Chicago and New York,

1916, 5 volumes).—One of the better types of subscription works.

Trimble, William Joseph.—The Mining Advance into the Inland Empire.—Bulletin of the University of Wisconsin, No. 638 (Madison, Wisconsin, 1914).

Wright, Robert M.—
1. Frontier Life in Southwestern Kansas.—Kansas Historical Society Publications, Vol. VII;
2. Dodge City the Cowboy Capital (Wichita, Kansas, 1914).

PERIODICALS

This is a selected list. Many others might be mentioned.

Allen, Richard M.—Harvard Men in the Range Cattle Business.—The Harvard Graduates' Magazine, Vol. II, December, 1893, pages 183-192. Gives an interesting account of some of the events described in this monograph that took place on the reservations of the Kiowa-Comanche and Cheyenne-Arapaho.

Andrews, E. Benjamin.—The American Ox and His Pasture.—Review of Reviews, Volume XXVII, January, 1903, page 61. Contains an interesting map giving the number of cattle in the various states.

Baker, Ray Stannard.—The Great Southwest, the Tragedy of the Range.—The Century Magazine, volume XLII (new series), August, 1902, pages 535-545. Interesting but of no great value.

Barker, Robert M.—The Economics of Cattle Ranching in the Southwest—The American Monthly Review of Reviews, Volume XXIV, September, 1901, pages 305-312. A good article and well illustrated.

Bauman, John.—On a Western Ranche.—The Fortnightly Review, Volume XLVII, April, 1887, pages 516-533. Interesting and valuable.

The Cattle Business.—The Nation, Volume XLI, July 2, 1886; July 16, 1885; August 6, 1885, and August 27, 1885, pages 15-17, 50-51, 113-114, and 172-174.

Chapman, Arthur.—The Cowboy of Today.—The World's Work, Volume VIII, September, 1904, pages 5272-5278.

Dale, Edward Everett.—
1. The Ranchman's Last Frontier.—Mississippi Valley Historical Review, Volume X, No. 1, June, 1923;
2. Those Kansas Jayhawkers.—Agricultural History, Volume II, No. 4, October, 1928;
3. The Romance of the Range.—West Texas Historical Association Year Book, Volume V, June, 1929;

4. Ranching on the Cheyenne-Arapaho Reservation.—Chronicles of Oklahoma, Volume VI, No. 1, March, 1928.

5. The Passing of the Range Cattle Industry of Oklahoma.—The Cattleman, Volume XI, No. 6, November, 1924. (In addition to the last two most of the others here listed have been reprinted in the Cattleman);

6. Romance Rode with Development.—The Cattleman, Volume XII, No. 10, March, 1926.

Duffield, George C.—Driving Cattle from Texas to Iowa, 1866.—Annals of Iowa, Volume XIV, April, 1924, pages 242-262.

Grohman, W. Baillie.—Cattle Ranches of the Far West.—The Fortnightly Review, volume XXXIV, October 1, 1880, pages 438-457. An English viewpoint that is interesting but not practicable.

Harger, Charles Moreau.—

1. Cattle Trails of the Prairies.—Scribner's Magazine, Volume II, June, 1892, pages 732-742. A well written article and a very valuable one by a man that evidently is familiar with his subject. One of the best.

2. Modern Methods in the Cattle Industry.—The Outlook, Volume LXXII, September 6, 1902, pages 39-47.

Hayes, A. A.—Cattle Ranches of Colorado.—Harper's Magazine, Volume LIX, November, 1879, pages 877-895.

Hoke, Charles E.—Beef in the Southwest.—Country Gentleman, Volume LXXVIII, No. 8, February 21, 1914, page 380.

Keese, G. Pomeroy.—Beef.—Harper's Magazine, Volume LXIX, July, 1884, pages 292-301.

King, Henry.—The Indian Country.—The Century Magazine, Volume VIII (new series), August, 1885, pages 599-606.

Love, Clara M.—History of the Cattle Industry in the Southwest.—Southwestern Historical Quarterly, Volume XIX, April, 1916, pages 370-399; and Volume XX, July, 1916, pages 1-18.

Lyman, A. W.—From Steer to Steak.—Kansas Magazine, April, 1872.

Mayo, Earl.—A Day's Work on a Cattle Ranch.—The World's Work, Volume VIII, January, 1902, pages 1628-1645.

Paxson, Frederic L.—The Cow Country.—The American Historical Review, October, 1926. Very valuable and scholarly as anything from this distinguished historian must be.

Roosevelt, Theodore.—Ranch Life in the Far West.—The Century Magazine, Volume XIII (new series), February, 1888, pages 495-510.

The Home Ranch.—The Century Magazine, Volume XIII (new series), March, 1888, pages 655-669.

The Round-up.—The Century Magazine, Volume XIII, (new series), April, 1888, pages 849-867.

Sheriff's Work on a Ranch.—Century Magazine, Volume XIII (new series), May, 1888, pages 39-51.

The Ranchman's Rifle on Crag and Prairie.—The Century Magazine, Volume XIII (new series), June, 1888, pages 200-212.

Snow, E. P.—Sheepmen and Cattlemen. — The Outlook, Volume LXXIII, April 4, 1903, pages 839-840.

The Sportive Cowboy.—The Atlantic Monthly, Volume LXVI, November, 1890, pages 710-711.

Speed, John Gilmen.—The Oklahoma Land Lottery.—The Outlook, Volume LXVIII, Part II, July 20, 1901, page 667. (*See also* page 852.)

Wilkeson, Frank.—Cattle Raising on the Plains.—Harper's Magazine, Volume LXXII, April, 1886, pages 788-795.

Wister, Owen.—The Evolution of the Cowpuncher.—Harper's Magazine, Volume XCI, September, 1895, pages 602-617.

Wyeth, N. C.—A Day with the Round-up.—Scribner's Magazine, Volume XXXIX, March, 1906, pages 285-290.

Zogbaum, Rufus Fairchild.—A Day's Drive with Montana Cowboys.—Harper's Magazine, Volume LXXI, July, 1885, pages 188-193.

MISCELLANEOUS

A Six Year Resident, Texas, the Australia of America.—A volume by an unknown author printed just before the Civil War.

Brand Books.—Several have been consulted including those of the Western Kansas Stock Growers' Association for 1884, the Cherokee Strip Live Stock Association, 1885, the Panhandle Live Stock Association, 1886, the Wyoming Stock Growers' Association, 1880-1890, and the Southwestern Brand Book of 1883, for western Kansas, Indian Territory and the Panhandle of Texas.

Cattleman Magazine (various files).

Constitution and Laws of the Cherokee Nation (St. Louis, 1875).

Dale, Edward Everett.—A History of the Range Cattle Industry in Oklahoma.—Manuscript of some 500 pages, prepared as a doctor's dissertation for the Department of History of Harvard. One copy is in the Harvard Library and a duplicate in the manuscript collections of the University of Oklahoma.

Gannett, Henry.—A Gazeteer of Texas.—United States Geological Survey Bulletin, No. 224 (Washington, 1904).

Hopkins Manuscript.—The Production of Beef Cattle in Iowa.—

Manuscript in the files of the Bureau of Agricultural Economics, Division of Statistical and Historical Research.

Letters and Statements, 1924-1926.—These are from many men engaged in ranching or who formerly had large live stock interests. Among them are Ike T. Pryor of San Antonio, R. M. Kleberg of the King Ranch, Murdo MacKenzie of the Matador, E. B. Spiller, and Eli Moore of the Texas and Southwestern Cattle Raisers' Association, Swenson Brothers of the S M S Ranch, George W. Saunders of San Antonio, president of the Old Trail Drivers' Association, F. M. Simpson, of the Producers' Commission Company of Kansas City, J. T. Botkin, and D. D. Leahy of Wichita, Kansas, the late J. A. Blair, former secretary of the Cherokee Strip Live Stock Association, and many others.

McArthur, Daniel E.—The Cattle Industry of Texas, 1685–1918.— Manuscript of some 300 pages written as a master's thesis for the University of Texas.

Memorial of the Cherokee Strip Live Stock Association to the President of the United States (Kansas City, 1889).

Mumford, Herbert, and Hall, Louis D.—Review of Beef Production in the United States.—Illinois Agricultural Experiment Station. Circular No. 169 (Urbana, 1913).

Oklahoma Red Book (Oklahoma City, 1912, 2 volumes).

Proceedings of the National Stock Growers' Convention (various years).

Read and Pell.—Reports from commissioners and inspectors, 1880, Volume XVIII, Serial 856, (British Document).—Report of a Parliamentary Commission consisting of Clare Read and Albert Pell, both members of Parliament, sent to America to study the cattle industry in the West with special reference to the amount of British capital invested in it.

Reports of the Wyoming Stock Growers' Association (1882 and years following).

Texas Almanac (various numbers).

Thompson, James Westfall.—Manuscript of several hundred pages on the history of the Live Stock Industry in the United States. Prepared by this distinguished historian during the period of the Great War. In the files of Bureau of Agricultural Economics, Division of Statistical and Historical Research.

Youngblood, Bonney.—An Economic Study of a Typical Ranching Area.—Bulletin No. 297 of the Texas Agricultural Experiment Station (College Station, Texas, 1921).

INDEX

Abilene, Kansas: cattle shipping point, 38 f.; advertised by McCoy, 41; loses position as cow town, 41; terminus of trail, 49

Arapaho Indians, home of: 20, 22, 123

Arizona: cattle country, 16; Texas cattle driven to, 51

Arkansas, losses of cattle in: 12

Arkansas River, trail crossing of: 49

Army Posts, as a market for cattle: 62

Associations, cattlemen's: established during Civil War, 11–12; formed in Texas, 52; growth of, 85–88, 105; *see aslo* Stock associations

Atchison, Topeka and Santa Fe Railway: building of, 27 f., 41–42, 121; *see also* Railways

Atlantic Seaboard, cattle shipped to: 8

Austin, Texas, population of in 1860: 10

Bad Lands, Dakota, Montana, and Wyoming: 16

Bandera, Texas, on cattle trail: 48

Barb wire: first use of, 108–109; effects of its use, 109; brings on fence cutting, 111; *see also* Fencing

Baxter Springs, Kansas: on cattle trail, 34 f.; as a cow town, 49

Beef contracts: secured by contractors, 45; with the Indians, 62–63; close supervision of, 63; prices paid, 63–64; importance of, 63–64; graft connected with, 63 f.; profits of, 64–65; prices paid, 78–80

Beeves: price of, 9; *see also* Cattle

Bell, Joseph, ranching operations of: 74

Big Horn, battle of: 25

Big Pasture, reserved to Indians: 146

Binkleman, George A., establishes ranch in Colorado: 72

Bismarck, North Dakota: terminus of Northern Pacific, 27; supply point for buffalo hunters, 27; railway to, 74

Black Hills: 16; gold discovery in, 75

Blizzards: in cattle country, 17; on drives, 48, 69

Blockade, restricts cattle shipments: 11

Boggy Depot, Oklahoma, on cattle trail: 34

Boskowitz, J. and A., purchasers of buffalo hides: 28

Branding, agreements for: 6

Brands: recording of, 83; importance of, 84

Breeding animals, purchase of: 171

Breeding ranches: 149 f.

Breeds, improvement of: 91, 148 ff., 152–53

Brownsville, Texas, population of in 1860: 10

Buffalo: area of, 10; on the plains, 20 f.; profits of hunting, 25; camps established, 26; slaughter of, 26–27, 62; slaughter of northern herd, 27 ff.; value of to settlers, 60; disappearance from northern plains, 75

Bureau of Animal Industry, statement of: 172–73

Cairo, Illinois, cattle shipped to: 36 f.

Caldwell, Kansas: 138 f.

California: size of farms in, 5; first drives to, 8; herds driven to during Civil War, 8, 11; gold rush to, 18, 26 f., 60; Texas cattle driven to, 51; emigration to, 60 f.

Canada: 15, 171

Canadian River: trail crossing of, 49; on trail, 52

[201]